André Maurois

AN ILLUSTRATED HISTORY OF
ENGLAND

Translated from the French by

Hamish Miles

With a Foreword by Sir Arthur Bryant

THE VIKING PRESS

NEW YORK

Condensed English text © 1963 by The Bodley Head Ltd., London
All rights reserved

Published in 1964 by The Viking Press, Inc.
625 Madison Avenue, New York, N.Y. 10022

Printed and bound in Italy by Istituto Italiano d'Arti Grafiche, Bergamo
Library of Congress catalog card number: 64-20410

CONTENTS

NOTE ON THE ILLUSTRATIONS

The reference in italics after each illustration is to the source from which the photograph was obtained. The reference in brackets is to the present location of the item reproduced.

The publishers gratefully acknowledge the assistance of the Illustrations Research Service in undertaking the preliminary research.

Foreword

'The history of England,' André Maurois writes, 'is that of one of mankind's outstanding successes. It is the history of how certain Saxon and Danish tribes, isolated on an island on the outer rim of Europe, merging with the Celtic and Roman survivors, became with the passing centuries the masters of one-third of the planet.' With sympathy and understanding, yet with the objectiveness and detachment of a lifelong observer who has been fascinated by English character and outlook ever since he served as a liaison officer with the British Army in the first World War, this brilliant French man of letters retells a familiar story in a new and original way.

Much of that story has been closely linked with that of M. Maurois's own country, whose language our rulers once spoke and so much of whose thought and culture, to our enduring gain, our ancestors inherited or acquired. Here, too, it is an advantage to see our past through such keen yet kindly foreign eyes. With generosity the author is quick to note, too, the debt of France to England, as when he writes of the eighth century:

'It was a strange paradox that the Mediterranean culture came to be preserved for the Gauls by Anglo-Saxon monks... When the Saracens were thrusting into the heart of France, when the classic age seemed to be ending in Europe, the Venerable Bede, a monk in this almost barbarian land, was writing in Latin his delightful ecclesiastical history of the English nation. Bede himself was the master of Egbert, who was in turn the teacher of Alcuin; and Alcuin it was who, summoned by Charlemagne, checked the intellectual decadence of France.'

In this illustrated edition of his history M. Maurois makes no attempt to chronicle detail, which, if it is to be made interesting, is only possible on a large canvas. Instead, he confines himself to the essentials of our past and the principles, spiritual and material, through following which we have prospered, served mankind and grown great, and, through ignoring which, we have from time to time — and deservedly — suffered punishment and disaster. In this he has been wise for it makes his volume as easy to read as it is delightful to the eye. Some things he sees which scarcely anyone else has noted, as, for instance, the effect of our precise geographical position on our culture:

'This accessible part of England lies exactly opposite the frontier which severs the Roman from the Germanic languages... and was thus destined to be open equally to the bearers of the Roman and Latin culture, and to those of the Teutonic... England characteristically combined elements from both these cultures, and out of them made a genius of her own... In this respect England differs profoundly from France or Italy, in both of which the Latin basis is always dominant, despite certain Germanic contributions, and also from Germany, where Latin culture was never more than an ornament, and often was indignantly rejected.'

Written before the last War but revised and abridged since, M. Maurois's book ends with a question mark. The modern world, he considers, confronts Britain and the Commonwealth with a problem more difficult of solution than any she has successfully solved in the past; personally, though otherwise agreeing, I should not have thought it more difficult than the problem — seemingly so insoluble — which faced England in the middle of the sixteenth century. Flanked by huge nations with populations and resources superior to her own, 'can Britain,' the author asks, 'remain one of the great World-Powers?... The British Empire as Kipling saw it no longer exists, but it has been replaced by something no less splendid or valuable. The essential change lies in the fact that the British peoples are no longer in a position to select their allies or to live in a state of isolation. It is for them to achieve a last compromise between the national independence which is so dear to their hearts and that international solidarity which is the condition of their survival.' This seems to me profoundly true.

ARTHUR BRYANT

I

Before the Norman Conquest

England up to 1066

'WE MUST always remember that we are part of the Continent, but we must never forget that we are neighbours to it.' Bolingbroke's words define the primordial facts of England's position. So close to the Continent does she lie that from the beach at Calais the white cliffs of Dover are plainly visible, tempting the invader. For thousands of years, indeed, England was joined up with Europe, and for long ages the Thames was a tributary of the Rhine. The animals which returned to roam the country after the Ice Age, and the first hunters who followed on their tracks, crossed from Europe on dry land. But narrow and shallow as the straits are which now sever the island of Britain from Belgium and France, they have nevertheless shaped a unique destiny for the country which they protect.

'Insulated, not isolated.' Europe is not so far away that the insularity of English ideas and customs could remain unaffected. Indeed, that insularity is a human fact rather than a phenomenon of nature. In the beginnings of history England was invaded, like other lands, and fell an easy victim. She lived then by husbandry and grazing. Her sons were shepherds and tillers of the soil rather than merchants or seamen. It was not until much later that the English, having built powerful fleets, and feeling themselves sheltered within a ring of strong sea defences, realized the actual benefits of insularity, which freed them from fears of invasion, and, for several centuries, from the military requirements which dominated the policy of other nations, and so enabled them safely to attempt new forms of authority.

By a fortunate chance, the most accessible part of England was the low-lying country of the south-east, which confronts the Continent. If the land had happened to slope in the other direction, if the Celtic and Scandinavian sea-rovers had chanced upon forbidding mountains on their first voyages, it is probable that few of them would have attempted invasion, and the history of the country would have been very different. But their vessels came with the inflowing tides deep into well-sheltered estuaries; the turfed chalk ridges made it possible to explore the island without the dangers of marsh and forest; and the climate, moreover, was more kindly than that of other lands in the same latitude, as Britain lies in a gulf of temperate winters produced by the damp mild mists of the ocean. Thus every feature of the coastline seemed to encourage the conqueror, who was also the creator.

This accessible part of England lies exactly opposite the frontier which severs the Roman from the Germanic languages (nowadays, the French from the Flemish), and was thus destined to be open equally to the bearers of the Roman and Latin culture, and to those of the Teutonic. History would show how England characteristically combined elements from both these cultures, and out of them made a genius of her own. 'Her east coast was open to Scandinavian immigrants, her south to Mediterranean influences reaching her through France. To the Teutons and Scandinavians she owes the greater part of her population, numerous traits of character, and the roots of her speech; from the Mediterranean peoples she received the rest of her language, the chief forms of her culture, much of her organizing power.' In this respect England differs profoundly from France or Italy, in both of which the Latin basis is always dominant, despite certain Germanic contributions, and also from Germany, where Latin culture was never more than an ornament, and often was indignantly rejected. England was thrice sub-

jected to contact with the Latin world — by the Roman occupation, by Christianity, and by the Normans — and the impress left by these Latin influences was deep.

Paradoxical as it may seem, it is true to say that England's position on the globe changed between the fifteenth and the seventeenth centuries. To the races of antiquity and the peoples of the Middle Ages, this mist-clad country represented the farthest fringe of the world: Ultima Thule, magical and almost inhuman, on the verge of Hell itself. Beyond those rocks battered by ocean billows lay, to the west, the sea that had no end, and northward the everlasting ice. The boldest of the bold ventured thither because they could find gold and pearls, and later wool; but how could they imagine the prodigies which the future held for these islands? Those were days when all human activity was founded, directly or indirectly, on the Mediterranean basin. It needed the barrier of Islam, the discovery of America, and above all the emigration of the Puritans, to shift the great traderoutes, and to make the British Isles, confronting a new world, into the most advanced maritime base of Europe.

Finally, it was in the eighteenth and nineteenth centuries that England's insular position, after allowing her to attain behind the shield of her fleet a higher degree of domestic liberty than Continental peoples could reach, enabled her through that same maritime instrument to conquer a world-wide Empire. The mastery of the seas, which solved the problem of national defence inherent in England's geographical situation, serves as one key to her political and imperial history. And the invention of the aeroplane is for her the most important and the most perilous development of our times.

The first page of England's history is not, as has often been said, a blank. It is rather a page inscribed with the letters of several alphabets to which we have no key. Time was when historians chose to portray the primitive Britons as overawed by the forests of the weald, haunted by gods and beasts, and wandering in small groups of hunters and shepherds who took refuge on the hills. But such monuments as those at Avebury and Stonehenge

STONEHENGE (WILTSHIRE). The circle of megaliths seen from the air. Stonehenge is ten miles from Salisbury; it dates from 1700-1400 B.C. and may have served as a sun-temple. The outer circle of standing stones, twenty feet high, is over a hundred feet in diameter. The stones were quarried 180 miles away. *Aerofilms Ltd.*

CELTIC BRONZE MIRROR found in a woman's tomb at Desborough (Northants) and dating from the Bronze Age. *British Museum.*

seem to prove the existence of a fairly numerous population fully two thousand years before the Christian era, customarily united for common action under an accepted authority.

The name of Iberians is generally given to these primitive inhabitants who peopled England after the disappearance of palaeolithic man and at the end of the Ice Age, bringing with them cattle, goats, and swine. They are supposed to have come from Spain, but whether Spanish or not, they were certainly of Mediterranean origin. The traveller returning from Malta is struck, at Stonehenge, by the resemblance between the megalithic monuments of two places so far apart. It is more than likely that in prehistoric times there existed in the Mediterranean, and along the Atlantic seaboard as far as the British Isles, a civilization quite as homogeneous as the European Christendom of the Middle Ages. This civilization was introduced into England by immigrants, who retained contact with Europe through traders coming in search of metals in Britain, and bartering the products of the Levant or amber from the Baltic. Gradually the islanders,

like the inhabitants of the Continent, learned new technical devices, the arts of husbandry, the methods of building long boats and manipulating bronze.

Between the sixth and the fourth centuries before the Christian era, there arrived in England and Ireland successive waves of pastoral and warrior tribes who gradually supplanted the Iberians. They belonged to a Celtic people who had occupied great tracts in the Danube basin, in Gaul, and to the north of the Alps. They probably began to move because shepherd races are doomed to follow their flocks when hunger drives these towards fresh pastures. Doubtless human causes also intervened: an adventurous chief, the desire for conquest, the pressure of a stronger people. These migrations were slow and steady. One clan would cross the Channel and settle on the coast; a second would drive this one further inland, the natives themselves being pushed always further back. These Celtic tribes had a taste for war, even amongst themselves, and were composed of tall, powerful men, eaters of pork and oatmeal pottage, beer-drinkers,

[9]

CELTIC WARRIORS AT A HUMAN SACRIFICE. Detail from the Gundestrup Vase now in Copenhagen. *Editions du Pont Royal.*

GLADIATORIAL COMBAT. This form of entertainment spread from Rome where it was very popular. This vase, supposedly from Colchester, 190 B.C. is in the museum at Colchester (Essex). *Fine Art Engravers Ltd.*

and skilful charioteers. The Latin and Greek writers depicted the Celts as a tall, lymphatic, white-skinned race, with fair hair. Actually there were many dark Celts, who in the Roman triumphs were sorted out and made to dye their hair, so as to produce prisoners in conformity with popular ideas for the parades in the metropolis. The Celts themselves had formed an ideal type of their own race, to which they strove to approximate. They bleached their hair and painted their bodies with colouring matter; whence it came about that the Romans later styled the Celts in Scotland, Picts (*Picti*, the painted men).

In this slow and prolonged Celtic invasion, two main waves are distinguished by historians: the first, of the Goidels or Gaels, who gave their language to Ireland and the Scottish Highlands; and the second, of the Bretons or Brythons, whose tongue became that of the Welsh and the Bretons in France. The evidence of Julius Caesar is our best source for the Celts' mode of life. They had nominal kings, it is true, with local influence, but no serious political sway. Every town or township — every family almost — was divided into two factions, the leading men of each giving protection to their partisans. These people had no sense of the State, and left no political heritage: both in England and France, the State was a creation of the Latin and Germanic spirits. The Celtic clan rested on a family, not a totem, basis, which

forges strong links but hampers the development of wider associations. In countries of Celtic origin the family has always remained the unit of social life. According to Caesar the rural community life with communal fields and pastures, so important later in English history, is essentially Germanic, and certainly would hardly have fitted in with the network of factions described by him. The most highly honoured class was the priestly one of the Druids, who approximate most closely to the Brahmans of India or the Persian Magi. In Caesar's time the most famous Druids were those of Britain, who foregathered every year at a central point, possibly Stonehenge, although their holy of holies was the island of Mona (Anglesey). The Druids taught ' that death was only a change of scene, and that life is continued with its forms and possessions in the World of the Dead, which consists of a great store of souls awaiting disposal...' This population of souls does not seem to have been confined to the human race, and they apparently believed in the transmigration of souls.

In Britain as in Gaul, the quick-witted, adaptable Celts were swift to imitate the Roman civilization when it had defeated them. But the Celts were not merely good transmitters of a foreign culture. They had their own artistic tastes, and the spiral ornamentation of their weapons, their jewels and pottery, show that they were more fanciful than the Romans ever were. They gave to European

BRONZE HEAD OF CLAUDIUS, Roman Emperor from 41 to 54 A.D. It was under Claudius that the successful Roman invasion of England took place in 43 A.D. This sculpture was found near Saxmundham (Suffolk). It measures twelve inches. (*British Museum*).

literature an oriental sense of mystery and a dramatic conception of fatality which are peculiarly their own. It is difficult, however, for a weak people, living within reach of a great military power, to keep its freedom. With Gaul subdued, Britain became the natural objective for the Roman armies. Julius Caesar needed victories to impress Rome, and money to reward his legions and partisans; and in these fabulous islands he hoped to find gold, pearls, slaves. Late in the summer of the year 55 B.C., he decided to carry out a short reconnaissance across the English Channel. The expedition was not too successful in spite of the Roman superiority in discipline and military science. The Britons, on the alert, were waiting in force on the shore and had mustered thousands of chariots. The legionaries, compelled to leap from their transports into quite deep water, were battered by the waves, and under their heavy load of arms could hardly get a foothold. Caesar had to order the galleys of archers and slingers to set up a covering barrage of projectiles; nevertheless, he soon realized that his small army was not secure. Heavy seas had already destroyed some of his transports, and the equinoctial tides were at hand. Taking advantage of a slight success to secure hostages and promises, he secretly raised anchor soon after midnight. He had saved his face. And on the strength of this inglorious expedition he sent the Senate a dispatch in such glowing terms that a *supplicatio* of twenty days was voted to celebrate his victory.

But Caesar was too much of a realist to disguise the failure to himself. He had learned much about the nature of the country, the harbours, and the British tactics, saw that a conquest would need cavalry, and decided to return in the following year (54 B.C.). This time he found the Britons united by the pressure of danger and obeying one chief, Cassivelaunus, whose territory lay north of the Thames. The Roman army advanced in that direction and, when Caesar reached the northern bank of the river, he entered dexterously on negotiations. Taking advantage of the smouldering jealousies of the Celtic chieftains, some of whom he incited against Cassivelaunus, he secured the submission of several tribes, defeated others in the field, and finally, treating with Cassivelaunus himself, fixed an annual tribute to be paid to the Roman people by Britain.

For a century after Caesar's departure, Britain was forgotten. But merchants came thither from Gaul, by now thoroughly Romanized, and the Imperial coinage was current. In the time of Claudius, various groups urged a conquest of Britain: generals with an eye on fame and gain, traders who declared that mercantile security required the presence of the legions, administrators who deplored

RUINS OF THE ROMAN THEATRE AT VERULAMIUM. This is the only Roman theatre discovered in England. Verulamium (St. Albans) was founded by the Romans after their invasion in 43 A.D. possibly on the site of the fortress of Cassivelaunus, Caesar's adversary. *Institute of Archaeology, St. Albans.*

TOMBSTONE OF RUFUS SITA. This Roman sculpture depicts a Thracian horseman attacking a Briton. *Gloucester City Museum.*

the bad influence wielded in Gaul by the Druids, whose centre of activity was still in Britain, and a host of officials hoping to find posts in a new province. In the year 43 A.D., accordingly, Claudius sent over an expedition of four legions, totalling about 50,000 men inclusive of auxiliaries and horsemen. With such a force the conquest appeared easy enough, and resistance did not prove serious until the mountain regions of Wales and Scotland were reached. From the island of Mona (Anglesey), a centre of Druidism, came forth a terrifying host of warriors in whose midst women with flying hair brandished blazing torches, whilst the serried ranks of white-robed Druids raised their arms in invocation of the gods. In the south-east, which seemed to be pacified, the conquerors were momentarily imperilled by a violent rising led by a queen, Boudicca or Boadicea, provoked by the injustices of the first Roman administrators. But it was ended by a massacre of the Britons. By the beginning of the second century all the rich plains of the south were in subjection.

Roman methods of occupation varied little: they built excellent roads, enabling the legions to move swiftly from place to place, and fortified centres to hold fixed garrisons. Most English towns with names ending in ' chester ' or ' cester ' were Roman camps (castra) in the time of the occupation. Veterans of the legions, after their term of service, began to retire to the small British towns of Camulodunum (Colchester) and Verulamium (St. Albans). Towns like Lincoln, Gloucester and York were originally only garrison towns. London (Londinium) grew large in Roman times because the conquerors made it a centre through which passed all the roads linking north and south, the principal one being Watling Street, running from London to Chester. The excellent harbour of London was used for bringing over supplies for the armies. In towns built in their entirety by the

HADRIAN'S WALL (NORTHUMBERLAND). ▶ In 123 A.D. the Emperor Hadrian built this wall from Solway Firth across the North of Britain to the mouth of the Tyne marking, for the benefit of the Picts and Scots, the northern frontier of Roman Britain. *J. Allan Cash.*

PICT WARRIORS fighting the Romans from their retreat in Scotland. Detail from the Cross of Aberlemno. *National Museum of Antiquities of Scotland, Edinburgh.*

Romans, the streets intersected each other at right angles, the baths, the temple, the forum, and the basilica occupying their traditional places. Before long the south of England was sprinkled with small Roman houses. To this new life the Celts, or some of them at least, adapted themselves. Had they felt a sense of constraint they might have been more rebellious; but Roman policy respected local institutions and allowed the native to move spontaneously into a civilization endowed with a great prestige. In any case, Roman immigration was not so large as to be oppressive: a few traders and moneylenders, some officers and functionaries. The soldiers soon lost their Italianate character. The children of legionaries by British women were brought up near the camps, and in due time entered the service themselves. Roman civilization, it has been said, was not the expansion of a race, but of a culture.

This method of peaceful penetration was employed with outstanding success by Agricola, the father-in-law of Tacitus (A.D. 79-85). Here was a new type of Roman administrator, far removed from the aristocratic pro-consuls who had founded the Empire with one hand and pillaged it with the other. Agricola kept control of affairs in his own hands, appointed honest men to the adminis-

tration, made a stand against the exactions of tax-collectors, and strove to encourage the Celts in Roman ways of living. Many Celts at this time became bilingual, but for the mass of the people the Celtic dialects remained the current speech.

Religion could not stem this Romanization of Britain. With contented tolerance the Romans annexed the unknown gods. The Druidic worship they harried, and almost completely destroyed, but this was because they saw in it a political danger. The Celtic god of battles, Teutates, became identified with Mars. In the larger towns they raised Temples to the Emperors, to Jupiter, to Minerva. Other legionaries were worshippers of Mithra, and London itself has disclosed a temple of the goddess Isis. Christianity was certainly known in Britain from the third century; as early as the fourth a bishop of London, Restitutus, is known to have attended the synod of Arles along with two others from that country.

The south and central parts of Britain were thus becoming part and parcel of the Empire. But in the north the Roman dominion made no headway. On the edge of rough heather moorlands lived the half-savage tribe of the Brigantes, and still farther north another Celtic group, the Picts, both equally refractory to all peaceful penetration. These dis-

GODS. This stone from Shorngrafton is exhibited at Housesteads, the best preserved of the forts along Hadrian's Wall. *Ministry of Works.*

sident, uncompromising tribes, attracted by the comparative wealth of the Celto-Roman townships, kept making profitable forays into the south, and easily escaped the pursuing Roman generals. Finally the Emperor Hadrian, who himself came to Britain in the year 120, abandoned the idea of subduing the north, and fortified the frontier by building between the Tyne and the Solway Firth a line of fourteen forts, joined at first by a continuous earthwork, and soon by a stone wall, to be permanently garrisoned.

After the third century the Roman Empire, despite certain impressive counterstrokes, was threatened by a threefold crisis, economic, religious, and military. Roman capitalism had blindly exploited the resources of the provinces; the conflict of paganism with Christianity had sundered emperors and citizens; and military power had collapsed. The system of the continuous frontier (a line of forts linked by a rampart) had broken down. In Britain it had seemed slightly more effective than elsewhere, the line of defence being short, and there the Pax Romana survived longer than in the Continental provinces of the Empire. The first half of the fourth century, indeed, saw in Britain the apogee of its Roman civilization. But there as else-

where the army ceased to be Roman. The garrison of the Wall consisted of local units which were stationed there permanently. The first Dacian cohort spent two centuries up there, and the soldiers settled down to a colonizing life. Gradually the British legions forgot their links with Rome: indeed a day was to come, about the year 384, when they proclaimed their own Emperor, raising to Imperial rank their popular and truly remarkable leader, Maximus, who went over to the Continent to war with pretenders from other provinces.

After this the Picts and Scots seem to have become bolder, and to combat them a British chief, Vortigern, summoned Saxon auxiliaries, Hengest and Horsa, to whom he offered land as payment for their swords. Having once set foot on the island, they turned against their master, and Frankish and Saxon barbarian invaders, attracted by this fruitful and ill-defended land, became more and more numerous. The year 418 is noted in the Anglo-Saxon Chronicle as that in which 'the Romans gathered together all the treasure that was in Britain. Hiding part of it underground, they bore away the rest into Gaul.' In our own day some of these treasures have been unearthed, caches of gold and silver objects. The discoveries of archaeology all

FL.
INTALI
COMORB.
FR

Maxuna Caesariensis.

Valentia.

Britania prima.

Britania secunda.

Flauia Caesariensis.

point to a land then in a state of terror. Villas and destroyed houses show signs of fire; doors have been hastily walled up; skeletons have been found uncoffined. The Venerable Bede describes these invasions: 'Public as well as private structures were overturned; the priests were everywhere slain before the altars... Some of the miserable remainder, being taken in the mountains, were butchered in heaps. Others, spent with hunger, came forth and submitted themselves to the enemy for food, being destined to undergo perpetual servitude if they were not killed even upon the spot. Some, with sorrowful hearts, fled beyond the seas. Others, continuing in their own country, led a miserable life among the woods, rocks and mountains.' Most of the Celts fled into the mountainous districts of the west, where they are still living to-day. To these fugitives the Saxons gave the name 'Welsh', that is, foreigners (German, *Welche*). Other Celts moved away towards Armorica, one of the most remote parts of Gaul, and there created Brittany.

These Saxons and Angles had violence in their temperament, and kept it. After fifteen centuries, notwithstanding the strict rules of a code of manners sprung from that very violence, their character was to remain less supple than that of Celts or Latins. In the days of those invasions they held human life cheap: war was their delight. But 'this native barbarism covered noble inclinations', and there was 'a quality of seriousness which saved them from frivolity. Their women were chaste, their marriages pure. The man who had chosen his leader was true to him, and loyal towards his comrades though cruel to his foe. The man of this stock could accept a master, and was capable of devotion and respect.' Having always known the tremendous forces of nature, more so than the dweller in gentler climes, he was religious. A sense of grandeur and melancholy haunted his imagination. The solitudes which he had known in the Frisian marshlands and the great coastal plains were not like those which engendered the harsh poetry of the Bible, but they prepared him to understand it. When the Bible came in time to his ken, the Scriptures filled him with a deep and lasting passion.

It is fairly easy to picture the landings of the Saxon bands. Sailing with the tide into an estuary, the barbarians would push on upstream, or follow a Roman road, to find a villa ringed by tilled fields, or the huts of a Celtic hamlet. But these Saxon peasants, hunters and woodmen refrained from occupying the Roman villa; the Roman townships were left abandoned. In a new land these Germans followed their old usage, and built their cabins from the felled trees. The head of the tribe, the noble, had a hall of tree-trunks built for him by his men. In parcelling out the land the band would follow the Germanic tradition. The village ('town' or 'township', from the Saxon *tun*, hedge or fence) would own the fields collectively, but every man would have his share marked out.

The cell of Anglo-Saxon life, then, was the village, a community of between ten and thirty families. It was administered by the *moot*, a small assembly meeting under some tree or on a hillock, and determining the partition of the fields, the number of cattle which might properly be grazed on the common meadows, and the payment of the communal herdsmen. Here, too, were appointed the village *reeve*, both mayor and administrator of the common domain; the *woodreeve*, who looked after the woods; and the ploughman, who had to turn over the common arable land. Generally the village had its *thane*, the noble war-chieftain with rights to levy dues in kind or labour. In those primitive times social classes were simple and ill-defined. Beneath the noble was the freeman, owing nothing to the noble for his lands except the *trinoda necessitas*, that is, service under arms, the upkeep of roads and bridges. Then came various classes, varying with locality and period, but with the common feature that the men belonging to them paid a rent, in kind or services; and lastly the slaves, who disappeared in the tenth and eleventh centuries.

It is probable that when the Anglo-Saxons arrived, each new tribe that landed had its chief or king, whose thanes were bound to him by personal loyalty. Gradually, wider states were formed, by conquest, marriage, or fresh clearances of the land. An embryonic central power contrived to impose that modicum of administrative structure without which it would have been impossible to muster an army or levy a tribute. In the seventh century England still had seven kingdoms. In the eighth, three survived: Northumbria, Mercia, and Wessex. By the ninth, there was only Wessex.

CORONATION OF KING ARTHUR, from a manuscript composed a considerable time later. King Arthur, a Celtic hero who died in combat c. 542, became a legendary figure with his Knights of the Round Table. (*Chetham Library, Manchester*, Ms 6712).

The King in each kingdom came always of one sacred family, but from its members the Witan, or council of elders, could within certain limits make a choice. This body was not a representative assembly, an anticipation of Parliament or the House of Lords; it was not even an assembly of hereditary peers. The King summoned to it the leading chiefs, and later, after the conversion of the Germans, the archbishops, bishops, and abbots. This council of elders, few in number, was also the supreme judicial body. It could depose a bad king, or refuse — especially in time of war — to entrust the realm to a minor. The monarchy was thus partially elective, though from within a definite family. The kingdom was divided into *shires*, the boundaries of these Anglo-Saxon divisions corresponding nearly everywhere to those of the present-day counties. At first the shire was primarily a judicial unit, with a court of justice to which every village sent its representatives several times a year. Before long the King was represented by a sheriff, whilst the *ealdorman* appeared as a local governor, at the head of military and judicial administrations. The shire was composed of *hundreds* (groups of one hundred families, or groups furnishing one hundred soldiers), and these in turn were made up of *tuns* or townships. In the sixth century, these divisions were vague, and became definite only after several centuries of organization.

There was a rude beauty in the religion of the Anglo-Saxons. It derived from the mass of legends recounted in the Edda, the Bible of the North. The gods, Thor, Freya (who gave their names to the days of the week), lived in Valhalla, the paradise to which the Valkyries, the warrior virgins, carried off men who died fighting in the field. But in transportation across the North Sea this religion lost much of its strength. In any case, from the sixth century, the kings of the Angles and Saxons knew that their racial brothers in Gaul and Italy had become converted to Christianity, and example encouraged them. These small Anglo-Saxon courts received the Christian missions with tolerance, often with respect.

ANGLO-SAXON KING PRESIDING AT THE WITAN, THE COUNCIL OF ▶ ELDERS. This 12th century manuscript shows the king majestically dispensing justice. (*British Museum*, Ms. Claudius V.IV).

cæp qþam þeapum phapao mœtte
þæþ þæt he þe ræþe ʒan up oþþam þ

théſtōde beanpe ta· þhim ſ ꝑ uni
t reoꞃon ꝼæᵹne oxan ꝿꝯꝓe

The conversion of England was the work of two groups of missionaries, one from the Celtic countries, Ireland in particular, and the other from Rome itself. After the departure of the Romans, Wales had remained largely Christian. In Ireland, St. Patrick — the Roman Patricius — had converted the Celtic tribes to the faith, and founded monasteries which later became the refuge of scholars from the Continent in flight from the barbarians and then from the Saracens. From these monastic centres there sallied forth saintly men (St. Columba, the most famous of them) who converted the Celts of Scotland. In the Celtic lands, Ireland, Wales and Scotland, a national Church with some degree of independence from the Roman had taken shape, striving to approximate to the primitive Church. The Irish monks were for many years solitaries living like those of the Thebaid in isolated huts; only the need for security made them accept the assembling of these huts within an enclosure, and the rule of an abbot. In Ireland neither monks nor secular priests were forbidden to marry. The churches remained bare, with no altars. The priests baptized adults on the river banks, and Mass was said in the vernacular, not in Latin. The priests lived as poor men, distributing in alms whatever gifts they received. And the date of Easter was fixed by certain old usages, so that the festival amongst the Celts did not coincide with the Roman Easter.

But meanwhile the Roman Church had found a leader. Pope Gregory the Great, a Roman aristocrat whose early career had taken him through lay dignities, had been able to ensure for the Papacy the provisional succession of the Western Empire. This great man of action was an artist: under his inspiration the Gregorian chant was evolved, as also were those superb ceremonies of the Church which so deeply impressed the barbarians. For the preaching of the faith in fresh countries, he used chiefly the monks. Early in that century, St. Benedict had founded the Benedictine Order, which combined intellectual with manual toil, and he had introduced perpetual vows, the novitiate, and the rule of elected abbots — reforms which had attracted the choice spirits of that generation into the monasteries. Gregory entrusted numerous missions to the Benedictines, and it was to one of their number, the Prior Augustine, that he entrusted the evangelization of England.

The Pope was to rely on women as well as on monks for the conversion of the pagans. The King of Kent had married the Christian daughter of the King of Paris, and allowed his consort to bring over a chaplain. It was to her that Augustine first turned, with his forty monks, alarmed at finding themselves in a land which they regarded as quite savage, and they were immediately welcomed in the capital of Kent, Canterbury. The Pope had given them sage counsel: they must, above all things, interfere as little as possible with the usages of the pagan folk. 'Firstly, let there be no destruction of the temples of idols. If

IMAGO HOMINIS

◊ACISHATheus

these temples be well built, it is good and profitable that they pass from the cult of demons to the service of the true God; for so long as the nation may see its ancient places of prayer, so long will it be more disposed to repair thither as a matter of custom to worship the true God.' This conciliatory method worked, and the Kentish King was converted. The Pope sent to Augustine the *pallium*, symbol of authority, giving him power to set up bishops in England, and advising him to choose Canterbury as his temporary archbishopric, and move to London as soon as London became converted. But nothing endures like the provisional, and Canterbury has ever since been the ecclesiastical capital of England.

The conversion of England to Christianity proceeded by local stages, but the headway made by the Church of Rome in England was to cause a clash with the old British Church of the unconquered west. Augustine, having received Papal authority over all the bishops of Britain, summoned the Celtic bishops and required of them three concessions: to celebrate Easter at the same time as other Christians, to use the Roman rite of baptism, and to preach the Gospel to the Anglo-Saxon pagans, which the Celts had always refused to do, because, in their hatred of invaders who had massacred their forbears, they had no wish to save their barbarian souls. The Britons yielded on none of these points and broke with Rome, declaring that they would recognize only their own Primate.

Finally King Oswy of Northumbria, a convert of the Scots, convoked a synod at the abbey of Whitby, where both parties should expound their teachings; and after a long and learned discussion, all present resolved thenceforth to give obedience to the Pope.

So, from the eighth century, the whole of England formed part of the Roman Church. Her Kings looked for support to the Church, not only as believers, but also because of their realization that

from this great body, inheritor of the Imperial traditions, they could derive the hierarchy, the organic form, and the experience which they lacked. Bishops and archbishops were for many years to be the Kings' natural choice as ministers. And the Church likewise upheld the monarchies, being in need of a temporal authority to impose her rules.

The Papacy, too, was strengthened by the foundation in England and Germany of new and obedient Churches. The Eastern Churches were disputing the supremacy of the See of Rome; the Church in France was occasionally too independent, but the English bishops spontaneously requested the constant intervention of the Holy Father, who dispatched to England virtual pro-consuls of the faith, men who stood in relation to ecclesiastical Rome very much as the great organizers of the provinces had stood to Rome as the centre of the Empire. The universality of the Church is nobly displayed in the spectacle of a Greek from Asia Minor, Bishop Theodore of Tarsus, and an Afri-

can, the abbot Hadrian, introducing to England a Latin and Greek library, and setting up in Northumbria monasteries which rivalled in their learning those of Ireland. It was a strange paradox that the Mediterranean culture came to be preserved for the Gauls by Anglo-Saxon monks. At the time when the Saracens were thrusting into the very heart of France, and when the classic age seemed to be ending in Europe, the Venerable Bede, a monk in this almost barbarian land, was writing in Latin his delightful ecclesiastical history of the English nation. Bede himself was the master of Egbert, who was in turn the teacher of Alcuin; and Alcuin it was who, summoned by Charlemagne, checked the intellectual decadence of France.

It was in 787 that the Anglo-Saxon Chronicle recorded the first arrival in England of three shiploads of Norsemen, coming from the 'land of robbers'. Gradually the strength of these enemy fleets increased. In 851, for the first time, the pagans wintered on the Isle of Thanet, and in that

BROOCH. Chased silver disc, Anglo-Saxon art of the 9th century. *British Museum.*

year, too, three hundred of their vessels sailed up the Thames estuary, their crews taking Canterbury and London by storm. In the years that follow, the 'pagans' are given their real name — the Danes; and the Chronicle speaks only of the movements of 'the army', meaning the army of these Norsemen, which at times mustered 10,000 men.

The tribes then inhabiting Sweden, Norway and Denmark, all of one race, were indeed pagans; they had barely been touched by the old Roman Empire, and not at all by that of Christian Rome. But they were not barbarians. Their painted ships, the carved figures of their prows, the literary quality of their sagas, and the complexity of their laws all show that they had been able to create a civilization characteristic of themselves. These Vikings obeyed the chiefs of their bands and were doughty fighters, but did not like fighting for fighting's sake. They gladly used guile instead of force when they could. In their warring and pillaging alike they were traders and, if they found themselves confronted

on the strand by too large a crowd of inhabitants, were quite ready to barter their whale-oil or dried fish for honey or slaves.

There may be matter for surprise in the swift success of these expeditions, originally composed of small bands, and attacking kingdoms which ought to have been able to put up an easy defence. But it should be remembered that the Vikings held the mastery of the sea. Neither Saxons nor Franks had tried to build a fleet. The ruler of the sea is immediately ruler of the islands and can use them as naval bases. The earliest Danish attacks were made on those rich monasteries which the first monks, in their desire for solitude, had placed on islands like Iona and Lindisfarne. The faithful had made gifts of jewels and gold to the monks. The Vikings sacked these treasuries, slew the monks, and occupied the islands. However near these might be to the mainland, the invaders were there impregnable. And in this way Thanet became their base on the English coast, as Noirmoutier did off

[29]

RECONSTRUCTION OF THE HELMET FROM SUTTON
HOO (SUFFOLK). 7th century. This is one of the
objects which came to light when the Sutton
Hoo ship-burial was unearthed. (*British Museum*).

the French coast and the Isle of Man in the Irish
Sea. It must also be borne in mind that mastery of
the sea enabled them to choose their point of attack.
If they found the enemy too strong at one point,
it was easy to re-embark and seek a better chance,
especially as the means of communication among
their victims were primitive and joint understanding
rare. How could a Saxon king oppose them? He
assembled the *fyrd* — a militia of freemen. But
they were a throng of peasants armed with boar-
spears — sometimes even, when the reserves were
called up, with pitchforks — slow to muster, difficult to feed, and unable to stay long under arms
because of the claims of their farming. They were
unworthy opponents for the northern warriors,
who were well armed, wore protective mail and
metal helmets, and wielded the battleaxe to rare
advantage. The only Englishmen capable of standing up to them were the King's companions (the
comitati or *gesiths*), but these were few in number,
and in any case the Danes were constantly improv-
ing their tactics. They soon learned, on landing,
to seize the local horses, equip a mounted body of
soldiery, and then hurriedly build a small fort. The
Saxon rustics and woodmen, who had never built
fortified towns and had lost their seafaring tradition,
and were disunited to boot, let the invader conquer
nearly the whole country. Ireland, then in the
throes of anarchy, was the first to be subjugated;
then Northumbria; then Mercia. Soon Wessex itself

was partly lost, and it looked as if the whole of
England would become a province of the Norsemen's empire.

The Danish invasions resulted directly in hastening the formation in Saxon England of a class
of professional soldiers. There might have been
three solutions to the problem of the country's
defence: (i) the *fyrd*, or mass levy of freemen, to
which the kings long resorted, in spite of the inad-
equacy already indicated; (ii) mercenaries, such as
were used by the later Roman emperors, and again
by Kings Canute and Harold; but the Saxon princes
had no revenues sufficient to maintain such an army;
and (iii) a permanent army of professional warriors,
paid by grants of land in lieu of money payments.
The last was the solution gradually adopted
throughout Europe between the end of the Roman
Empire and the tenth century, because, in default
of strong States, no other method was possible. It
was formerly taught that feudalism was imported
into England by the Normans during the eleventh
century; in point of fact, feudalism was originally
not a deliberately selected system, but the outcome
of manifold natural changes. At the time when
the Saxon tribes reached England, peasant and
fighting-man were one and the same. The freeman
was free because he could fight. When warlike
equipment, after the Danish forays, became too
burdensome for the average peasant, soldiering
could not be anything but the profession of one class.

How came the free husbandman to admit the superiority of that class? Because he could not dispense with it. Attachment to a superior has great advantages in times of trouble: not only is he a well-armed captain, but he defends the title-deeds of his men. So long as the central State is strong — as the Roman Empire had been and the Tudor dynasty was to be — individuals count upon that State and admit their duties towards it. When the State weakens, the individual seeks a protector nearer at hand and more effective, and it is to him that he owes military or pecuniary obligations. A personal bond replaces the abstract. In the welter of the small English kingdoms, endlessly warring with each other and being laid waste by piratical raids, the hapless peasant, the churl or *ceorl*, could maintain his land or preserve his life only by the aid of a well-armed soldier, and agreed to recompense him in kind or services or money for the protection he could give. Later, this working practice was to engender a doctrine: ' No land without a lord.' But in origin feudalism was not a doctrine, but rather, as it has been described, a disintegration of the right of property together with a dismemberment of the rights of the State.

A further effect of the Danish invasions was to end the rivalries between the Anglo-Saxon kingdoms. Pressure from without always imposes a sense of unity on peoples of the same culture, although rent by old grievances. Some of the Anglo-Saxon kings had already styled themselves kings of the whole of England: they were not so powerful as their Norman successors proved to be, but they prepared the ground for the latter. In contrast with Continental developments, they were already turning their nobles into an aristocracy of service rather than of birth. The thanes held their lands from the king because, as warriors, administrators, or prelates, they were his servants. With the king they were nothing, but without them the king could do nothing. He took important decisions only with them, in his Council. The Saxon king was not absolute, any more than the Saxon kingship was absolutely hereditary. And finally, after the conversion to Christianity, the king was the sacred chief, protected and counselled by the Church. He was bound, more than any man, to respect the Church's commands. The image of the just sovereign, duly taking counsel with his wise men for the common weal, was to be firmly engraved upon the English mind, even before the Conquest, by great Saxon sovereigns like Alfred.

Alfred is a sovereign of legend, whose legend is true. This wise and simple man was at once soldier, man of letters, sailor and lawgiver, and he saved Christian England. He had all the virtues of devout kings, and his adventure partakes of the fairy-tale and the romances of chivalry. Like many a romantic hero, he was the youngest son of a king, Æthelwulf, and in those days of invasion he was brought up with the din of battle in his ears and the memory of three of his brothers slain. An excellent horseman and great hunter, he also knew from childhood the desire for learning. ' But, alas ! what he most longed for, training in the liberal arts, was not forthcoming according to his desire, for in that day good scholars were non-existent in the realm of Wessex.' In childhood he had made a pilgrimage to Rome, where the Pope ' hallowed him as king ', and then, back in England, won distinction alongside of his brothers in the struggle against the Danish ' army '. When the last of his family had been slain, Alfred was chosen as King by the Witan, in preference to his nephews, who were too young to rule in time of war.

The first year of his reign saw him in battle against the Danes, but having a mere handful of men he was worsted. He purchased peace from the invaders by payment of a tribute, as the Saxon and Frankish kings had so often done. But success in blackmail was bound to encourage the aggressor in his devices. The Danes occupied the north and the east of the country, and with this conquest behind them a fresh horde, under the pagan king Guthrum, again invaded Wessex. Panic reigned at first. Alfred had to flee almost alone into the Isle of Athelney, where he and his companions built a small fort in the marshes. Near this spot, during the seventeenth century, a beautiful jewel of enamel, gold and crystal, was unearthed, bearing the inscription ' *Ælfred mec Heht gewyrcan* ' (Alfred Fashioned Me). For a whole winter the King remained hidden in the swamps, and the Danes believed that they were masters of Wessex. Towards Easter he left his hiding-place and, at the place known as ' Egbert's Stone ', secretly convoked the *fyrd* of Somerset, Wiltshire and Hampshire. The Saxon peasants were overjoyed to find their king alive, and marched at once with him against the Danes, who were pursued to their strongholds, besieged, and forced by starvation to surrender. Alfred spared their lives, but insisted that the 'army' should evacuate Wessex, and that Guthrum and the leading Danish chiefs should be baptized. Three weeks later Guthrum and twenty-nine other chiefs received baptism, Alfred himself being their sponsor. A pact was then signed, fixing a frontier between Wessex and the Danelaw. The Danes thereafter remained masters of the east and north, and Alfred was able to reign in peace over the territories south of that line.

Alfred's mind was at once original and simple; he transformed the land- and sea-forces as well as justice and education. Increasing the effectives of the army, he summoned to the rank of thane all freemen possessing five hides of land, and those merchants of the ports who had made at least three voyages on their own account, requiring from this lesser nobility services of knighthood. The Anglo-Saxon armies had always been handicapped by their short term of service. Alfred created classes which could be called upon to relieve each other in turn. He ordered the restoration of the fortifications of the old Roman towns, and had the very modern idea of setting up two echelons for defence, mobile and territorial. Knights living near a burgh, or fortified town, were to proceed thither in time of war, whilst those living in the open country formed the mobile force. He created a fleet, the vessels of which, though few, were of his own design and more trustworthy than the ships of the Vikings. He composed a code which incorporated the various rules of life then accepted by his subjects, from the Mosaic commandments to the laws of the Anglo-Saxon kings.

Alfred was hard put to it to revive the pursuit of learning in a country where it had been ruined by wars and woes. He said himself that, when he came to rule his kingdom, it probably contained no man south of the Thames who could translate his prayers into English. The king set up great schools where the sons of nobles or rich freemen might learn Latin, English, horsemanship and falconry. He likewise commanded the preparation of an Anglo-Saxon Chronicle, which should record the chief happenings of each year, and is so valuable to us to-day.

After the death of this great monarch, the prestige of the Anglo-Saxon sovereigns was further enhanced by his successors, trained in his school. They first recovered Mercia, then Northumbria, from the Danes. King Athelstan (924-941) could truthfully style himself 'King of all the Britains'.

ALFRED THE GREAT (848-900). The first king to reign over all England, so the scribe here affirms, he protected the country from the Danish invaders. He was a scholar and has been regarded as the founder of Oxford University. (Corpus Christi College, Cambridge, Ms. 26 fº 129). *Courtauld Institute of Art*.

The Danes settled in East Anglia intermingled with the Anglo-Saxon inhabitants, and began to adopt their language. But peace in England depended on two conditions: a strong king and the cessation of invasions. The piratical forays had apparently slowed down because the Norsemen, in their own lands, were engaged in internal struggles to create the kingdoms of Norway and Denmark. When this period of conflict ended, voyages of adventure were resumed, all the more actively as many malcontents wished to escape from the new-made monarchies. The Anglo-Saxon Chronicle, through the second half of the tenth century, shows the same baleful process at work as in the earlier onslaughts. This new invasion coincided with the reign of an inept king — Ethelred. Instead of defending himself, he reverted to the cowardly method of buying off the invaders for a heavy tribute, to pay which he had to levy a special tax, the Danegeld, a land tax of three or four shillings on each hide of land. The Danes' appetites, of course, were whetted; they became more and more exigent; and after the death of Ethelred's son, Edmund Ironside, who had tried to fight but was murdered, the Witan could find no solution but that of offering the crown to the leader of the invaders, Canute, the twenty-three-year-old brother of the King of Denmark. 'The whole country,' says one chronicler, 'chose Canute, and submitted of its own accord to the man whom it had lately resisted.'

The choice turned out well. Canute had been a stern, even a cruel, foe, but he was intelligent and moderate in his ideas. A foreigner wishing to become an English king, he began by marrying the Queen Dowager, Emma of Normandy, a woman older than himself but who linked him to his new kingdom. He made it clear at once that he would draw no lines between English and Danes. What was more, he put to death those of the English nobles who had betrayed his adversary, Edmund Ironside. How could a man who had deceived his master become a loyal servant? He disbanded his great army and kept only two-score ships, the crews of which, some 3200 men, formed his personal guard. These were the ' housecarls ', picked troops who, contrary to feudal usage, received payment in money and not in land. To pay them Canute continued to levy the Danegeld, and bequeathed to the Conqueror this land-tax, which the people themselves accepted. In 1018, at Oxford, Canute summoned a great assembly at which Danes and English pledged respect to the old Anglo-Saxon laws. An astonishing figure, this princely pirate who transformed himself at the age of twenty-three into a conservative and impartial king. A convert to Christianity, he showed such piety that he declined to wear his crown, and had it suspended above the high altar at Winchester as a sign that God alone is King.

King of England in 1016, and King of Denmark by the death of his brother two years later, Canute conquered Norway in 1030 and, at the cost of surrendering the English rule over much country north of the Tweed, he received the homage of the Scottish king at about the same time. Once again England found her lot involved with the Nordic peoples. But the Anglo-Scandinavian empire lacked the breath of life. Made up of stranger nations, and divided by dangerous seas, it existed only through one man. Canute died at forty, and his creation perished with him. After some struggles between his sons, the Witan again showed its power of choice by reverting to the Saxon dynasty and choosing as King the second son of Ethelred, Edward. These alternations buttressed the authority of the Witan, and royalty, a mere elective magistracy, lost much of its prestige.

The Rollo who obtained the Duchy of Normandy from Charles the Simple in 911, by the verbal agreement of Saint-Clair-sur-Epte, sprang from the same race as the conquerors of the Danelaw. But after a century these two stems of a single breed had diverged so widely that Danes in England were calling Danes in France 'Frenchmen'. The English Danes had encountered a European civilization which was still feebly rooted, and they left their mark upon it; but the Norman Danes, confronted by Rome in the form of France, had imbibed the Latin spirit with surprising speed.

Normandy had no great vassals. None of its lords became strong enough to withstand the Duke, who was directly represented in each district by a viscount; and a viscount was not a mere bailiff of royal domains, but a real governor. The Duke of Normandy levied money taxes and had a genuine financial administration known as the Exchequer. Of all his contemporary sovereigns, he approximated most closely to the head of a modern State.

KING CANUTE (995-1035) AND QUEEN AELGYFU. Crowned by an angel, the Danish king places a golden cross on the altar of Newminster Abbey, Winchester, at the church's dedication. Christ, with the Blessed Virgin and St. Peter, presides at the ceremony. (*British Museum*, Ms. Stowe 944, *Liber vitae* of Newminster, 1016-1020, f° 6).

The Normans adopted the ceremonial and hierarchy of Continental chivalry much sooner than did the English. And in England, feudalism had developed in Europe through the need for local defence, but by the eleventh century it was regulated with more precision. Under the Duke of Normandy stood the barons, who in turn had power over the knights, a knight being the owner of land the tenure of which involved military service. At his baron's summons, the knight had to present himself armed and mounted, and to remain in the field for forty days. The baron himself had to answer his Duke's call to arms, bringing with him the knights dependent on him.

But how came it that a Duke of Normandy, in the eleventh century, conceived the idea of making himself King of England? After the death of Canute's ineffectual progeny, the Witan had proclaimed as king the natural heir of the Saxon sovereigns, Edward, named the Confessor by reason of his great piety, of whom his biographer naïvely remarks that he never spoke during divine service unless he had a question to propound. Edward the Confessor seems to have been a gentle, virtuous man, but childish and lacking in will. Despite a vow of chastity he took in marriage the daughter of the most powerful of his *ealdormen*, Godwin, formerly a local lord but who had become predominant in Wessex. Edward's upbringing in Normandy had made him more Norman than English; he spoke French; he was surrounded by Norman consellors; he chose a Norman, Robert of Jumièges, as Archbishop of Canterbury. He was visited by his cousin from Rouen, William the Bastard (later

to be known as the Conqueror), who always maintained that Edward, during this visit, promised him the succession to the throne. Edward could not in fact offer a crown which was dependent, not on himself, but on the choice of the Witan; but it is possible that he made the offer to William, as he also did, apparently, to Harold, son of Godwin, and to Sweyn, King of Denmark. The kindly busybody Edward has been compared to a rich uncle who promises his fortune to several nephews. He had vowed to make a pilgrimage to Rome, but received a dispensation from the Holy Father on condition that he founded an abbey. He accordingly built one at Westminster, and moved his own residence near to this, from its old position in the City of London. This act of piety of the Confessor's had great and unpredictable consequences, for the removal of the royal palace from the City fostered an independent spirit among the citizens of London which, in time, exercised a great influence on the nation's history. Edward the Confessor died in the summer of 1066, leaving memories cherished by his people.

William the Bastard, Duke of Normandy, was the natural son of Duke Robert and the daughter of a tanner in Falaise, Arletta by name. Acknowledged by his father, he succeeded him. A man of dogged will, he knew how to hide his feelings and bide his time in days of failure. When his resolve to marry Matilda, daughter of Count Baldwin of Flanders, was countered by the Pope's ban on a union within forbidden degrees of kinship, William was patient, and then forced the marriage. He stormed against Lanfranc, the prior of Bec, for

WILLIAM THE CONQUEROR'S SHIPS UNDER CONSTRUCTION. Shipwrights at work on Viking-type vessels, as depicted in the famous Bayeux tapestry, woven c. 1077. (Musée de la Reine Mathilde, Bayeux) *Louis Laniepce, Editions du Chêne.*

KING EDGAR OFFERING UP THE FOUNDATION CHARTER ▶ OF THE ABBEY AT WINCHESTER. The king (944-975) is flanked by the Blessed Virgin and St. Peter while Christ is enthroned above. (*British Museum*, Cotton Ms. Vespasianus A. VIII, f° 2 v°).

venturing to condemn this defiance of a pontifical decree, but then made use of the same Lanfranc to negotiate a pardon from the Pope, which in the end he obtained. During the parleys this highly skilful prior of Bec had become intimate with the most powerful man in Rome, the monk Hildebrand, who was later to become Pope Gregory VII. Two ambitions were coming into harmony: William aspired to the crown of England, and in this great project the Pope could help him; Hildebrand hoped to make the Pope the suzerain and judge of all the princes of Christendom, and this candidate for a throne offered pledges to Rome which a lawful king would have declined to give.

What claims had William to the English crown? Genealogically, none. The Duke of Normandy's only relative in common with Edward the Confessor had been a great-aunt, and he himself was a bastard. Besides, the English crown was elective, and at the disposal only of the Witan. Edward's promise was a poor agreement, as Edward had promised to various claimants something which he had no right to pledge. But Lanfranc and William, who always subtly lent a moral covering to their desires, had engineered a diplomatic machination against the only possible rival, Harold, son of Godwin, and brother-in-law of Edward. The hapless Harold had been made prisoner by the Count of Ponthieu after being shipwrecked on his coast, but was freed by William and conveyed to Rouen. There the Duke let him understand that he had full liberty, on the sole condition that he should do homage to him and become in the feudal sense 'his' man. In this ceremony Harold had to give an oath, the exact details of which are unknown. It may have been to marry William's daughter, or to support William's claim to the English throne. Whatever it was, he swore something which afterwards was held against him.

When Edward died, however, the Witan showed no hesitation between a bold and well-beloved lord, Harold, and a mere child, Egbert's only descendant, Edgar the Atheling. Within twenty-four hours Harold, the elected King, was crowned in the new Abbey of Westminster. There had been no question at all of William. But immediately a well-staged propagandist campaign was launched in Europe, and especially at Rome, at the instigation of William and Lanfranc. The Duke of Normandy called upon Christendom to take cognizance of the felonious act whereof he was the victim, and because he had undertaken to adopt the ideas of Hildebrand and to reform the Church of England he was supported by Rome. The Pope declared in William's favour, and, in token of his blessing on the enterprise, sent him a consecrated banner and a ring containing a hair of St. Peter.

For so difficult a campaign the ordinary forty days' service of the Norman knights would not have sufficed. Harold's house-carls formed an excellent and dangerous body of troops. Everything looked hazardous. But William had the knack of transforming an act of international brigandage into

◀ KING EDWARD THE CONFESSOR (1001-1066) giving instructions to Harold who was to succeed him. Like most western kings at this period he wears a lily-crown and a sceptre to match. From the Bayeux tapestry. *Mansell Collection, London.*

BATTLE OF HASTINGS, confronting the Normans (*Franci* in the tapestry) and English, October 1066. The English take flight, as the final inscription on the tapestry records. *Louis Laniepce, Editions du Chêne.*

a real crusade. And a profitable one: to all his Norman vassals he promised money and lands in England. Adventurous barons came from Anjou, from Brittany and Flanders, even from Apulia and Aragon. It was a slow mobilization, but that mattered little as the fleet had to be built before embarkation could be started. Early in September 1066, the fleet of 750 vessels was ready. For a fortnight longer William was delayed by contrary winds; but as often happens in human history, this unwelcomed delay brought him an easy victory. For in the meantime there had arrived on the Northumbrian coast the King of Norway with three hundred galleys. At the bidding of the traitorous Tostig, Harold's brother, he too had arrived to claim the crown of England. Harold, who was awaiting William off the Isle of Wight, had to hasten north with his house-carls. He inflicted total defeat and destruction on the Norwegians, but on the morrow of his victory learned that William had landed unopposed on the shore of Pevensey, on September 28.

By forced marches Harold came south. Things were starting ill for him. His guard had been broken by the clash with the Norwegians. The north-country thanes had done their fighting and showed little ardour to follow him. The bishops were perturbed by the Papal protection granted to William. The country contained a 'Norman party', formed of all the Frenchmen introduced by Edward the Confessor. The only battle of the war was fought near Hastings, where two types of army were confronted. Harold's men formed the traditional mounted infantry of their country, riding when on the move and dismounting to fight. The Normans, on the other hand, charged on horseback, supported by archers. In the ensuing massacre Harold himself fell.

William's subsequent military and diplomatic moves throw light on his character. Instead of attacking London directly, he encircled the town, surrounding it with a belt of ravaged country, and awaited the inevitable surrender. Instead of proclaiming himself King of England, he waited for the crown to be offered to him, and even then made a show of hesitation. He tried to 'put his possible adversaries in the wrong', and wished to appear in all men's eyes as the lawful sovereign. At last, on Christmas Day, 1066, he was crowned in the Abbey of Westminster.

II

The French Kings

William I to Henry III, 1066-1272

THE POSITION of William in England on the morrow of his coronation was very ambiguous. He sought, *de jure*, to be the lawful sovereign, sprung of the old royal stock, preserving continuity, reluctant to innovate; *de facto*, he was a conqueror, with a train of five or six thousand grasping knights to whom he had promised land, which would have to be provided at the expense of existing landowners. But how were these few Normans, isolated on foreign shores in a time of slow and difficult communications, to maintain themselves and rule? The conquerors had a number of advantages. In William they had a born leader, who brought from Normandy sound experience in sovereignty; local opposition they met, but no national resistance; and above all they had an impressive mastery in armed force. After the defeat of Harold's house-carls, no army in England could again oppose the feudal cavalry of the Normans. Further, they were skilled in the building of strongholds, either on hills or, in flat country, on artificial *mottes*, which before the days of cannon were impregnable. It was not long before the hapless English peasants, in all the march counties, were giving forced labour to raise these earthen mounds and crenellated towers which would then keep them in subjection. On these artificial *mottes* the first building had to be of wood, because the soft earth could not support a heavier structure; but stone replaced this when the earth had become more solid. But William, a prudent monarch, authorized such building only to house royal garrisons, as at the Tower of London or in the remoter regions of the north and west, where he installed trusty men. The lords of the central parts were forbidden to own fortified castles, and William was a man to make his veto respected.

It was characteristic of the Conqueror to affix a mask of justice to the most arbitrary actions. To distribute the promised demesnes to his Normans, he had to rob the vanquished; but he robbed them with due propriety. He first deprived traitors of their land, traitors being those who had fought for Harold — a legal fiction which just held water because he, William, declared himself to be the lawful sovereign. He then took advantage of the numerous revolts, and annexed new territories for the Crown. With appalling severity he crushed a rising in the north, burning villages far and near, and then raised the superb castle of Durham to dominate that ravaged land, flanking it with a cathedral worthy of his abbeys at Caen. In the end, the last of the Saxon rebels, Hereward the Wake, was overcome, and he organized the kingdom. For himself he kept 1,422 of the manors which had become 'lawfully' vacant, and this ensured him unrivalled military power and wealth. Other domains were much smaller. The unit of land was the 'knight's fee', which sent one knight to the king in time of war. William created numerous domains counted as from one to five knights' fees, the holders of which were to form as it were a feudal 'plebs', which the great lords could not draw into league against the king. The greater domains themselves were not in single hands, but made up of manors scattered throughout the country. Thus, from the first, there was no suzerainty comparable to that exercised in France by a Count of Anjou or a Duke of Brittany. After conquest and partition, the country was held by about five thousand Norman knights, who were at once landed proprietors and an army of occupation. In principle the loyal English had the same rights as these Frenchmen; in practice, all important posts were held by Normans. The indispensable Lanfranc, summoned from Caen, became Archbishop of Canterbury.

WILLIAM THE CONQUEROR CROWNED IN WESTMINSTER ABBEY. The coronation took place on Christmas Day, 1066, and was recaptured by a Flemish artist working c. 1470. (*British Museum*, Ms. 15 E. IV, f° 23 b). *Hachette.*

HEDINGHAM CASTLE (ESSEX). The massive style of architecture imported by the Normans is evident in this aerial photograph. *Aerofilms Ltd.*

The Norman king had a Court, the *Concilium* or *Curia Regis*, which corresponded roughly to the Saxon Witan. Three times a year, as Alfred or Edward the Confessor had done in days gone by, William 'wore his crown' at Westminster, Winchester and Gloucester, and there held 'deep converse with his wise men'. But whereas the Saxon Witan in the days of the powerful *ealdormen* had been masters of the king, the Norman Council generally confined itself to listening and approval. Barons, bishops and abbots attended, not as a national duty, but as a feudal duty to their suzerain. These convocations were irregular: sometimes the Council consisted of a hundred and fifty prelates and magnates, at others the king was content to consult on some question with only those of his counsellors who happened to be present when it arose. This lesser Council also varied in composition. But the presence of the sovereign sufficed to make any decision valid.

The Norman Conquest was not followed by a ruthless breach with the past. On the contrary, William the Conqueror, who regarded himself as the heir of the Saxon kings, was glad to make appeal to their laws and judgments. He preserved all such of the Saxon institutions as served his plans. The *fyrd* was to become a useful weapon against the barons when the peasantry came to regard themselves as allies of the Crown — an alliance which was soon reached. In the Saxon sheriffs the Norman king recognized his viscounts, and found an instrument of government. He therefore appointed a sheriff for each shire, entrusting him with the collection of taxes, the administration of the court of justice in the shire (which now was called the county), and in general with the representation of the central power. The sheriff punished abuses of power and noted signs of popular discontent. The whole policy of the Norman monarchs was one of checking the barons by securing the support of the freemen, until later the people and barons in unison came to curb the power of the Crown. That alliance was a factor in the growth of parliamentary institutions.

It would be misleading, not to say crude, if we conceived the image of a royal power constantly concerned with checkmating rebellious lords. Hostility could not have been a normal relation between

William and his companions, as he needed them and they needed him. Some of the baronage may have been turbulent, but most of them were loyal, and helped the king to suppress rebellion. A period of general revolt, as at the time of Magna Carta, meant that the king had overstepped his rights, and that the barons were acting in self-defence, sometimes with the support of the knights and burgesses. But these troublous times were brief, and although they fill the pages of history with their hubbub, they must not blind us to the long, tranquil years during which king, nobles, and common people behaved as members of a united body, and during which a civilization was being unobtrusively built up.

For a king to be able to impose his will on a warlike nobility impatient of all tramels, two conditions are essential: the sovereign must have armed force, and must possess an assured revenue. In his opposition to the barons William could count on the main body of the knights, on his own vassals, and before long on the *fyrd*. At Salisbury, in 1086, he took oaths of homage directly from the vassals of his vassals, so that a troth pledged to the king outweighed any other loyalty.

As regards revenue, the Norman king was well provided. He had, to start with, the revenue of his private domain. William's lands brought him eleven thousand pounds annually, twice as much as Edward the Confessor had enjoyed, and to this were added the feudal revenues (' reliefs ') due from vassals; ' aids ' in the case of crusade, ransom, marriage of the suzerain's daughter, entry into chivalry of an eldest son; ' wardship ' of the property of minors; the Danegeld, a legacy of the Saxon kings; payments made by burgesses of towns, and by Jews; and finally, fines. The exchequer accounts show that under William's successors these fines were numerous, and sometimes curious. We read how Walter de Caucy paid fifteen pounds for leave to marry when and whom he might choose; how William de Mandeville gave the king twenty thousand marks to be able to marry Isabel Countess of Gloucester; how the wife of Hugo de Neville gave the King two hundred pounds for leave to lie with her husband (who must have been a prisoner of the king). Lastly, the king sold liberties: under Stephen, London gave a hundred silver marks to choose her sheriffs; the Bishop of Salisbury gave a palfrey to have a market in his city; some fishermen paid for the right to salt their catch; and the profits of justice increased with the prestige of the Royal courts.

The Conqueror had previously pledged his word to the Papacy for the reform of the Church in England. With the help of Lanfranc, even greater as statesman than churchman, he kept his word. The ignorant and licentious clergy had lost the respect of the faithful; priests wore lay clothes and drank like lords; bishops used unlawful means of procuring advancement. Orders came from Rome, where Hildebrand had become Pope Gregory VII in 1073, that Lanfranc should compel the celibacy of the clergy, that the investiture of bishops should remain in Papal hands, and that the King of England, who owed the throne to him, should do him homage. Lanfranc and William moved cautiously. It would have been dangerous to impose strict celibacy on the Saxon priests; allowances would have to be made for the customs and moral standards of this newly acquired country. Lanfranc disallowed the celebration of further marriages of priests, forbade bishops and canons to have wives, but authorized parish priests already married to remain so. He admitted that only Rome could depose bishops, but maintained the elective principle, and that of investiture by the Crown.

The King, however, writing a ' firm and respectful ' letter, declined to regard himself as the Pope's vassal. The conflict between Church and State was already taking shape.

William's prompt affirmation of his conqueror's authority over nobles and ecclesiastics laid the foundations of a great monarchy. But he was not an absolute sovereign. His coronation oath bound him to maintain the Anglo-Saxon laws and usages; he had to respect the feudal rights granted to his companions; he feared and revered the Church. William the Conqueror could not conceive the idea of absolute monarchy as it was later envisaged by Charles I or Louis XIV. The Middle Ages did not even imagine a State in the modern sense of the word; a country's equilibrium, as they saw it, was not ensured by a central keystone, but by a network of coherent and mutually strengthening local rights.

The economic unit of feudalism was the manor, just as its political unit was the knight's holding of land, sending a single horseman to the King's

WILLIAM THE CONQUEROR PRE-
SENTING FIEFS TO HIS NEPHEW,
ALAIN LE ROUX, COUNT OF
BRITTANY. The count subsequently became Duke of Brit-
anny and Count of Rich-
mond. This illustration is
from a 13th century manu-
script. (*British Museum. Reg-
istrum honoris* of Richmond,
Faustina B. VII, fº 42 vº).

army. The size of the manor varied, but in many cases it corresponded to a present-day village. Frequently manors were separated by intervening forests or heaths, connected to their neighbours only by tracks which winter made impassable. In the centre was the hall, later the castle, belonging to the lord of the manor and surrounded by his farm or private land. When the lord held several manors, he went from one to another to make use on the spot of the dues paid to him in kind. In his absence he was represented by a seneschal or bailiff. The communal fields and meadows preserved the same aspect as in the times of the Saxon masters. The villeins were obliged to have all their corn ground by the lord's mill. The peasants were headed by the reeve of their own election, who, caught between the bailiff and the villagers, led a difficult life. Many local disputes were judged by the manor court, which was held every three weeks in the hall, or under an oak tree traditionally so used, and was presided over by the lord of the

manor or his representatives. In principle only trifling offences were there dealt with: few manors had been granted the right of trying more serious crimes. Theoretically a manor was supposed to be self-sufficing, having its own cordwainer, its wheelwright, its weavers. The weavers spun the wool. Nothing was bought from outside but salt, iron or steel tools, and millstones. To pay for these imports the manor exported wool and hides. All other produce was locally consumed, except where a market was near at hand.

The position of the villeins might seem to our own day to be none too happy. The villein was bound to the soil, and could not go away if he were discontented. He was sold with the property. Even an abbot did not scruple to buy and sell men for twenty shillings apiece. The villein could give his daughters in marriage only with the lord's consent, and had to pay for that. If he died the lord could claim a death-duty of the best head of cattle, or the most handsome object, left by the dead man; and after the lord, the parish priest had the right to claim his share of the heritage. Furthermore, the lord could levy an annual 'tallage', of varying value, from his serfs, exacting from them about half of the peasants' time. Finally, every lord was bound to respect manorial usages, the traditional rights of the village which the peasants themselves undertook to keep alive. At a later date all these rights and obligations were inscribed in the manorial records. About the middle of the thirteenth century it became customary to hand to tenants on their request a copy of the pages in that register touching upon their lands and rights. Those in possession of such copies were termed 'copyholders', in contrast to the 'freeholders', whose property was absolute and unencumbered.

An outstanding grievance of the native English against the Conqueror and his Normans was the creation of royal forests. As Duke of Normandy, William had had vast forests where he could hunt the stag and boar. As King of England he wished to provide for his favourite pastime, and not far from Winchester, his capital, he planted the New Forest, thus destroying (according to the chroniclers) sixty villages, many fertile fields and chur-

ches, and ruining thousands of inhabitants. The figures seem exaggerated, but those royal forests were certainly a lasting grievance. In the twelfth century they covered a third of the area of the kingdom, and were protected by ruthless laws. In William's day anyone killing a hind or a stag had his eyes put out. To kill boars or hares meant mutilation. At a later date, the slaying of a deer in the royal forest was punished by hanging.

At first the Conquest hardly changed the lot of the small Saxon towns. Those which resisted were dismantled; here and there King's men razed houses to make room for a Norman keep; but, as amends, the Conqueror's peace allowed merchants to grow rich. The liberties of London had been prudently confirmed. New craftsmen came over from Normandy in the train of the armies, among them Jewish traders. The position of these last could only be precarious in a Christian community. As their Sabbath did not coincide with the Christians' Sunday, they could not easily undertake farm work, or even shopkeeping; and as ordinary livelihoods were thus barred to them, they sought refuge in money-lending, a trade forbidden to Catholics by the Church. Doubly hated as enemies of Christ and as professional creditors, these hapless crea-

SCENES FROM 12TH CENTURY LIFE. On the left, a king and his ministers supervise the weighing out of gold; on the right, a king and queen, enthroned, receive petitions. (*Trinity College, Cambridge*. 12th century manuscript R. 17. I, fᵒ 230).

THE ST. NICHOLAS FONT. The font, in Winchester Cathedral, is adorned with bas-reliefs depicting scenes from the life of St. Nicholas, sculpted in dark marble from Tournai by Belgian artists. *National Buildings Record*.

tures, living in special quarters, the Jewries, were the natural victims of any wave of popular anger. Their sole protector was the King, to whom they belonged, body and goods, like serfs. The royal city of Winchester was the only one in which a Jew could be a citizen, and was styled the English Jerusalem. The title deeds of Jews were kept in a special room of the Palace of Westminster, and their debts, like the King's, were privileged. In return for this protection, the king called for money from the Jews when he required it.

For twenty-one years William reigned over England with effective firmness, 'wearing his crown' thrice a year, at Christmas and Easter and Whitsun, combating the overweening barons, hunting the stag, and crossing occasionally to Normandy to guard against the encroachments of the King of France. But during one of these campaigns, when he had just regained Mantes, this great man was mortally injured. His horse stumbled, and a blow from the pommel of his saddle bruised him internally, from which he died. He was buried in the Church of St. Stephen at Caen, in only a small concourse. Of his three sons, whom he had not associated with his rule, the second was his favourite; and to him, William Rufus (so called because of his red complexion), he left the English crown. To Robert, the eldest, whom he held in scant esteem, he reluctantly bequeathed Normandy, declaring that with such a sovereign the Duchy would fare ill. Henry, the youngest, received only 5000 silver marks. Rufus embarked for England with a letter from his father to Lanfranc, who agreed to crown him at Westminster. This time there was no election by the Council, and the barons simply accepted their king from the archbishop. That was a sign of the growing power of the Church.

William Rufus was no fool, but he was a boor. This fat, clumsy, brutal youth, stammering his sarcasms, cared only for soldiers. At a time of universal piety he flaunted his dislike of priests, and took a crude delight in blasphemy. His delight was in the Christmas and Easter banquets that he gave his barons, to heighten the splendour of which he employed the London craftsmen for two years building Westminster Hall, then regarded as the most magnificent building in the country and destined, in the reconstructed form in which Richard II left it, to become the seat of the Courts of Justice. The Court of William Rufus was 'a Mecca of adventurers', and to maintain the hundreds of mercenary knights from overseas he levied taxes contrary to usage, in spite of his coronation oath to respect the laws of the land. 'But who can keep to all he promises?' he said cynically.

Conflict became inevitable between the Roman Church, as reorganized by Gregory VII, and the lay monarchies. The Pope's ambition, to reform the Church so as to fit it for reforming the world, was a noble one. The clergy, he felt, had lost their prestige through excessive contact with secular society. If a churchman were dependent on lords or kings, he could not combat sin or impiety with the same uncompromising courage as if his allegiance were only to his spiritual heads. This was the underlying significance of the so-called conflict of investitures which disturbed England and Europe. A bishop had two aspects; he was a Prince of the Church, and as such depended only on the Pope and God; but he was also a temporal lord, the owner of great fiefs, and so had to do homage to the king, his suzerain. Many bishops felt humiliated by this temporal subordination, but if they had refused homage after their election, the king, for his part, would have withheld the episcopal lands. A Papal surrender in this matter of the investitures would have endangered the Church, by placing it in the hands of creatures of the lay power. If the king yielded, he would be encouraging within his realm a rival power which he could not control. The conflict of investitures may not have been the first clash of Church with State, as the State did not yet exist; but it was a clash between Church and Monarchy, both claiming to be creations of the same God.

During his lifetime, Lanfranc's prestige maintained the balance. After his death in 1089, the King tried not to replace him, and did not nominate an Archbishop of Canterbury. He thus retained the archiepiscopal revenues, a device which he found so profitable that when he died eleven great abbeys and ten bishoprics were vacant. But as regards the see of Canterbury the strongest pressure was put upon William by the Church, and by the barons, to make him appoint Anselm, prior of Bec-Hellouin. Anselm was a saintly man, to whom earthly life appeared as a swift, empty dream,

GEOFFREY, COUNT OF ANJOU AND
MAINE (1113-1151), known also
as Geoffrey Plantagenet because
of the broom-sprig (genêt) he
was known to sport on his hat.
His son by Matilda, the antago-
nist of King Stephen, became
Henry II. The lions on the shield
were to figure in Edward I's coat
of arms. Limoges champlevé
enamel from his tomb in St.
Julien's Cathedral, Le Mans,
c. 1155. (Musée Municipal du
Mans). *Rhys Dorvyne - Hachette.*

meaningless except as preparatory to eternal life. Only a grave illness made the King consent in a moment of fear to invest Anselm, himself openly reluctant. But Anselm had the firmness as well as the modesty of a saint, and was resolved to have the dignity of the Church respected in his own person. Between King and Archbishop began a struggle, now hidden, now open. Rufus did not disguise his hatred of this Archbishop who looked him in the eyes and blamed him for his vices. Anselm challenged the King by recognizing Pope Urban, against whom the Germanic emperor had tried to set up an anti-Pope, and after this defiance had to flee the country. Once again the see of Canterbury was left vacant and the King drew its revenues, but he had uneasy dreams, and for all his sarcasms was concerned about his salvation. He had no time to ensure it, for in the year 1100, when hunting in the New Forest, he was killed by an arrow piercing his heart.

Prince Henry, the Conqueror's third son, left his brother's body where it lay and hurried off to Winchester to secure the keys of the royal treasury. He arrived just in time, as almost immediately there appeared the treasurer, William of Breteuil, who claimed it in the name of Robert, Duke of Normandy, the lawful heir. But at headlong speed Henry arranged his own proclamation as king by a small group of barons, and was crowned by the Bishop of London in default of an archbishop: all of which was irregular, but accepted. Robert was far away, a foreigner, and ill-famed. Henry was reported to be energetic and instructed, especially in matters of law. Furthermore, he won popularity immediately on his accession by granting a charter, by which he pledged himself to respect ' the laws of Edward the Confessor, to abolish the evil customs introduced by his brother Rufus, never to leave ecclesiastical benefices vacant, and to raise no more irregular feudal taxation.' These first actions of his roused confidence; he recalled Anselm, and, to crown all, married a wife of the blood royal — Edith-Matilda, daughter of Malcolm III of Scotland and a descendant of Ethelred. This ' native ' marriage delighted the Anglo-Saxon people, who gladly hailed the King's eldest son as ' the Atheling ', the ancestral style of the firstborn of the Saxon kings. After this marriage, which augured well for the fusion of the two races,

Henry's position in England was so strengthened that revolt on the part of Robert's partisans was useless. In 1106 Henry conquered Normandy by a victory at Tinchebrai, an English victory gained on Norman soil — a revenge, so to speak, for Hastings. He made a peace of compromise with the Papacy, after long discussion of the investitures, renouncing his claim to hand personally to the bishop the ring and crozier, but winning his counterclaim, that the duly invested bishop should do homage to the sovereign for his temporal fiefs.

After his victory over the insurgent barons, Henry I enjoyed a tranquil reign, and he took advantage of the calm to organize his realm. He was conspicuous as a jurist, and, thanks to him, the royal courts of justice were developed at the expense of the feudal. Nearly every crime was henceforward regarded as a breach of the King's Peace, and accordingly brought before the King's courts. The jury, as yet in its infancy, an institution borrowed by the Normans from the Franks, represented an ancient method of determining facts by the evidence of those who were capable of knowing the truth. Gradually the Norman and Angevin kings came to muster a jury to decide questions of fact in all criminal cases. Then individuals requested the service of the royal jury. Step by step the feudal jurisdiction of the lords was supplanted by local courts, presided over at first by the sheriff and then more and more by judges of the royal court, with a jury's assistance.

The central administration, meanwhile, was becoming more complex. There were a Justiciar, a Treasurer, and a Chancellor. Originally the Chancellor was only the head of the royal chapel, but as the clerks of this chapel could write, they were entrusted with the copying and editing of documents, with the result that the importance of their chief was speedily enhanced. He was given charge of the Royal Seal. (It was not until the days of King John that, side by side with this, the Privy Seal, entrusted to the Keeper of the Privy Seal, was established). Financial affairs were administered by the Court of Exchequer, which met at Winchester at Easter, Whitsun and Michaelmas. All the sheriffs of the country had to submit their accounts to it, and they sat there at a large table — the Chancellor, the Bishop of Winchester, and a clerk to the Chancellor who, in the absence of

BAMBURGH CASTLE (NORTHUMBERLAND). Bamburgh was the capital of Saxon Bernicia, cradle of many kings. A fort existed on the site, 150 feet above the sea, in 547 and was rebuilt in 1150. *Aero Pictorial Ltd.*

the latter on other duties, came in time to take his place and became known as Chancellor of the Exchequer. (The covering of the table was marked out with horizontal lines crossed by seven vertical lines, for pence, shillings, pounds, tens of pounds, hundreds, thousands, and ten thousands of pounds. This squared design gave the name ' Exchequer ').

The King's Peace and the new dynasty had never been so strong and secure when an unpredictable accident ruined all hopes. William the Atheling, the heir to the throne, was returning from Normandy with a band of his friends, in a vessel called the *Blanche Nef*, which sank as a result of the faulty steering of a drunken pilot. When King Henry was told next day, he fell in a swoon of grief. At no price would he leave his kingdom to Robert's son, William of Normandy, whom he hated, and in 1126 he named as his successor his daughter Matilda, widow of the German Emperor Henry V. To ensure the loyalty of the barons, he

made the Great Council do homage to her. Then, to protect the frontiers of Normandy, he married the future Queen of England to Geoffrey of Anjou, the Duchy's most powerful neighbour. This foreign marriage was not liked by the English, many of whom regretted having plighted their oath to a woman. It was obvious that the death of Henry I would bring troubles, and when he died there followed nineteen years of anarchy. Another claimant rose against Matilda — Stephen of Blois, grandson of the Conqueror through his daughter Adela. The citizens of London, with a small band of barons in Stephen's pay, proclaimed him King, and the country was split into partisans of Matilda or of Stephen. Everywhere fortified castles sprang up, unsanctioned by the Crown. The city of London, copying new Continental customs, assumed extensive powers of self-government. The untrammelled lords became simply bandits, employing the peasants on forced building labour and

CANTERBURY CATHEDRAL (KENT). Since St. Augustine converted King Ethelbert in 597 and founded this episcopal see, Canterbury has been the seat of the English Primate. For many centuries it was the goal of pilgrimage to the shrine of St. Thomas à Becket, murdered within its walls by Henry II's barons. The style is perpendicular, a form of late Gothic. *Radio Times Hulton Picture Library.*

filling their completed castles with hardened and harsh old soldiers. Resistance was met with monstrous tortures: men were hung head down and roasted like joints, and others thrown, like fairytale heroes, into dungeons crawling with vipers and toads. But strangely enough, these bandit noblemen, fearful of damnation, were at the same time endowing monasteries. Under Stephen alone, over one hundred monastic houses were built. Land passed out of cultivation; towns were put to sack; religion was the only refuge left. Never had men prayed so much; hermits settled in the woods; Cistercian monks cleared forests in the north, and London saw new churches rising everywhere. At last, in 1152, Matilda's young son, Henry, whose father's death had left him Count of Anjou, came to an understanding with Stephen. The Church this time usefully arbitrated, and formulated a treaty which was signed at Wallingford and confirmed at Westminster. Stephen adopted Henry, gave him a share in the administration of the realm, and made him his heir. Peace and unity throughout the land were sworn to by Stephen and Henry, the bishops and earls and all men of substance. In 1154, Stephen died and Henry became king.

Henry Plantagenet, who thus became Henry II of England, came of a powerful family with a dark history. His Angevin ancestors included Fulke the Black, who was reputed to have had his wife burnt alive and forced his son to crave his forgiveness crouching on all fours and saddled like a horse. One of his grandmothers, the Countess of Anjou, had the name of being a witch, who once flew off through a church window. Henry himself was a hard man, of 'volcanic force', but cultivated and charming in manner. A stocky, bull-necked youth, with close-cropped red hair, he had taken the fancy of Queen Eleanor of France when he came to do homage to King Louis VII for Maine and Anjou. She obtained a divorce, and two months later, at the age of twenty-seven, married this lad of nineteen, to whom she brought as dowry the great Duchy of Aquitaine, which included Limousin, Gascony and Périgord, with suzerain rights over Auvergne and Toulouse. Through his mother, Henry II already owned the Duchy of Normandy, and through his father, Maine and Anjou; he was becoming more powerful in France than King Louis himself. Of his thirty-five years on the throne he was to spend only thirteen in England. He was in France continuously from 1158 to 1163. In fact, he was an emperor, viewing

England as only a province. He was French in tastes and speech, but this Frenchman was one of the greatest of English kings.

Like his ancestor the Conqueror, Henry II was helped by being a foreigner in England. He had energy, he was zealous for order, and he came to a country whose feudalism had become anarchy; he would hew the living rock and restore the Norman order. The rebels dared not resist the master of so many provinces abroad, from which he could bring armed forces if need be, and Henry forced them to pull down or dismantle the castles built without licence. Taxes were again collected and the sheriffs were made subject to dismissal. The feudal term of forty days' service was inadequate for the Angevin ruler's campaigns in Aquitaine and Normandy, and for this was substituted the tax known as scutage, which enabled him to pay mercenaries. This left many of the English nobility to become unused to war, and they took to jousts and tourneys instead of real fighting. The bellicose lord hardly survived, except in the Border counties, and thereafter it was in the counties palatine, facing Scotland and Wales, that all the great risings broke out.

When the young King from abroad came to the throne, Theobald, Archbishop of Canterbury, was eager to see a trusty man at the King's side, and commended to him one of his clerks, Thomas Becket, who won Henry's favour and was in time made Chancellor. Becket was a pure-blooded Norman of thirty-eight, the son of a rich City merchant. Of gentle upbringing, he had become clerk to Archbishop Theobald after the ruin of his family. As Becket's gifts seemed administrative rather than priestly, the kindly-disposed Archbishop handed him on to the King, and immediately the sovereign and servant became inseparables. Henry valued this young minister, a good horseman and falconer, able to bandy learned jokes with him, and astoundingly able in his work. But success made the Chancellor proud and powerful. Campaigning in the Vexin in 1160, he took seven hundred horsemen of his own retinue, twelve hundred more hired by himself, and four thousand soldiers: a veritable private army. Becket himself, notwithstanding his priesthood, dismounted a knight in single combat during this campaign.

On Theobald's death, Henry II resolved to give the see of Canterbury to Becket. There was some grumbling from the monks to whom the election properly belonged; Becket was not a monk, and seemed to be more soldier than priest. The Chancellor himself, showing the King his lay vestments, said laughingly that Henry was choosing a very handsome costume to put at the head of his Canterbury monks. Then, when he had accepted, he warned the King that he would hate his Archbishop more than he would love him, because Henry was arrogating to himself an authority in Church matters which he, the Primate, would not accept. There is much that is remarkable in this great temporal lord who turned ascetic immediately on becoming an archbishop. Henceforth he devoted his life to prayer and good works. On his dead body were found a hair shirt and the scars of self-discipline. The see of Canterbury had made the gentle Anselm into a militant prelate, and of Becket, the King's servant and Chancellor, it made a rebel, then a saint.

The line of conflict between King and Church lay no longer on the question of investitures, but on the analogous one of the ecclesiastical courts. In separating civil and religious courts, the Conqueror and Lanfranc had wished to reserve for the latter only cases of conscience. But the Church had gradually made all trials into religious cases. If property rights were violated, this became perjury, a case of conscience. Accused parties were only too glad to have recourse to this milder jurisdiction, which sentenced men neither to death nor mutilation, seldom even to prison, as the Church had not its own prisons, but to penance and fines. The clerks were answerable only to tribunals of their own category, and so a murderous clerk nearly always got off easily. This was a grave matter when even a lawyer's scrivener was a clerk in the ecclesiastical sense. Any scamp might enter the minor orders and avoid the law of the land. Furthermore, the court of Rome reserved the right of calling an ecclesiastical case, and then the fines were not paid to the Exchequer. If this intrusion into lay matters had not been checked, the King would no longer have been master in England. Henry II insisted that a clerk found guilty by an ecclesiastical court should be degraded. After this, being a layman again, he could be handed over to the secular arm. Thomas refused, arguing that a man could not be twice punished for one crime. The

King was angered, and summoned a council at Clarendon, where, under threat of death, Becket signed the Constitutions of Clarendon, which gave the victory to the King. But the Archbishop did not hold himself bound by a forced oath. Pope Alexander gave him dispensation. Condemned by a court of barons, Thomas proudly left England, bearing his crozier, beaten but not tamed, and from his haven at Vézelay began to hurl excommunications at his foes.

Powerful as Henry II was, he was not strong enough to face an excommunication with impunity, or to risk his kingdom being placed unter Papal interdict, which would mean seeing his people deprived of the sacraments. In a time of universal faith, the popular reaction might well have swept away the dynasty. But compromise was difficult. The King could not drop the Constitutions of Clarendon without humiliation; and the archbishops refused to recognize them. In the end Henry met Becket at Freteval, made a show of reconcil-

iation, and required him only to swear respect for the customs of the realm. But Becket had hardly landed in England when there reached him, at his own request, Papal orders to turn out those bishops who had betrayed their primate during his disgrace. Now, it was a law established by the Conqueror that no subject was entitled to correspond with the Pope unless by royal leave. The King heard this news when feasting at Christmas near Lisieux. He was furious, exclaiming that his subjects were spiritless cowards, heedless of the loyalty due to their lord, letting him become the laughing-stock of a low-born clerk. Four knights who overheard him went off without a word, took ship for England, came to Canterbury, and threatened the Archbishop. He must absolve the bishops, they declared. Becket, the soldier-prelate, replied boldly and proudly. And a little later the altar steps were smeared with his brains, his skull cleft by their swords.

When the King learned of this crime, he shut himself up for five weeks in despair. He was too

EFFIGY OF ELEONOR OF AQUITAINE, WIFE OF HENRY II. This late 12th century sculpture is in the abbey of Fontevrault (Maine-et-Loire). *Frédérique Duran.*

MARTYRDOM OF ST. THOMAS A BECKET. From ▶ an English Psalter, c. 1200. Four barons killed the archbishop on 29 December 1170, in execution of what they took to be King Henry II's wishes. Henry VIII had the saint's tomb at Canterbury destroyed. (*British Museum.* Harleian Ms. 5102, f° 32).

clever to be blind to the danger. The people might have wavered between the King and the living Archbishop, but with a martyr they sided unreservedly. For three hundred years the pilgrimage to Canterbury was an enduring feature of England's life. All the King's enemies were heartened, and rallied. To parry the most urgent, he mollified the Pope by renouncing the Constitutions of Clarendon, and then promised to restore to the see of Canterbury its confiscated wealth, to send money to the Templars for the defence of the Holy Sepulchre, to build monasteries, and to combat the schismatic Irish.

But his own wife and children rose against him. He treated his sons well: the eldest, Henry, he had had crowned King of England during his own lifetime, and to the second, Richard, he made over the maternal inheritance of Aquitaine and Poitou. Now they both refused his request to hand over a few properties to their youngest brother, John, and at Eleanor's instigation took the head of a league of nobles against their father. In this peril Henry II showed his energy. He returned forthwith from the Continent to crush the revolt. After landing he came through Canterbury, dismounted, walked to the tomb of Becket, knelt for a long time in prayer, and divesting himself of his clothes submitted to discipline from three-score and ten monks. After this he triumphed everywhere; the nobles gave in, his sons did him homage. When order was restored the question of the ecclesiastical courts was apparently settled. Henry maintained his claim to try clerks charged with treason and offences against the laws of his forests. Those accused of other serious offences (murder and crimes of violence) were now left to the bishops' courts. And to reach this halting settlement the two outstanding men of the time had ruined two lives and a great friendship.

The history of England has this essential feature — that from the time of Henry II the kingdom had achieved its unity. The task before her kings was easier than it was for those of France. Thanks to William the Conqueror, no English lord, however great, was the sovereign of a petty territory with its own traditions, history, and pride. The Saxon kingdoms dropped into oblivion. Wales and Scotland, which would have been difficult to assimilate, were not yet annexed. The Church, despite Becket's resistance, seemed by the end of the reign to be in submission to the King, who controlled all ecclesiastical links with Rome, supervised the selection of bishops, and patiently sought to reconcile the monks of Canterbury and the bishops, who disputed the right of electing the Archbishop. The Primate, indeed, was now his servant. In fact, one century after the Conquest, the fusion of conquerors and conquered was so complete that an English freeman could hardly be distinguished from one of Norman origin. Both languages existed side by side, but corresponded to class divisions rather than racial differences. The cultured Saxon made a point of knowing French. Mixed marriages were frequent. ' A strong king, a weak baronage, a homogeneous kingdom, a bridled Church ' — these things enabled Henry II to make his court the single animating centre of the country.

That court was one of the most lively in the world. The King had a cultivated and inquiring mind, and gathered men of learning and erudition round him, such as the theologians Hugh, Bishop of Lincoln, and Peter of Blois, great linguists like Richard FitzNeale, author of the *Dialogus de Scaccario*, historians like Giraldus Cambrensis. Queen Eleanor had vanished, a captive rebel. The King had many mistresses, the most famous of whom was Fair Rosamund. Henry II was interested in happenings in all the courts of Europe, and travellers bringing news were always welcome guests of his. The court still moved from one royal domain to another, now in England, now in France, consuming its revenues in kind. Peter of Blois has described the King's retinue, a swarm of mummers, laundresses, wine-sellers, pastrycooks, prostitutes, buffoons, ' and other birds of like plumage '. Nevertheless, a solid order was coming to birth. Everywhere the King's jurisdiction was encroaching on private justice. It was Henry's aim to hold his own court of justice in every part of the realm, the local image of the *Curia Regis*. This was indeed a necessity, as the latter was continually on the move, and the hapless litigant had perforce to follow it. From 1166 onwards, judges set off from the court to cover definite provincial ' circuits ', at fixed annual dates. Their journey was ceremonious, their persons were treated with deep respect. They were preceded by a writ addressed to the sheriff, bidding him convoke the lords, lay and clerical,

SAINT HUGH OF LINCOLN. He was a Burgundian nobleman who came to England and was consecrated Bishop of Lincoln in 1186. He was a theologian at Henry II's court and his special concern were the enclosed orders. From a 15th century manuscript. *Mansell Collection.*

the reeve and four freemen of each village, and also twelve townsmen from each town, to assemble on a given day. On his arrival, the judge presided over this body, causing it to nominate a jury, composed as far as possible of knights, or, failing these, of freemen. The system of itinerant judges soon engendered the Common Law, identical and universal in application. Feudal and popular courts had followed local usage, but a judge moving from county to county tended to impose the best usage on all. Local customs were not destroyed, but were cast, as it were, into the melting-pot of the Common Law. The central court of justice recorded precedents, and thus, very early, a body of law took shape in England which covered the majority of cases.

All in all, a 'good peace' prevailed through most of the country in the twelfth century, and this was in great measure due to the King. Judges were honest only when a strict sovereign kept them in hand. If a king showed weakness, or became weakened by adventures abroad, a reaction from the barons would be the inevitable result. But on Henry II's death England could show the strongest government in Europe.

King Henry's end was tragic. He would gladly have shared his empire between his sons, but they hated each other and they all betrayed him. The two eldest, Henry and Geoffrey, died before their father, Geoffrey leaving a son, Arthur of Brittany; the third, Richard, plotted against his father with the new King of France, Philip Augustus, a cold, able young man, firmly resolved to regain his suzerainty over these Angevins and making skilful use of their dissensions. Henry II, the saddened and lonely old King, cared now only for his fourth son, John. He had left England and Normandy to Richard, and wished to keep Aquitaine for John: a plan which infuriated Richard, who, more closely linked with his mother, Eleanor of Aquitaine, than with his father, attached more importance to that province than to all the rest of the kingdom. Suddenly he did homage to the King of France for all his father's Continental territories, from the Channel to the Pyrenees. Henry II, caught in Le Mans by Philip Augustus and his own son, had to flee from the blazing town, which was the city of his birth and the burial-place of his father, the Count of Anjou. He left it, blaspheming against

God, and fled at a gallop by the footpaths, with his own son Richard chasing him. At Chinon the King was so ill that he had to halt, and there he was rejoined by his Chancellor, who returned from a mission to Philip Augustus bearing a list of the English traitors whom he had found at the French court. It was headed by John, his favourite son. Seeing his father in danger, John too had turned traitor. 'You have said enough!' cried the King. 'I care nought now for myself nor for the world!' After which he became delirious, and died of a haemorrhage. Henry II had been a great king, a cynic, a realist, and stern, but on the whole a well-doer. His reign had lasted from 1154 to 1189.

A statesman (it has been said) was now succeeded by a knight-errant. Richard I, styled by some Coeur de Lion or Lion-heart, and by Bertrand de Born of Périgord 'Richard Yea-and-Nay', inherited certain traits from his father: the violence of the Plantagenets, their immoderate love of women, and their courage. But Henry II's aims had been practical and cautious. Richard pursued adventure and despised prudence, in a life that seemed a frenzy of violence and fury. A poet and troubadour, friendly with all the warrior squires of Périgord, he wished to play the romantic knight in real life. The great chivalrous episode of Richard's reign was the Third Crusade, in which he took part with Philip Augustus of France. England had hardly been affected by the First and Second, to which some single adventurers, but no sovereign, had gone. Towards the end of Henry II's reign the victories of Saladin and the fall of the Kingdom of Jerusalem had so deeply impressed Christendom that the King raised heavy contributions, through the Saladin tithe, which was notable as the first direct taxation imposed on all property, movable and immovable, and no longer only on land. But this tax was intended to subsidize foreign armies rather than to send Englishmen to the East. Henry II promised to go himself, but he never embarked: there was nothing enthusiastic or romantic in Henry II. But Richard was different: having once received his father's inheritance, he drained the treasury dry, sold a few offices and castles, and took ship.

Richard and Philip Augustus, outwardly friends but actually rivals since Richard's succession to his father, set off together for Jerusalem. By the time

illuftris rex anglie a ierofolimis rediens capi pfentat augufto.

Rex anglie d'morte machiois accufat. quod abnegas
fe enfium manu excufaturu pmittit.

tande uenia petes ut abfoluat

THE ARREST OF RICHARD THE LIONHEART
BY THE DUKE OF AUSTRIA. Driven ashore
on the Dalmatian coast by a storm,
Richard tried to steal through the Duke's
lands in disguise. The Duke, however,
found him out and kept him prisoner
for a year, as Richard had insulted him
at the Siege of Acre. The King was
finally ransomed for 100,000 pounds.
(« Petrus de Ebulo - Liber ad honorem
Augusti. » *Burgerbibliothek*, Berne, cod.
120, II f⁰ 129).

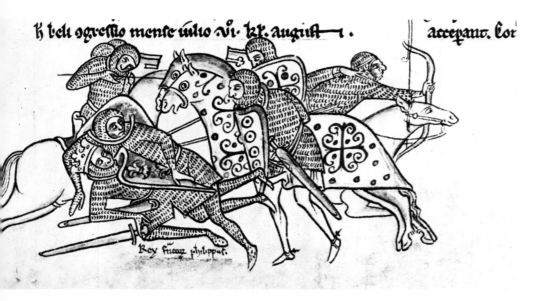

they left Sicily they had quarrelled. Richard lost much time in waiting for the small fleet which the Cinque Ports should have fitted out for him. (These five ports of Hastings, Dover, Sandwich, Hythe and Romney played the same part for the navy as did the knights' fiefs for the army: the King granted the Cinque Ports valuable privileges in return for their furnishing him with ships in time of war.) King Richard's expedition gave him the chance of showing his courage, but did not free the Holy Sepulchre, and he roused hatred by his insolence and cruelty. In the meantime Philip Augustus, who had gone home, was preparing war against his rival.

Richard was regarded by the crowned heads of Europe as a dangerous man, and on his way home from the Crusade was treacherously made prisoner by the Duke of Austria and handed over to the Emperor Henry VI, who ignored the Crusaders' privilege and kept him in captivity. News reached England that her King was a prisoner, and that his ransom would be one hundred thousand pounds. To raise this vast sum, the ministers who did their best to replace an absentee sovereign tried hard to spread the burden over all classes of society (1193). They demanded scutage of twenty shillings for each knight's land, a quarter of every layman's revenue, a quarter of the clergy's temporal goods, and one-tenth of the spiritual revenues. The churches were asked for their plate and jewellery, monastic Orders

for one year's wool shearings. Normandy had to pay the same taxes. In spite of these overwhelming dues, the sum raised was insufficient. But the Emperor agreed to give King Richard provisional liberty. In the King's absence his brother John had tried to seize power, but had been repulsed by the energy of Hubert Walter, Archbishop of Canterbury, who showed himself as good a soldier as he was a minister.

Richard was welcomed back with enthusiasm and pomp by the citizens of London. But instead of showing proper gratitude for this surprising loyalty, he at once proclaimed fresh taxes. The plight of the realm was dangerous. Philip Augustus had invaded Normandy; Aquitaine was in revolt, Anjou and Poitou were drifting towards France. To defend Normandy Richard built one of the greatest fortresses of the time, Château-Gaillard, which commanded the valley of the Seine. 'I shall take it, be its walls of iron!' cried Philip Augustus. 'And I shall hold it,' retorted Richard, 'be they of butter!' He had not time to keep his word. One of his vassals, the Viscount of Limoges, found a gold ornament, probably Roman, in a field near his castle of Chalus; Richard maintained a claim to it as King. A quarrel over this trifling incident grew into a war and, whilst besieging Chalus, Richard was struck by an arrow. The wound festered and the King died in his tent on April 6, 1199. His body was buried at Fontevrault, and his

Neustria Johis fuit inofensa sub armis
Quo moriente, gallis possessa reliquit

Johannes Rex genuit videlicet

heart in his 'faithful city of Rouen'. This absentee King was to lie for ever far from his realm: he hardly belongs to English history.

Medieval peoples forgave their kings much, because the worst king was better than the shortest spell of anarchy. The Norman dynasty had conquered the English with the aid of their barons, and then their barons with the aid of the English. King John succeeded in uniting all his subjects against himself. There had been greatness in Henry II and Richard; but John was merely odious. This betrayer of his father and brothers was suspected throughout Europe of having caused the murder of his nephew, Arthur of Brittany, who might have disputed his succession. Philip Augustus, his Continental suzerain, summoned him before his court, and then, after delays, declared him guilty of felony and deprived him of all his French fiefs. With feudal right thus on his side, the King of France proceeded to take back his domains from John,

one by one. Normandy was reoccupied by France in 1204; in 1206 he lost Anjou, Maine, Touraine and Poitou. Ten years after the death of Henry II the Angevin empire had virtually come to an end. There remained Aquitaine, but this proved difficult to keep because the English barons, who had always been ready to fight for Normandy, where they held fiefs, were very reluctant to pursue an adventure in Gascony, of little utility to themselves, and in the service of a hated king.

At war with the King of France, and quarrelling with the English baronage, John Landless also got into difficulties with the Church. The Archbishops of Canterbury generally acted as chief ministers to the King, and the sovereign quite naturally claimed the right of choosing his Primate. But, as we know, the bishops of the realm and the monks of Canterbury both laid claim to this right. Under John, all three parties appealed to Rome, and Pope Innocent III responded unexpectedly by appointing over the heads of King, monks and bishops, his own candidate, Stephen Langton, a priest admirable for character and learning, who had been long resident at Rome. John was furious, and refused recognition to a prelate whom he declared to be known only because he had always lived among his enemies; and he confiscated the properties of the archbishopric. The Pope countered by the customary sequence of pontifical sanctions. He placed England under an interdict; the church bells were dumb, and the dead were left without Christian burial. The faithful were in sore torment. But the strength of the royal institution was such that no rebellion took shape. A year later the Pope excommunicated King John. Finally he deposed him, and authorized Philip Augustus to lead a crusade against this contumacious England. The position was becoming dangerous. Already the Scots and Welsh were becoming active on the Borders. The King yielded. He humbled himself before the Papal Legate, and received Langton with a respectful, hypocritical welcome. Then, feeling secure in the saddle again, he tried to fabricate a Continental coalition with the Count of Flanders and Otto of Brunswick against Philip Augustus. Something unknown in baronial history happened when his barons refused to follow him. John had to postpone his departure, and kept his allies placated with subsidies. Next year (1214) this coalition was shattered at Bouvines, a battle which was at once the triumph of the Capets (whom it enabled to unify the kingdom of France), and the safeguard of English liberties: because, if John had returned home victorious at the head of his Brabant mercenaries, he would have taken cruel vengeance on the English lords for their refusal to serve. Only Gascony and the port of Bordeaux were left of his French possessions.

A clash was now inevitable between John and the baronage. They had endured the despotism of Henry II, a powerful, victorious king who held such wide popular respect that none dared resist him. But why should they have tolerated the abuses of a defeated king so universally despised? In 1213 Archbishop Langton, the brain of the conspiracy, had quickened feeling by a secret gathering of barons to whom he read the forgotten charter of Henry I, which promised respect for the rights and usages of the King's subjects. At another meeting the barons swore on the relics of St. John that they would grant peace to the King only if he gave his oath to observe this charter. In 1215 they addressed an ultimatum to John, and declared their ' defiance ' (*diffidatio*), which a vassal had to signify to an unworthy suzerain before taking arms against him. The King tried to persuade the freemen to his side and to bring in mercenaries, but was forced to realize that the whole country was against him. The citizens of London welcomed the small baronial army with enthusiasm. Conflicts between manor and village were now less frequent. The Papal interdict had left a deep mark on a religious people, and this appeal to ancient liberties was welcome to all classes. The capital was in rebel hands, the whole administration at a standstill. Without his Exchequer, John had no revenues. He had to yield. The King agreed to meet the barons on the meadow of Runnymede, between Staines and Windsor, and there signed the Great Charter.

The importance of Magna Carta has been sometimes exaggerated, sometimes underrated. It should be remembered, first and foremost, that this was a document drawn up in 1215, that is to say, at a period when modern ideas of liberty had not even taken shape. When the King in the thirteenth century granted the privilege to a lord of holding his own court of justice, or to a town of electing its own officials, these privileges were then styled ' liberties '. The Great Charter declared in general terms that the King must respect acquired rights. The barons did not regard themselves as making a new law; they were requiring respect for their former privileges, and the wording of their text enabled future generations to read into Magna Carta these principles: that there exist laws of the State, rights pertaining to the community; that the king must respect these; that if he violates them, loyalty is no longer a duty and the subject has a right of insurrection. The true significance of the Charter, therefore, resides in what it implies rather than what it is: it marks the end of the untrammelled monarchy of the Anglo-Norman period. To succeeding generations it was to become, in the modern sense, a ' charter of English liberties ', and until the fifteenth century every king had to swear, several times during his reign, that he would respect its text.

No sooner had King John accepted its terms than his thoughts turned to evasion. He approached Pope Innocent III, with whom he had been reconciled, seeking dispensation from his oath to respect the accursed Charter; and the Pope, outraged by this armed rebellion inspired by an archbishop of his own choosing, excommunicated the citizens of London. On Langton's advice they rang the bells and said Mass as if nothing had happened. Papal authority over England, too distant a country, was weakening. Philip Augustus took advantage of events to try to have his son Louis, whose wife was a niece of John, proclaimed King of England. John, he said, had been condemned to death for the murder of Arthur of Brittany, and so had lost his rights to the throne: the lawful heir to the English crown was Louis of France. In 1216 Louis landed in Kent, and set out with the support of numerous English barons in search of the King. But fate speedily ended this drama. John died on October 19, 1216, from a surfeit of peaches and fresh cider.

The change from feudal to parliamentary control that slowly emerged in medieval England after Magna Carta had its birth in the establishment of new communities. Feudal law protected the warrior landlord, and indirectly his serfs. But a gradually prospering society, untroubled now by invaders, could not remain a nation of soldiers and farmers.

The burgesses, craftsmen, monks, traders, students, and all who did not fit into the feudal framework, could only find security in association.

During the Saxon invasions most of the smaller Roman towns had fallen into decay, but a few survived. London, Winchester, York and Worcester, for instance, had never ceased to be towns. In the thirteenth century London had about 30,000 inhabitants, but the other towns were very small. Encased within its walls, a medieval town could not expand; its houses were small, its streets narrow. Thatched roofs frequently caused fires. Dirt was prevalent. The first public well in London dates from the thirteenth century, and its water was reserved for the poor to drink, as all who could drank beer. Ordure lay in the streets, and the stench was vile. Occasionally some contagion carried off part of the population. Every town was partly rural: even within its walls London had its kitchen gardens, and the mayor was constantly forbidding citizens to allow pigs to wander about the streets.

In the thirteenth century the French invented the *commune* or free town, a kind of conspiracy of townsmen under a vow of mutual protection. The name and the idea at once crossed the Channel. When the town attained the status of a tenant-in-chief it found its place in the feudal structure, having its own court, presided over by the mayor,

A JEW FROM COLCHESTER, 14TH CENTURY. This characteristic profile is depicted on the Forest Roll of Essex (E 32.12 m 3 d.) The Jews were well established in commerce. *Public Records Office.*

◀ FOURTEENTH CENTURY SHIPS as they appear on the municipal seals of Hythe and Hastings. (Paris, Archives Nationales). *Giraudon.*

and its own gallows, raising its own taxes, and being in due course summoned to Parliament. Towns, in France as in England, came to have their own seals, arms and mottoes, because they were themselves lords. The individual, in the Middle Ages, only participated in the governance of the country if he were a noble, but the *communities* were independent powers, and as such recognized by the law. The House of Commons emerged, not as a House of Communes, but a House of Communities — of counties, towns, and universities. England did not pass from the personal and feudal bond to a patriotic and national bond, but rather to a bond between the King and the 'States' or Commons of the realm.

In a medieval town people weve grouped in their several quarters according to their vocations: a street of butchers, another of armourers, another

of tailors. The gild or corporation had the twofold object of protecting its members against outside competition, and of imposing on them rules to safeguard the consumer. The Middle Ages did not admit the idea of competition, nor that of the open market. To buy in advance simply to sell again was an offence, and to buy wholesale so as to sell retail likewise. If one member of a gild made a purchase, any other member, if so minded, could buy also at the same price. No stranger was entitled to settle in a town to practise his calling without licence. Gild membership was an hereditary privilege. Merchants, of course, were not saints, and had countless tricks for evading the control of gild or municipality. Bakers kneaded loaves of short weight in which case they were punished in the pillory, the fraudulent loaves being strung round their necks. A seller of bad wine

[65]

had the residue of the stuff poured over his head. Rotten meat was burnt under the nose of its vendor, that he might smell it for himself. But gain is as strong a stimulant to fraud as to laborious toil. Notwithstanding strict rules, merchants grew rich. In 1248 the prosperity of London outraged the feelings of King Henry III, who, having had to sell his plate and jewels to make up deficiencies of taxation, learned that they had been bought by merchants of his capital. Throughout the Middle Ages the political strength of London was great. Its armed citizens, and the bands of apprentices ever ready to join in a riot, were a contribution to the armies, now checking, now upholding the sovereign.

The trading methods of the Middle Ages were later severely judged by nineteenth-century economists, and the corporations, like all such bodies of men, were bound to cause abuses. But the system had great advantages in its day. The suppression of middlemen and the ruling-out of speculation made rural life excellently stable, until the middle of the fourteenth century. If a rich man wished to build a great house or a church, he might rent a quarry, cut timbers from his own trees, buy winches, and become his own contractor. If a burgess wanted a silver cup, he bought the metal, agreed with a silversmith for the style of its engraving, and weighing the finished article, obtained back the unused portion of his silver. The gild protected both vendor and buyer against the excess of competition. It was a regulative instrument.

Foreigners were not themselves entitled to engage in retail trade, but must deal with English merchants, burgesses of a town. The league of Flemish towns, and the famous Hanseatic League (Hamburg, Bremen and Lübeck), had their own warehouses in London. That of the Hansa towns, the Steelyard, was fortified, and the celibate German merchants lived there together under a corporate rule, like Templars or Knights of St. John. The French merchants of Amiens and Corbie also maintained collective organizations in London. These foreigners, however, were authorized to attend the great fairs. To hold a fair was a seigniorial privilege granted to certain towns and abbeys, its object being the double one of enabling English producers to find more buyers than there were in the town markets, and allowing the country-dwellers to obtain goods not to be found in their small local towns. For the great Stourbridge fair a veritable town of wood used to arise, and men came to it from as far off as London. The Lombard money-changers were there with their balances; Venetian merchants spread out their silks and velvets, their glass and jewellery. Flemings from Bruges brought their lace and linen. Greeks and Cretans displayed their raisins and almonds, and a few rare coco-nuts, highly prized, the shells of which were mounted in tooled silver. The Hamburg or Lübeck merchant paid with Eastern spices for the bales of wool clipped on English grazings. Noblemen bought their horses and furred gowns. Exchequer clerks moved about, collecting the import duties. In this way did commerce and industry begin to develop in medieval England.

From the eleventh to the thirteenth centuries, Christendom was like a spiritual Empire. The clerks of all countries in Europe spoke Latin; the Church taught one single faith; the Crusades were joint enterprises of the Christian kings; the militant orders, such as the Templars, were international armies. Although communications were slower than in our day, intellectual contacts seem

to have been then more close and more frequent than now. A famous master, whether Italian, French or English, attracted students from every country, and was understood by them because he taught in Latin. In England the taste for classic studies was never wholly extinct. The Irish monasteries kept the torch alight during the Saxon invasions; then came the noble period of Northumbrian culture; and when the Danes had destroyed the School of Bede and Alcuin, Alfred rescued what he could of the classical culture. The Normans had elementary schools where the children learned Latin hymns, and sometimes how to read; monastic schools provided for postulants to the secular clergy; and grammar schools, often likewise under the tuition of monks, taught Latin grammar — often with the aid of bodily punishments. But ignorance was deep, even amongst the clergy, in the thirteenth century. In 1222 Archbishop Langton bade the bishops examine the priests of their dioceses and make sure that they understood the Scriptures.

The first university in England was that of Oxford, which for a long time had been one of the chief towns of the kingdom. Before the foundation of the university itself, eminent masters were teaching in the churches. Oxford became a real university when Henry II, at loggerheads with Becket, recalled the English clerks from Paris. As for Cambridge, numerous students and masters migrated there from Oxford in 1209, in protest against the injustice of the Mayor of Oxford, who had caused three innocent students to be hanged for the murder of a woman. In Scotland, the first university was that of St. Andrews, founded early in the fifteenth century.

The students of Oxford and Cambridge in the Middle Ages were not young men of good family coming there to learn the gentlemanly life and make acquaintance with the cream of their generation, but poor clerks preparing for ecclesiastical or administrative careers. Some were so poor that they owned but one gown between three of them, and ate only bread and soup. Shielded by 'benefit of clergy', these clerks often enough lived an unholy life of quarrelsome violence and loose morals. The colleges were founded to give the protection of a stricter discipline to those young men who had previously lodged with townspeople. Study did not thrive. Roger Bacon complained that students preferred the inanities of Ovid to the wisdom of Seneca. Soon even Ovid went unread, and the teaching of classical Latin died. As in Paris, the fashionable training after the rediscovery of Aristotle by Edmund Rich was in dialectics and logic.

The medieval spirit was metaphysical, not positive. But here and there, in a few minds, the sense of scientific method had been quickened by contact with Arabic science through the Crusades, and by reading of the classics. The most famous of these early European savants was Roger Bacon, 'the prince of medieval thought', as Renan called him.

RUINS OF FOUNTAINS ABBEY, YORKSHIRE. It was ▶ an important Cistercian monastery founded in 1132 in a secluded valley by a stream. *Radio Times Hulton Picture Library*.

AN OUTDOOR CLASS IN RELIGIOUS INSTRUCTION. The teacher is King Solomon. The headgear of the man on the right marked him, according to the conventions of the day, as an Oriental. (*British Museum*, Royal Ms. L 5. D. III, fº 285.)

He went from Oxford to Paris, where he taught geometry, arithmetic, and the art of observing with instruments. He certainly had an intuitive awareness of the critical method.

The universities played an important part in the political awakening of England. At Oxford, students from Scotland and the southern counties, from Wales and East Anglia, met and mixed. Classes, like districts, mingled freely. The spirit of Oxford was independent, and when Simon de Montfort opened his bold fight against absolutism, the students enrolled in his party. Any political or religious quarrel might start a university riot. Before long the Church had to reckon with the danger to unity of faith presented by this body of young rhetoricians, so easily beguiled by any new doctrine. And to recover its grip on the universities, the Church had to make use of new religious orders.

Popular faith during the thirteenth century remained simple and strong, but the Church frequently fell below men's expectations. Notwithstanding the stern measures of Gregory VII, many of the lesser clergy in England were still married or living in concubinage. Vows of poverty were no better observed than those of chastity. Simony was prevalent: churches, livings, preferment, all were bought and sold. The parish priests, who should have received the tithes paid by the faithful, were often robbed by an abbey which took over, with the rectorial rights, all the larger tithes (corn and wool), leaving the hapless vicar only the lesser

tithes of vegetables and fruit. The monks may not have been so vicious as the satirists depicted them, but they were far from being models of virtue. In vain did St. Bernard forbid the Cistercians to raise over-ornate buildings: their magnificent abbeys in England are proof at once of their excellent taste and ineffectual rule.

Two Orders of thirteenth-century origin gave a better response than the older monastic orders to men's constant need for fervour — the Franciscans and the Dominicans. These 'mendicant' Orders were composed not of monks, but of friars, who were ready to leave the monastery and live in the world, amongst their fellowmen, in absolute poverty and with total rejection of worldly goods. When the Dominicans and Franciscans reached England in 1221 and 1224 they quickly began a wide range of activity to combat ignorance and disaffection. Papal prestige had been affected by an excessive use of excommunication. Men remembered that London had defied the interdict of Rome and forced its priests to celebrate the Mass. To retain her hold over England, the Church would have to find new missionaries who could influence the common people. Her great part in the formation of English society had sprung from the fact that she was the only link between the rude peasantry and the culture of the outside world. This mission had to be completed. The isolation and ignorance of villagers were a tragic aspect of the Middle Ages. But could the parish priest secure

a bond? He was equally ignorant and hardly less isolated. The monk, again, lived a conventual life which, even if it might be holy, was still self-centred. The mendicant monk, moving from town to country, but living at other times with his brethren and renewing his stock of ideas, could fulfil this function. And he did so.

For a long time the rule of absolute poverty was observed by the Franciscans, and it is easy to imagine the effect on the common people of Orders so whole-hearted in their rejection of this world's riches. They soon became the fortunate rivals, in the universities, of the secular clergy. Monks and priests eyed askance these mendicant friars, whose bare feet and wretched victuals were a silent condemnation of rich living and abbatial abundance. But the poor students welcomed them with a trust not extended to a comfortably placed clergy. At Oxford the Franciscan school attained a splendid reputation. It produced the three greatest minds of the time — Roger Bacon, Duns Scotus, and William Ockham — and raised the University of Oxford to the level of the Sorbonne. These first mendicant Orders were joined by two others during the century — the Augustinians and Carmelites. Then, as time went on, like the monks before them, the four Orders of friars neglected the disciplines which had been their greatness. In the fourteenth century the 'begging brothers', too plump, too well-fed, were a favourite target of the satirist, and they lost their dominion over the poor. Actually most of the brothers were good-hearted men, but the contrast between precept and practice could only provide fuel for the indignation of the pure of heart. Besides, in a country which had become aware of its national originality since the end of the Norman and Angevin empires, these friars, being representative of the latest wave of Continental ideas and claiming to depend directly on the Pope, were a vexation to many of the faithful. The conflict between the Church of Rome and the Church of England was not yet ready to break out, but from that time the deep causes of rupture lay sown in the most exacting consciences: and there they were to germinate.

When the death of King John in 1216 left as lawful king a boy of nine, Henry III, the barons who had rallied to Louis of France from hatred of John, now instantly rallied to the Crown. A sense of nationality was becoming strong in this nobility, foreign though its own origins were. The loss of Normandy had severed the Norman barons from the domains in France, and tied them more closely to England. During the King's minority the security of the country was assured by sound soldiers, William the Marshal and Hubert de Burgh, and at last, in 1227, the young King came of age. Henry III was neither cruel nor cynical like his father. His piety and simplicity recalled rather Edward the Confessor, whom he held in great admiration, and in whose honour he rebuilt Westminster Abbey. But he was ill equipped to rule England at that juncture. At a time when all the essential forces of the country were trying to impose checks on the royal power, Henry stood for absolutism. In a period of nationalism, he was not English. Having married Eleanor of Provence, he had gathered round him the Queen's uncles, one of whom, Peter of Savoy, built the Palace of Savoy beside the Thames below Westminster. Also, the devout young King, in gratitude to the Pope for protection during his minority, acknowledged himself as vassal of the Holy Father, and encouraged Roman encroachments at the expense of the English clergy. Anger was rife amongst the native clergy, and there was a rising tide of hostility towards Pope and King.

For thirty years the unpopularity of Henry III waxed slowly greater. Seven confirmations of the Great Charter did not bring him to observe it. Unable to renounce the great Angevin dreams, he tried to reconquer a French empire, and was beaten at Taillebourg in 1242. The limits of England's patience came when he accepted from the Pope — who, on his own diplomatic chessboard, was playing the King of England against the Emperor — the Kingdom of Sicily for his second son, Edmund. This onerous gift had to be conquered, and for this expedition the barons refused all aids, unless the King would accept reforms. The Great Council met at Oxford in 1258; contrary to custom, the barons attended it armed. They insisted on his accepting the Provisions of Oxford, which entrusted the governance of the realm to a reforming council, which would control the Exchequer and appoint the Justiciar, the Treasurer, and the Chancellor.

The King gave his word, but soon fell back on his father's tactics and obtained Papal release from

his pledge. The barons protested, and it was agreed that both sides should accept the arbitration of the saintly King Louis of France, whose prestige in Europe stood very high. The King and his son, Edward, went themselves to defend their cause at the conference at Amiens. Louis decided for them, and declared the Provisions of Oxford null and void, as running counter to all his political ideas, and confirmed Henry's claim to employ foreigners as counsellors or ministers. The judgment, however, a somewhat obscure pronouncement, upheld Magna Carta. The more conservative barons accepted the award of Amiens, but a younger and bolder party maintained that the arbitration was contradictory, that it was impossible at once to confirm Magna Carta and annul the Provisions which were its application, and that the struggle should continue. This party was headed by the most remarkable man of the time — Simon de Montfort, Earl of Leicester.

This champion of English liberties was a Frenchman; but his paternal inheritance had included the earldom of Leicester, formerly confiscated by King John. It had been restored to him by Henry III, who became intimate with him, and in 1238 Montfort had married the King's sister, to the indignation of English feeling. The brothers-in-law quarrelled. Henry was impatient and frivolous, Simon impat-ient and in earnest, and there was endless bickering. Montfort soon took the lead in the reforming faction. He was a close friend ot the great Bishop Grosseteste, and his enthusiasm was infectious. Impressed by the evils besetting the realm, the Earl of Leicester was the soul of the aristocratic opposition which sought to control the royal authority at the Council of Oxford. After the award of Amiens the great rebel totally defeated the royal troops at Lewes, where he had against him his nephew Edward, and part of the baronage, but had on his side the younger nobility, the London burgesses, enthusiastic if ill-armed, the students of Oxford, and especially the excellent Welsh archers, who were thus indirectly defending the independence of their Principality. Simon counted strategy among his gifts. He captured the King and heir-apparent, and in 1264, resolving on a reform of the realm, summoned in the King's name a Parliament which was to be attended by four trusty knights from each county, elected to handle the affairs of the kingdom along with the prelates and magnates. Till then parliament had been a debate of the Council, and the Council itself had remained a court of law, composed of the greater barons, collectively convoked by the sheriff. The knights had been present simply as bearers of information, and had not formed part of the Council. Now

[71]

Simon de Montfort, the real head of the government, placed power in the hands of a council of nine members, appointed by three Electors; the latter could be deprived of their function by the Council. Simon de Montfort was certainly far from imagining what the British Parliament would one day become, and it is anachronistic to view him as the first of the Whigs. But this great man understood that new forces were rising in the land, and was determined to lean more strongly on the new classes.

The celebrated Parliament of 1265 included two knights from each county, and two citizens from each city or borough, the latter being summoned by a writ dispatched, not to the sheriff, but directly to the town. This time all the elements of the future Parliament were brought together: lords, county members, borough members.

There was one man at least who watched with interest and reluctant admiration the new policy carried out by the Earl of Leicester. This was Edward, the heir to the throne. Inferior in character to his uncle, devoid of the zealous idealism which made Simon a noble figure, Edward was better equipped for success. Simon de Montfort, obsessed by the greatness of his plans, refused to allow for the pettiness of men. Edward was uninventive, but superior in practical application. Having escaped, he rallied the barons from the western and northern borders, fell upon Montfort and, applying the tactical lessons received from him, defeated the Earl at Evesham. Montfort dispassionately ad-mired the manoeuvre that was his undoing. For a whole morning he fought heroically, and then was slain. His enemies mutilated his corpse, but Edward allowed the Franciscans to bury what remained; and for many years the relics of Simon de Montfort were venerated by the people as those of a saint.

With Simon de Montfort vanished the last of the great Frenchmen who helped to fashion England. Before long the sons of the Norman nobles were learning only English. Godric and Godgifu had won. But the part played by these Norman and Angevin kings had been a great one. When William the Conqueror landed, he found a country of settlers, a crude local justice, a licentious and contumacious Church. His vigour, the vigour of Henry I, the vigour of Henry II, had established a new country. Many of the institutions imposed or preserved by these kings are extant to-day — the jury, the assizes, the Exchequer (at any rate in name), and the universities. Even the perfidious King John and the weak Henry III played quite useful parts. The Great Charter, granted by the former and confirmed by his heir, proclaimed the transmutation of feudal usage into national law respected by the King. The period between 1066 and 1272 is one of the most fruitful in English history. The Norman colony founded by the five thousand adventurers of the Conquest developed on lines so original that, during subsequent centuries, after one last effort to unite the two realms of France and England, it cut every link with the Continent.

III

The Peak and Decline of Feudalism

Edward I to Richard III, 1272-1485

THE NORMAN Conquest had raised a double barrier of language and grievance between patricians and plebeians, between the village and the castle. But quite suddenly the two civilizations thus set forcibly in juxtaposition became merged. On Edward I's accession this fusion was almost complete, and it was symbolized in the person of the new King. Although directly descended from the Conqueror, Edward I bore the old Saxon name of the Confessor and was an English monarch. His main objective was no longer to reconquer Normandy or rebuild the Angevin empire, but to unify Great Britain by bringing first Wales, then Scotland, to submission. English was to him as natural a speech as French. Under his rule the English speech, which since the Conquest had been following an underground course amongst villeins and artisans, emerged again into the light of day. At the time of Simon de Montfort it was used in an official document and by the end of the fourteenth century the teaching of French in England's schools had ceased. Like the language, the institutions of Edward I are a prefiguration of modern England. His laws exerted an enduring mark on the social structure of the country. And despite his sincere piety, Edward's attitude towards the Pope was to be that of the 'national and insular' head of a State.

Such modernism and insularity were the more surprising as the King remained temperamentally feudalistic, and in his tastes was a Plantagenet. A vigorous, superbly built man, he delighted in the hunt and tourney. He would make no concessions in the forest laws. His homeward journey from the Crusade was like the wandering of a knight-errant of romance. On the way he redressed wrongs, attacked a brigand in Burgundy, and fought with the Count of Châlons. When he conquered Wales he asked for King Arthur's crown, and staged a banquet of the Round Table. Towards the King of France, his suzerain for Gascony, he was at pains to observe with punctilio the code of an irreproachable vassal. He did homage, and sub-missively accepted his lord's decisions. His motto was ' *Pactum Serva* ' — *Keep Troth*. It may have turned out that he changed his mind, after thus pledging his word; and he then showed wonderful skill in twisting texts to reconcile promises and desires. The revolt of the barons taught him that the age of despotism in England was over, that the monarchy could now be consolidated only by gaining the support of these new classes.

It was under Edward I that there first appeared a Parliament composed of two Houses, but the creation of parliamentary institutions was not a deliberate act. Against unforeseen difficulties a series of expedients was set up by the sound sense of the kings, the power of the barons, and the resistance of the burgesses. From these clashes Parliament was born. Summoned by the king as an instrument of government, it became, first for the barons and then for the nation, an instrument of control. Its origin lies in the Great Council of the Norman sovereigns, the shade of which still haunts the Palace of Westminster to-day. As we enter the House of Lords, the throne reminds us that the King presides over this assembly. In practice he does so only when he comes there to read the Speech from the Throne. On the Woolsack sits the Lord Chancellor. Why is he there? Because it is he who convokes this House, in the name of the king. And whom does he convoke? The right to be summoned to the Council remained ill-defined until the fourteenth century. A peer of the realm is, literally, a gentleman entitled to be judged only by his peers, or equals; but there were thousands of such gentlemen in 1305, whereas the

Council then consisted of only seventy members, five being earls and seventeen barons, the rest being ecclesiastical or royal officials.

After Simon de Montfort and his disciple Edward I, the custom grew up of consulting in grave emergency not only the baronage, but representatives of the 'commons': two knights from each shire, two citizens from the principal towns. This convocation had a double object: the King had realized that a tax was more acceptable if the taxpayer had previous warning; and as the difficulty of communications made it almost impossible to gauge the state of public opinion, he thought it well to explain occasionally how matters stood in the kingdom to men who came from all the counties and could then create a favourable atmosphere by their reports and descriptions. At first this method was not a new privilege granted to the knights and citizens; indeed, it was only a convenient way of impressing them and extracting money.

Besides, these deputies for shires and towns took no part in the Council's deliberations. They listened in silence. It was a Speaker (then a Crown officer) who advised the Council of their assent or dissent. But they soon took to discussion among themselves, and towards the end of the century the chapter-house of the monks of Westminster was allotted as their place of meeting. These first meetings of the Commons, it should be remembered, were secret; they were tolerated, but had no legal standing.

The convoking of the different 'Estates' of a kingdom (military, priestly and plebeian), in order to obtain their consent to taxation, was not peculiar to England in the fourteenth century. But the primordial structure of English society soon caused the Parliament to assume a different form from that of the States General in France. In England, as in France, the king began by asking each of the three Estates to tax itself; but this he soon dropped, because the threefold division did not

correspond with the actual mechanism of England. First: the bishops belonged to the Council, not as bishops, but as tenants-in-chief and feudal lords, and so the rest of the clergy ceased to be represented in Parliament. The priesthood preferred to vote its taxes in its own assemblies, the Convocations of Canterbury and York, and their abstention headed England towards the system of two Chambers. Second: the knights might have sat with the bishops and barons, but in the county assemblies and assize courts they had found themselves in constant touch with the burgesses, with whom, through marriage and a new mode of life in agriculture and commerce, they were more at ease. Like the burgesses, they were convoked by the sheriff, and were likewise representative of communities. From this union of the petty nobility with the burgesses was born the House of Commons.

Edward was the first Plantagenet to bear an English name, and also the first to try to complete the conquest of the British Isles. Ever since the Celts had fled before the Saxon pressure into the hills of Wales and Scotland, they had maintained their independence and continued their internecine bickerings. The Saxon Kings in time adopted towards them the passive method of Hadrian, that of wall-building, and about the end of the eighth century built Offa's Dyke, designed to hold back as well as possible the dwellers in the Welsh mountains. At the time of the Conquest, Norman adventurers carved out domains for themselves in the Welsh valleys, where they built *mottes* and keeps, and the malcontent tribes fled into the hills. There they preserved their own language and customs. Poetry, music, and the foreign occupation, imbued the Welsh with a real national sense. In the mountainous region of Snowdon the tribes united under a Welsh lord, Llewelyn ap Iorwerth, who styled himself Prince of Wales. He had dexterously played the double role of national prince and English feudal

BEAUMARIS CASTLE, ANGLESEY, built between 1293 and 1330 by order of Edward. I. It could serve as a port, for it had access to the sea. *Ministry of Works.*

lord, supported the barons at the time of Magna Carta, and so ensured himself of their support. His grandson, Llewelyn ap Griffith Gruffydd (1246-82), took up the same attitude in Simon de Montfort's day, and gave powerful aid at the victory of Lewes. When Edward was still only Earl of Chester, he had made unavailing efforts to impose English customs on the Welsh, who rebelled and repulsed him. The young Edward ruined himself in this struggle, but it taught him to understand Welsh methods of fighting, and especially the value of their archers, who used a long bow, the range and strength of which were much greater than an ordinary bow; and it taught him that against them it was useless to bring up feudal cavalry, whom they routed with their arrows. These lessons he was to remember.

Henry III had given him Ireland as well. But there all military enterprise seemed useless. Ireland, the ancient cradle of the Saints, had been partially taken from the Christian Celts by the invading Danes, who had however only occupied the ports on the East coast while the Celtic tribes in the interior of the island continued their feuds. When the Church in Ireland ceased to be part of the Church of Rome, the country became quite detached from European affairs. It lived on the margin of the world. When Henry II sought the Pope's pardon after the murder of Becket, he sent over to Ireland Richard de Clare, Earl of Pembroke, known as Strongbow. But here, as in Wales, the Normans had

only established themselves within the shelter of their castles. Round Dublin lay an English zone known as the Pale, beyond which the English had no hold. Norman barons owning castles beyond the Pale acquired, after a few generations, the language and manners of the Irish themselves. These barons, who enjoyed sovereign rights, desired the coming of an English army no more than did the native-born tribes. Theoretically they recognized the suzerainty of the King of England; actually, they maintained a regime of political anarchy. England, it has been said, was too weak to conquer and rule Ireland, but strong enough to prevent her from learning to govern herself.

On Edward's accession, Llewelyn in Wales made the mistake of supposing that he could continue his role in England as arbitrator between sovereign and barons; but Edward I was not Henry III, and soon tired of the Welshman's tricks. In 1277 he prepared an expedition into Wales under his own leadership. Broad roads were cut through the forests; the Cinque Ports supplied a fleet, which hugged the coast in touch with the army, ensuring its food supplies. Llewelyn with his brother David and their partisans were surrounded in Snowdonia, and had to surrender as winter approached. Edward then tried a policy of pacification, treating Llewelyn and David with courtesy, and set about administering Wales on the English model. He created counties and courts, and sent thither itinerant judges

[77]

to apply the Common Law. The Welsh protested and clung to their ancient usages, but Edward was narrow as well as strong and refused to tolerate customs which he regarded as barbarous. He maintained his laws, and a rising followed. Llewelyn and David broke their troth, and the King, ruthless to the faithless, this time fought them to the death. Llewelyn was killed in battle, and David was hanged, drawn and quartered. In 1301 the King gave his son Edward, born in Wales and reared by a Welsh nurse, the title of Prince of Wales, which has remained the title of the ruling sovereign's eldest son. Although English laws and customs were there and then introduced, the Principality remained outside the kingdom proper, and did not send representatives to Parliament. It was Henry VIII who in 1536 made England and Wales one kingdom.

Edward I had conquered the Celts of Wales, but against those of Scotland he failed. There a feudal monarchy had established itself, and a civilization analogous to the Anglo-Norman. One Scottish province, that of Lothian, had English inhabitants; many barons had property on both sides of the Border; a fusion seemed easy enough. When King Alexander II of Scotland died, leaving the throne to a granddaughter living in Norway, Edward wisely suggested marrying her to his son, and so uniting the two kingdoms. The idea seemed congenial to most of the Scots, and a ship was sent to Norway to bring her across, but the delicate child did not survive the wintry crossing. She died at sea, and immediately the great Scottish lords were disputing the Crown. Two of them, John de Baliol and Robert Bruce, both kinsmen of the dead king, and both of French descent, seemed to have equally good claims. Edward was chosen as arbitrator, and awarded the kingdom to Baliol, who was crowned at Scone. But the English King, carried along by this appeal to his authority, insisted that the new King and the Scottish nobles should acknowledge his status as suzerain.

The Scots had supposed that such a suzerainty would remain nominal. When Edward declared that a litigant losing his case in a Scots court could henceforth appeal to the English tribunals, Baliol made alliance with the King of France, then opposing Edward in Gascony, sent his defiance to the King of England, and refused to obey a summons from his suzerain; Edward thereupon marched into Scotland, made Baliol prisoner, carried off the Stone of Destiny from Scone — traditionally the pillow of Jacob — and fashioned it into part of a sumptuous chair which ever since has been used at coronations of the Kings of England.

Whenever Edward I was victorious he began with acts of mildness. As in Wales, so now in Scotland, he embarked on the enforcement of the English laws which he liked and admired. He

AN ARMED CAMP IN THE EARLY 14TH CENTURY. Isabel of France and her troops. She married Edward II and had his favourite, Despenser, done to death by quartering — see background. (Flemish manuscript in the *British Museum*. Royal Ms. 15. E. IV, f° 316 v°).

EDWARD III WITH PHILIP VI OF FRANCE. The English king pays homage for his French territories to the King of France, decked out in fleurs-de-lys. (*Bibliothèque nationale, Paris*. «Grandes Chroniques de France», copy belonging to Charles V. Ms. fr. 2813, f° 357 v°).

encountered an unexpected resistance, not from the barons, but from the Scottish people, who rose in revolt under Sir William Wallace. In vain did Edward win the day at Falkirk in 1298; in vain did he hang his prisoners, even Wallace himself; in vain did he spread ravage and desolation across the Border country. In days gone by the Romans had been forced to admit that a victory in Scotland was never more than a prelude to defeat. Lines of communication were too long, the climate was too harsh, the country too barren. In 1305 Edward imagined himself master of the whole country; but in 1306 Robert Bruce headed a fresh revolt of Scotland, and was crowned at Scone.

By now the King of England was an infirm old man. This last Scottish campaign finished him. Feeling death near, he bade his sons farewell, asking that his heart be sent to the Holy Land with a hundred knights, that his body should not be buried until the Scots were beaten, and that his bones be carried into battle, so that in death as in life he might lead his army to victory. The epitaph for his tomb he had composed himself: '*Edwardus primus Scotorum malleus hic est. Pactum Serva.*'

Pactum Serva — no pledge was ever kept less loyally than that of Edward II to his father. He instantly abandoned the conquest of Scotland, and when events forced him to resume the attempt, was beaten at Bannockburn in 1314. He was a strange man, a mixture of vigour and effeminacy, who had an entourage of curious favourites, grooms and young workmen, being particularly attached to a young Gascon named Piers Gaveston, whose flippancies infuriated the court as much as they amused the King. Edward II took no interest in the affairs of the kingdom, his tastes being only for music and

[79]

manual work. When he married he instantly abandoned his wife for his friend Piers. The anger of the barons at last rose to boiling-point, and they murdered Gaveston. Then Queen Isabella, who had taken a lover, Roger Mortimer, Earl of March, headed a revolt against her husband and captured him. The Parliament of 1327 forced him to abdicate in favour of his son, who was proclaimed King as Edward III. The deposed King died later in the year, horribly murdered by his guards in Berkeley Castle. For some years the real power was wielded by the Queen Mother and Mortimer. But the young Edward III was a different man from his father. He soon rebelled against the tyranny of Mortimer, arrested him, and put him to death (1330). Thereafter he strove to be a strong ruler, as strong as his grandfather, the Hammer of the Scots.

A decisive war between England and France had become almost inevitable. Destinies and provinces had been mixed and confused by the hazards of feudal inheritance. The King of England, himself half-French, was in lawful possession of Gascony and Guyenne, both necessary to the King of France for the completion of his kingdom. The latter was supporting Scotland against the English King, who would have to subdue that nation if he were to feel secure in his own island. Such a situation could not last. It is customary to say that the immediate cause of conflict was the candidature for the French throne of Edward III, as the son of Isabella of France, and therefore a grandson of Philip the Fair. But when the legal experts, on the pretext of applying an ancient Frankish law, called the Salic Law, chose the nearest heir in the male line, Philip of Valois, son of a brother of Philip IV, Edward of England was so little inclined to wage a war in defence of his rights that he agreed to come to Amiens and do homage to his rival in respect of Gascony. This he did, contrary to feudal custom, wearing his crown and a robe of crimson velvet embroidered with gold leopards; but Philip was content with a mild protest, and Edward returned to England satisfied with the honours paid to him.

If he assumed the title of King of France in 1340, adding the lilies of France to the leopards of England on his arms, this was done at the request of the burghers of Flanders. It came about thus: England's chief product was wool, and the chief urban occupation of the Flemings was the weaving and finishing of cloth. Agricultural England and industrial Flanders lived in symbiosis. Accordingly, when the King of France showed signs of coveting Flanders and imposed a French count on the country, the English merchants were perturbed. But the merchants of Ghent felt scruples about declaring war on their suzerain, the King of France,

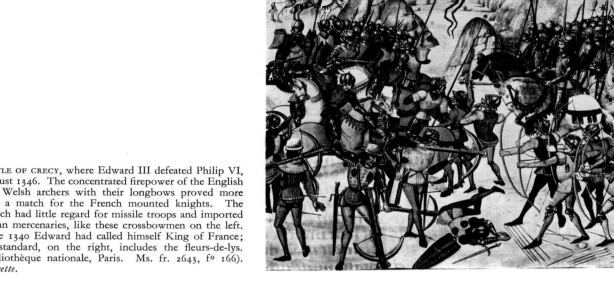

NAVAL WARFARE IN THE 14TH CENTURY. Probably an episode in the Battle of Sluys, 1340, in which the English defeated the French. *Mansell Collection.*

BATTLE OF CRECY, where Edward III defeated Philip VI, August 1346. The concentrated firepower of the English and Welsh archers with their longbows proved more than a match for the French mounted knights. The French had little regard for missile troops and imported Italian mercenaries, like these crossbowmen on the left. Since 1340 Edward had called himself King of France; his standard, on the right, includes the fleurs-de-lys. (Bibliothèque nationale, Paris. Ms. fr. 2643, fº 166). *Hachette.*

which were all the more troublesome because they were pledged to pay two million florins to the Pope if they committed this breach of faith. Their leader, Jacob van Artevelde, found the means of reconciling respect for treaties with their violation. He advised the King of England to join the arms of France to his own, and thus it was the ally of the Flemings, no longer their enemy, who became for them the real King of France and the object of their oath.

The Hundred Years War, then, was a dynastic war, a feudal war, a national war, and above all an 'imperialist' war. Further, it should be added that this war was popular in England because it led the armies into a rich country which provided abundant booty. Edward III and his barons were ' the flower of chivalry ', but the blazonry of their shields signalized a pillager's progress. It is curious to note, so early in her history, that the main characteristics of England's policy are already discernible, imposed upon her by her situation as well as by the nature of her people. Firstly, we find England in need of mastery of the sea, without which she can neither pursue her trade, nor send troops to the Continent, nor keep touch with those already sent. From the earliest days of this war the sailors from the Cinque Ports had the upper hand, and they were victorious at the battle of Sluys.

So long as England kept her naval superiority, she was easily victorious. Secondly, we see England able to send abroad only comparatively small armies, and seeking to form Continental leagues against her adversaries, backed by her money. Thus, at the start of the Hundred Years War, the English King tried to unite against France not only with the Flemings, but also with the Emperor.

Failing to form this coalition, Edward was about to make the move of attacking in Guyenne, when Sir Geoffrey of Harcourt pointed out that Normandy lay undefended. Hence, in 1346, came the landing at La Hogue, with 1000 ships, 4000 knights, and 10,000 English and Welsh bowmen. It was a heartrending sight, this passage of an army through that rich province where war had not been seen for several generations, and whose inhabitants had lost the art of defence. The sole plan of the English Kings at this juncture was to lay waste Northern France as widely as possible and withdraw through Flanders before the King of France had mustered an army. But beyond Rouen Edward found all the bridges on the Seine destroyed, and he could cross only at Poissy. This gave Philip time to summon his vassals, and he awaited the English in a position between the Somme and the sea. At that moment the invaders felt themselves lost. But their victory at Crécy (1346), as later at Poitiers

(1356), astounded them, and filled them with boundless pride. In 1347, too, they seized Calais, which gave them control over the Channel, and they kept the town for two hundred years, after expelling nearly all the inhabitants and replacing them with English.

Why were the English consistently victorious in these campaigns? The success of the feudal regime had been sanctioned by the predominance of horsemen cased in steel as shock-troops. Feudalism was to collapse before the royal artilleries, and before two forms of popular infantry — the English bowmen, and the Swiss pikesmen and halberdiers. It was not until the end of the thirteenth century that the bowmen took an important place in the English armies. Edward I had discovered during his Welsh campaigns that the long bow quickly shot a projectile which carried a hundred and sixty yards, and could pin to the saddle the thigh of a horseman wearing a coat of mail. By an Assize of Arms he had then made the use of the long bow compulsory on all small landowners. Tennis, bowls, skittles and other games were made illegal, so that practice with the long bow should become the only pastime of able-bodied subjects. So it was fairly easy, when the King needed bowmen for his campaigns in France, to recruit them, either from volunteers or by requiring a certain number from

each county. The victories of Edward III were due to superiority in armament.

It is erroneous to picture the King of France, at the outset of this war, as more 'feudal' than his adversary. No sovereign could have been more feudal than Edward III, who rejoiced in all the stagecraft of chivalry, was punctilious in courtesy, sighed for fair ladies, vowed to create the Round Table anew, and to this end built the great round tower of Windsor Castle and founded the Order of the Garter, consisting of two groups of twelve Knights, one commanded by the King himself, the other by his son, the Black Prince. But for all his relish in the game of chivalry, which was like that of his grandfather, Edward III was a realist sovereign and proved a good administrator. His taxes came in freely, especially when the waging of a popular war was in the forefront. Even the peasantry in England had hated the French for three centuries past, because of ancestral memories rooted in the Conquest and the long domination of a foreign nobility and a foreign tongue. In France, on the contrary, hatred of England in the countryside was not engendered until this war. The King of France could not at first count upon his people against the invader. The villager was indifferent. The King could not fall back on borrowing from rich merchants, nor on confiscating wool. Many

THE BLACK PRINCE. Edward, Prince of ▶ Wales, son of Edward III, settled at Bordeaux when his father made him Prince of Aquitaine, and defeated the French king, John the Good, at Poitiers, 1356. His bronze effigy is in Canterbury Cathedral. *British Travel and Holidays Association.*

SOLDIERS PILLAGING A HOUSE. A frequent scene during the Hundred Years' War. (*British Museum.* Ms. C, VII, fº 41 vº).

of the provincial Estates refused to vote the taxes, and when they did so the taxpayers showed marked resistance. Lacking money, the King of France could not muster troops. Whether he wished it or not, he had to be content with the feudal cavalry, already out of date and contemptuous of infantry. Even after Crécy the French nobles refused to admit the idea of a villeins' victory.

After the battle of Poitiers in 1356, when the King of France, John the Good, was made prisoner by the Black Prince, the eldest son of Edward III, the lesson was at last learned. The French army refused to fight in the open, and shut itself up inside strongholds. It could then smile at an adversary not armed for siege warfare. The peasants began to weary of the invasion. They harried the English, and did not hold captured lords to ransom, as professional soldiers did, but killed them if the opportunity arose. The English army wandered hither and thither, powerless to show fight, and the long-drawn campaign caused grumbling. At last, in 1361, the King of England made peace at Brétigny, and after asking for the whole realm of France, was content with Aquitaine, the county of Ponthieu, and Calais. It was a bad peace, as it did not solve the only grave question, which concerned the sovereignty of the English over provinces no longer wishing to be English. In Périgord and Armagnac there were murmurs, justifiable enough, that the King of France had no right to hand over his vassals. This resistance held the seeds of future wars; it foreshadowed the final liberation of France.

The start of the Hundred Years War was a time of seeming prosperity for England. Purveyors, armourers and shipbuilders made fortunes. Soldiers and their families were enriched by the pillage of Normandy. The King's need of money enabled towns and individuals to buy privileges cheap. For

a century past the lot of the villein had been rapidly changing. The system of dues payable by labour had been burdensome to the peasant, preventing him from tilling his own land. In the thirteenth century new methods had made their appearance: either the villein himself paid a substitute, who did the ordained work for him on the land of the domain; or he paid his lord a sum of money with which the bailiff hired agricultural workers. It was almost the 'farming' system of later centuries, except that the peasant's payment represented, not the rent of a piece of land, but the buying-out of an old servitude.

The real farmer soon appeared. Certain lords, instead of exploiting a portion of land and entrustnig the management to a more or less honest steward, who feathered his own nest at their expense, found it simpler to divide up the domain and rent out the land. The peasant, for his part, found it advantageous to cultivate one continuous piece of enclosed land, rather than the scattered strips hitherto allotted to him in the common fields. The rent paid was called in Latin the *firma*, a firm sum, whence the words 'farm' and 'farmer'. Thereupon two classes soon developed in English rural life: one, the farmers, almost landowners, free on the land they rented, half-way between the knight and the villein; the other, the agricultural labourers, who had freed themselves from serfage, either by purchase, or by taking sanctuary for a year and a day in a town protected by a charter. The battle of Crécy was followed by a scourge which depopulated England and made the restoration of serfage less possible than ever. What exactly these epidemic plagues were, which so long ravaged the world, is unknown. The name may have covered widely different maladies, from cholera and bubonic plague to a virulent influenza. Hygiene was poor, contagion swift, terror universal. The plague of the fourteenth century was called the Black Death because the body of the victim became covered with black patches. Coming from Asia, it attacked the island of Cyprus about 1347. In January 1348, it was raging in Avignon, and by August was moving from the coast of Dorset into Devon and Somerset. The mortality, though exaggerated by terrified recorders, was enormous. There were villages where the living were too few to bury the dead, and the dying dug their own graves; fields lay waste and the unherded sheep wandered over the countryside. Probably one-third of the population of Europe perished about — twenty-five million human beings. In England the pestilence was particularly long drawn out. Checked in 1349, it fastened its grip again in the following year and reduced the population of the kingdom to about two and a half million.

Such rapid depopulation was bound to have profound economic consequences. The peasantry found themselves suddenly richer, the communal fields being shared amongst fewer numbers. Scarcity of labour made workmen grasping and recalcitrant. The landlords, unable to find labourers to work their land, tried hard to let it off for rent. The number of independent farmers increased, and in the confusion of the landlords they obtained advantageous leases. Some barons granted exemption from rent through fear of seeing their farmers

abandon them, and others sold for a song land which became the property of the peasants. Many gave up agriculture and turned to sheep-breeding. This change seemed unimportant, but it was the first remote cause of the birth of the British Empire; because the growth of the wool trade, the need for outlets for this trade, and the need for preserving the mastery of the seas, were all in time to transform an insular policy into an imperial and naval policy.

But while the ordinary landlord was growing poorer and thereby weaker, a few of the greater barons became virtually petty princes. Intermarriage made them a close caste, linked with the royal family. The Kings of England then began to accumulate for their sons, by appanage and marriage, very extensive domains. The Black Prince married the daughter of the Earl of Kent; Lionel, another son of Edward III, became Earl of Ulster; another, John of Gaunt, married the heiress of the premier ducal house of Lancaster and owned ten fortified castles, the most famous of which was Kenilworth, seized from the family of Montfort. The Earl of March likewise had fully ten strongholds, and the Earls of Warwick and Stafford two or three apiece. Lord Percy, Earl of Northumberland, held the northern Borders for the King, but also for himself. These great lords all maintained their own companies of soldiery, no longer as vassals, but as mercenaries whose services they hired to the King for his wars in France. In the intervals of these campaigns these restless veterans would pillage farms, steal the horses and rape the women, and even seize manors. Parliament vainly ordered the magistrates to disarm them. But it needed a very bold sheriff to do that to these brigands.

War and pestilence were bursting asunder the feudal framework; but that of gild and corporation was likewise becoming too constricted. Until the fourteenth century wool, the country's chief product, had been shipped to Flanders for clothmaking. A few crude cloths were manufactured in England for common use, but the fine secrets of the craft were confined to the weavers of Bruges and Ghent. Then a chance turned up of transferring this industry to England. The Flemish burghers quarrelled with their overlord. The King of France supported him, and many of the craftsmen of Flanders, in defeat, had to leave their own country.

Crossing to England, they brought with them their traditions and manufacturing processes. Edward III sought to shelter this budding industry; in 1337 he forbade both the importation of foreign cloth and the export of wool. This brought ruin to Flanders, as it was impossible to procure large quantities of wool except from England. When war with France began, Edward could not maintain the embargo in its full rigour, because he had political reasons for placating his Flemish allies, but he imposed a protective tariff. Thereafter cloth-weaving became England's leading industry.

The coming of the Flemish weavers furthered the establishment in England of real capitalist enterprises, notwithstanding the gilds. The textile industry, of course, is a highly complex one, and the number of processes necessary to produce the finished article from the crude wool is high. The wool had to be picked, carded, spun, woven, and dyed; the fabric had to be scoured, fulled, napped, cropped, burled, and finally given lustre by pressing. Medieval ideas required that each of these stages should be carried out by a separate corporation, so that a very complex process of selling and buying had to take place alongside the process of production. To carry out one order, the agreement of fifteen corporations might have to be obtained. It was tempting for a fuller or a merchant-draper to buy wool, to spin and weave it as he chose, and supervise all the operations until it was finally sold. But such concentration of work offended all the gild principles. To escape these trammels, contractors soon began to establish themselves in country districts (much in the same way that, in the twentieth century, certain industries are seen moving away from towns so as to be free of certain trade union regulations). This new type of employer, buying the raw material and selling the finished product, was soon building his manufactory. In the fourteenth century there were two manufacturers at Barnstaple each paying tax on an output of a thousand rolls a year. Under Henry VIII, Jack of Newbury came to have a couple of hundred crafts carried on in one building, with six hundred workmen in his employ.

The day was coming when large-scale commerce proved more tempting to the adventurous young Englishman than wars of chivalry. But within the fences of a thirteenth-century corporation the

THE MERCHANT ADVENTURERS' HALL, YORK.
A fine example of a 14th century timbered
hall. It was here that the Yorkshire wool
merchants transacted their business. This
engraving was made in 1912 by E. Ridsdale
Tate. *Country Life*.

future of a master-craftsman was assured but cir-
cumscribed. His prices for buying and selling were
controlled, and he could not make a fortune quickly. Now the great English merchants at the close
of the Middle Ages no longer submitted to these
over-prudent rules and gradually supplanted the
Hanseatic League in European commerce. The
Lombard and Florentine bankers, who had replaced the Jews, had themselves to give way to
English bankers. With large-scale capitalism came
the inevitable collusion between wealth and political power. During the old age of Edward III, his
fourth son, John of Gaunt, Duke of Lancaster, was
surrounded by unscrupulous financiers. Richard
Lyon, a wealthy London merchant, was through
him introduced to the Privy Council, and became
the head of a real 'gang'. When all English wool
had to pass through the 'staple port', which at
that time was Calais, and there be cleared through
the customs, Richard Lyon contrived to ship his
bales to other ports where no duty was paid. He
thus made a vast fortune. With Lord Latimer,
the Duke of Lancaster's close friend, he 'cor-
nered' certain forms of merchandise arriving in
England and fixed prices to suit himself, making
some foodstuffs so scarce that the poor could hardly live. Such behaviour was in total opposition
to the medieval spirit, which believed in fixed
prices with moderate profits, and viewed as criminal any agreement tending to raise the price of

foodstuffs. But this spirit was dying; the King was
now in the grip of merchants; they were entering
his Parliaments and becoming the sole replenishers
of his Exchequer, and henceforth it would be for
them that England's foreign policy was shaped.

And now, at the close of the fourteenth century,
when a whole world, once great, was in disintegration, the Church seemed to be one of the most
stricken organs of the body politic. In England
it was still producing a few great men, but they
were administrators rather than priests. A bishop
who owned thirty of forty manors was adept at
checking the accounts of his stewards, and at ser-
ving the King at the head of the Chancellory or
Exchequer. With souls he was hardly now concerned. Amongst the better clerks, a few uneasy
consciences felt that the Church was moving away
from the doctrines of early Christianity, that a
priest's duty was to imitate evangelic poverty, and
that even if he had to render unto Caesar the
things that were Caesar's, this was no reason for
forgetting that God is above Caesar.

In England at this time the parish priests were
as poverty-stricken as the bishops and monks were
rich. In principle the priests had to live on their
tithe and raise from that both alms and the upkeep
charges of their churches. But a custom had
grown up amongst lords holding a living of 'ap-
propriating' its revenue, that is to say, allotting
it to a bishop or an abbey, with the result that

GEOFFREY CHAUCER. The «father of English poetry», sketched in a margin of the Ellesmere manuscript (now in the U.S.A.). He was on Edward III's expedition to France, 1359, went on diplomatic missions to Italy, where he may have met Boccaccio — another spinner of tales — and became a knight for the shire of Kent. Born c. 1340, he died in 1400. *Mansell Collection.*

the vicar received only a minute sum. Some priests let their rectories to farmers and did not even live in the parish. Their meagre perquisites were taken from them by the mendicant Orders, whose friars traversed the countryside charged with the duty of saying Masses in the convents. Chaucer drew a cruel picture of the friar going from village to village, entering every house, familiar with every housewife on his round, asking meal, cheese, beef, or ' any other thing as we have not the right to choose ', and then, for remembrance in his prayers, noting the name of his benefactress in his ivory tablets, cheerfully effacing all the names when he left the village. And it was not only the friar who thus competed with the priest; the country was also overrun with ' pardoners ', who came from Rome bearing a letter sealed with the pontifical seal, entitling them to grant remission of sins and indulgences to those who bought relics. Chaucer, whose anger was always roused by false religion, describes the pardoner preaching a sermon on the text that greed is the root of all evils — *radix malorum cupiditas* — and then selling to the villagers permission to kiss a morsel of crystal containing a bone and some scraps of cloth.

John Wycliffe (c. 1320-1384), a bold spirit, a Reformer long in advance of the Reformation, teacher of the Bohemian Hussites, a Puritan before the word was thought of, had started his career as an adherent of the ' Caesarean ' Church. In Crown employment he had been sent as ambassador to Bruges, and then became one of the most famous theologians in the University of Oxford. Startled by the immorality of the times, he reached the conclusion that the Church's virtues could only be recovered if her wealth were removed and her primitive poverty restored. His ideas became bolder. In his book, *De Dominio Divino*, he expounded the view that God is the sovereign of the universe, and grants power in fief to the temporal heads. His power is thus delegated to fallible beings, be they Popes or Kings; to all of these the Christian owes obedience. But every individual Christian holds from God Himself a fraction of *dominium*, and to the tribunal of God he must make direct appeal if God's vicegerents on earth do him a wrong. Man can be saved, not by ceremonies, indulgence, penitences, but by his merits, that is to say by his works.

Up to this point Wycliffe had been simply a rather bold teacher, tolerated by the Church because he was supported by the Duke of Lancaster and the University of Oxford. He became indisputably a heretic when he denied transubstantiation, the dogma of the Real Presence. This was an attack on the miracle of the Mass, and a doctrine which the Pope could not admit without imperilling the whole edifice of the Church. Wycliffe was condemned and repudiated the Papal authority, teaching in his later years that the Bible is the sole fount of the Christian verities. To spread the Scriptures more widely, he had the Bible translated into English, to replace the Latin and French versions which were not understood by the common people. He then formed a group of disciples, who were to live as humbly as the first Franciscan friars. Wyclyffe's ' poor priests ' were at first men from the university resolved to devote their lives to the salvation of the Church; later on this hard life seemed too exacting for young men of wealth and education. Wycliffe did not allow them to own any money, nor could they carry, as the friars did, a bag in which to put gifts — they could accept only food, and that only when they needed it. Wearing long robes of undressed wool, tramping barefoot, they went from village to village tirelessly preaching the doctrines of Wycliffe. Soon they were recruited only from amongst the poor. It is easy to imagine the force exerted in the countryside by ardent young men preaching poverty and equality. And after the Black Death this seed fell upon fruitful ground.

Nothing makes it easier to gauge the difference between the severity of the Church towards heretics after the fifteenth century, and its relative tolerance in the days when it was still sure of its strength, than the fact that Wycliffe, although condemned as heretical in 1382, remained until his death in 1384 Rector of Lutterworth, and was not personally disturbed. Archbishop Courtenay even had difficulty in preventing the Wycliffites from continuing their teaching at Oxford. Proud of its traditional independence and strong in the support of its students, the university stood out. Its masters inclined to regard themselves as professors rather than ecclesiastics. To make them yield, the King himself had to summon the Chancellor and threaten to deprive the university of its privileges. The

Wycliffites thereupon submitted, and for a long time Oxford ceased to be a centre of free thought.

In the country at large the 'poor priests', the Lollards (or mumblers), as the orthodox Catholics styled them, proved to be more staunch disciples of Wycliffe than the Oxford masters. They were favourably received, and shielded from the bishops, not only by the common people, but by many knights who were annoyed by the wealth of the Church. The bishops, indeed, had difficulty in obtaining the support of the sheriffs and of civil justice against the heresy. When the King promised this support, the Commons at first protested. They yielded when the ruling classes began to think that Lollardry was a social danger, threatening property as well as orthodoxy. In 1401 the statute *De Heretico Comburendo* was passed, confirming the Church's right to have heretics burnt by the common hangman. Persecutions began, the victims at first being chiefly poor people, tailors and tanners, whose crime was sometimes the denial of the Eucharist, sometimes the mustering of friends by night to read the Gospels in English, sometimes refusal to observe such ecclesiastical ordinances as were not in the Scriptures. Threats of torture caused many to retract. Others stood fast.

A long series of victories on land and sea marked the opening of Edward III's reign. Fifteen years after the Treaty of Brétigny, humiliation and discontent were rife in the land. The old King was going to pieces in the arms of the fair Alice Perrers, one of his Queen's women of the bedchamber, on whom he lavished crown jewels. The Black Prince was stricken with illness, and after prolonged struggles had been forced to leave his post in Aquitaine, borne on a litter, slowly dying. The King's son, John of Gaunt, the formidable Duke of Lancaster, had joined hands with Alice Perrers and was ruling the country with the support of a band of double-dealers. Nearly all conquests were lost again. France had found a great king in Charles V, who had refashioned a navy, and whose generals, men like Du Guesclin and Clisson, realized that in this war the only way to success was never to give battle except when sure of victory. Finally, and most important, England no longer held that mastery of the sea which made her invulnerable so long as it was hers. The clumsiness of the Black Prince, a better soldier than diplomat, had brought together the King of Castile and the King of France. Their fleets controlled the Gulf of Gascony and the Channel. Not only was an English fleet destroyed at La Rochelle, but French vessels sailed scatheless up the Thames and French flotillas sacked the coastal towns and burned the fishing villages.

In the general confusion and dismay only one body showed courage — the House of Commons. The division of Parliament into two Houses was now an established practice. The House of Commons contained regularly two hundred burgesses, representing a hundred boroughs, and seventy-four knights, representing thirty-seven counties. The

latter, though fewer, were dominant and decisive, because they represented a real force. It was they who, in the so-called 'Good Parliament' of 1376, boldly called Lancaster and his faction to account, insisted on the dismissal of Alice Perrers, and invited the King to ensure the maritime defence of the country. But once the session was over, the Duke cast the Speaker into prison; Alice Perrers, who had sworn to see the King no more, returned to his side; the bishops, who had sworn to excommunicate this woman, did not raise a finger; and when Edward III died in 1377, all the work of the Good Parliament had been undone.

As the Black Prince had died before his father, the lawful heir was Edward's grandson, Richard II, called Richard of Bordeaux: a handsome, intelligent lad, who could not reign in person for some years yet. His dangerous uncles, the Dukes of Clarence and Lancaster, were to become his counsellors, perhaps his rivals. From the first years of his reign (1377) Richard II had opportunities of showing a surprising courage and presence of mind; within four years came a rising which might well have turned into revolution. Ever since the Black Death, a latent agitation had been hatching in the rural districts. Not that the peasants were more wretched than before; on the contrary, for a full decade wages had risen while prices sank. But men had ceased to believe in the system which held them as serfs. The Wycliffites had preached to them of the scandalous riches of the abbots. The villages in 1381 saw numerous secret meetings, and there were mysterious messages circulated from county to county, through the lay and clerical agitators who preached the reform of the Church and the revolt of the peasants. Bitterness was heightened by the Statute of Labourers. Daily in one manor or another the peasants came into conflict with a lord or his bailiff, who tried to force them to do harvesting for two or three pence a day. The penalties provided against the recalcitrant by this absurd law drove from their fields men who had hitherto been peaceable labourers and now became vagabonds, wandering in the woods, demoralized by their uprooting. The immediate cause of the revolt was a tax which the Crown very clumsily sought to levy a second time because the first round of the collectors had not produced enough money. When the peasants saw the King's

men again, and when the latter tried to arrest defaulters, a whole village blazed with anger and chased them off. Then, alarmed by their own action, the peasants made off into the woods. In a few days Kent and Essex were ablaze. The rebels sacked houses and killed those sent to enforce the law. Their fixed idea was to destroy the written records of their servitude. In the manors which they seized they burnt registers and deeds. The nobles, strangely powerless in organizing a stand, fled before them, and soon the outlaws and peasants were entering the towns. The townspeople received the insurgents fairly well. At Canterbury the citizens and rustics joined hands in paying off some old scores and beheading certain much hated men. Then the shapeless army marched on London. The young King was there, said by the rebel leaders to be sympathetic, of whom the worthy people knew nothing beyond that he was a boy and had to be protected against his uncle, John of Gaunt, the most hated lord of all. On the way they slew Simon, Archbishop of Canterbury and Lord Chancellor, who fell into their hands, and also the Grand Prior of St. John's.

The King and his followers took refuge in the Tower of London. The town itself would have been easy to defend; the bridge could have been opened in its middle. But one alderman sympathetic to the rebels let them enter, despite the determination of the Mayor to stand fast for order. Instantly the streets were a scene of horror. The peasants had thrown open the gaols, and, as always happens in revolutions, a swarm of rogues emerged from the shadows to pillage and kill. A block was set up in Cheapside and heads fell fast. A whole settlement of Flemings was needlessly slain, merely for being foreigners. John of Gaunt's palace of the Savoy was burnt. Only the young King was spared by the populace. Nobody knew why, but he was the idol of all these hapless men, and stood to gain by the fact. He arranged a meeting with the rebels at Mile End, in a field outside the town, and there made a feint of granting all their demands. Thirty clerks set about drawing up charters of liberation and sealing them with the royal seal. The peasants believed in parchments, and as each group received its charter, it left the field in triumph and returned to London, bearing royal banners which had also been distrib-

RICHARD II OF ENGLAND MEETS CHARLES VI OF FRANCE, his prospective father-in-law. In fact a month later, November 1396, he married Charles' daughter, Isabel. The scene of the meeting is near the Field of the Cloth of Gold, where Henry VIII would meet Francis I. (Bibliothèque de l'Arsénal, Paris). *Giraudon.*

uted. But Richard's councillors had never intended to uphold the validity of concessions forced by pillage and murder. They were playing for time. And fresh crimes obliged them to take up the offensive rapidly.

Soon, however, from all sides knights and burgesses were arriving to rally round the King. A new meeting-place was fixed with the rebels at the horse-market at Smithfield. The boy-king rode into it on horseback, followed by the Lord Mayor and a full escort; at the other end were the malcontents, armed with their bows. Their leader, Wat Tyler, on horseback. came up to the royal procession. The man was insolent, and suddenly the Lord Mayor, who carried weapons under his robe, lost his temper and felled Tyler with a blow on the head. When he dropped, the King's men clustered round him, so that the bands at the other end of the open space should not see him. But they had seen already, and at once lined up for battle, stretching their bows; the young King then made an unexpected and heroic gesture which turned out well. Quite alone, he left his followers, saying: 'Stay here: let no one follow me.' Then he crossed towards the rebels, saying to them: 'I will be your captain. Come with me into the fields and you shall have all you ask.' The sight of the handsome lad coming over to them so confidently disarmed the insurgents, who had neither chief nor plan. Richard placed himself at their head and led them out of the City.

But the young King was leading them to a cruel end. For the repression was to be as bloody as the rising. When the peasants' army was disbanded and the labourers back in their villages, the judges went from county to county, holding assizes of death. In London, on the block which they had themselves set up in Cheapside, during the days of butchery, the guilty, and many innocent men too, were beheaded. The ruling classes became permanently afraid: their dread even reached the point of forbidding the sons of villeins admission to the universities. The knights and the liberal burgesses lost all authority in Parliament. But the spirit of independence in the English people did not die, and in the end it triumphed. Under the Tudors, the serf system was abolished, and then, 'under James I, it became a legal maxim that every Englishman was free.'

The boy-king whose courage the nobles and burgesses had admired on Smithfield market, whom the peasant bands had followed with veneration,

became a fanciful adolescent, and after a stable period of tolerant rule, Richard took swift steps to discredit and remove the foremost of his old enemies; he seized a favourable moment to pack a Parliament with his own men, secured an independent income from customs for the rest of his life, and had his own supporters confirmed in the control of affairs. Success turned the head of this able but somewhat unbalanced king. He became openly despotic, and his opponents were able to recruit fresh strength among those hitherto friendly or neutral. He exiled his cousin Hereford, John of Gaunt's son, and, on the old Duke of Lancaster's death, confiscated the son's inheritance. This was a direct provocation to revolt. Lancaster spent some time in Paris, preparing a *coup d'état*, and when he set foot in England, Richard found himself quickly deserted on every hand, and finally thrown into prison. Parliament, as heir to the Great Council, elected Lancaster to be King, and he was

forthwith crowned by both archbishops under the style of Henry IV.

Through the sixty years of this Lancastrian dynasty the power of Parliament, so much threatened by Richard II, continually increased. The first of the Lancastrian kings, Henry IV, knew that he was a usurper, and never ventured to thwart the Commons. The second, Henry V, spent much of his reign abroad and bequeathed the crown prematurely to a young child, Henry VI, who on reaching adolescence was to become a feeble, simpleminded sovereign. Thus, over a long period, the weakness of the sovereign, his absence, or his fears, made Parliament the real controller of events.

After a long truce Henry V reopened the war with France in 1415. His real aim was to make a foreign war to occupy the turbulent spirits of his own country. The religious agitations of the Lollards were turning into civil war. The stake no longer sufficed to deter the most resolute heretics.

[94]

DRAWING UP A TREATY. A twenty-eight-year truce was arranged between England and France on 9 March 1396. This symbolic scene shows Richard II and Charles VI with their respective heralds waiting as a chancellor, surrounded by four dukes, prepares the document. (*British Museum.* Harleian Ms. 4380, fᵒ 10 vᵒ).

THE ARREST OF THOMAS, DUKE OF GLOUCESTER. He led the opposition of the barons to his nephew, Richard II, whose guardian he was. He was arrested in 1396 as he left Court, and was imprisoned at Calais where he was murdered, having confessed to treason in favour of Henry of Lancaster. (*British Museum.* Ibid. fᵒ 134).

Henry himself had high ambitions; he dreamed of ending the Avignon schism and undertaking a crusade at the head of a Western league. Finding France torn between the factions of Orleans and Burgundy, and ruled in the name of a mad King by an unloved Dauphin, he cynically revived the claims of Edward III to the French throne. Now, whatever might have been the rather dubious claims of Edward III, those of Henry V, who was not even the most direct heir of his great-grandfather, were virtually none. So well did he know this that, after one opening diplomatic move, he asked only to be given the hand of Catherine, daughter of Charles VI, together with Normandy, Touraine, Anjou, Maine and Ponthieu. War became inevitable.

The second part of the Hundred Years War is astonishingly like the first. It looks as if a sort of obsession drove Henry V to imitate the campaign of his great-grandfather. He had only 2500 men-at-arms, their followers, and 8000 bowmen: in all, with servants and transport, not more than 30,000 men. After seizing Harfleur, the great arsenal of the west, in spite of a spirited defence, he sent a challenge to the Dauphin and decided to march towards Calais and across the Somme at Blanche-Tache, the ford of Crécy. It was a bold undertaking, but the French nobles, he argued, were divided and would doubtless leave him the week he needed to reach Calais. But finding the ford defended, Henry moved upstream and met the French army at Agincourt. A furious battle ensued, in which the chivalry of France, who for all their gallantry had remained blind to the precepts of Du Guesclin, were shattered by Henry's bowmen and hacked to pieces by his men-at-arms. Ten thousand Frenchmen perished in one of the bloodiest battles of the Middle Ages (1415).

After this, thanks to the Burgundian treachery which opened the gates of Paris to him, Henry was

left master of northern France. He married Catherine at Troyes, and there signed a treaty whereby he was recognized as heir to the French throne after Charles VI, and as Regent during the latter's lifetime. He was to rule with a French council, and to preserve all the ancient customs. His title, while Charles VI still lived, was to be Henry V, King of England and Heir of France; but a few years later, in 1422, he died in the forest of Vincennes, probably of dysentery, leaving a son one year old. Henry had led the English to fresh victories, and his private virtues were genuine. He was generous, courteous, sincerely religious, chaste, and loyal. But his moderation, conspicuous in a stern age, did not prevent him from being ruthlessly cruel when the interests of country and Crown seemed to require it. His good side and his bad had appealed equally to his people.

After Crécy, where feudal routine was defeated, France had produced a realist soldier in Du Guesclin. After Agincourt, France was saved by the sound sense and the faith of Joan of Arc. When the infant Henry VI, still in the cradle, became King of England in 1422, the game seemed to be lost for the French Dauphin. Charles VI died two months after his foe; Henry's uncles, the Duke of Bedford, regent in France, and the Duke of Gloucester, planned to have the child consecrated as King of France at Rheims, as soon as he was old enough to speak the sacred formulas. From 1422 until 1429 the Dauphin Charles wandered

through his few surviving provinces, without a kingdom or capital, without money or soldiers: 'the King of Bourges', he was called derisively. Bedford, master of the north of France, undertook the conquest of the centre and laid siege to Orleans. Charles had thoughts of withdrawing right into Dauphiné. It seemed to be the end.

And yet the English domination in France was frail and artificial. It rested, not on real strength, but on the divisions of Frenchmen, and the first blow made it collapse. The story of Joan of Arc is at once the most amazing miracle in history and the most logical sequence of political acts. The plans dictated to Joan by her voices were simple to the point of genius: 'Give the Dauphin self-confidence; set Orleans free; have Charles crowned at Rheims.' St. Joan's life (1412-1431) was too short to let her accomplish more than these three acts; but they sufficed. With Charles crowned, Henry VI could never be the lawful King of France. Once started, the people followed. The feelings roused by the victories of Joan and Dunois, the pity and horror provoked by her trial and martyrdom, filled France with hatred of the invader. In vain did Bedford have Henry crowned at Notre-Dame in Paris, in vain the Burgundian faction and the Sorbonne (whose consultations had sanctioned the burning of the Maid) welcomed the young English King with lavish pomp. The Dauphin gained ground. The house of Burgundy quarrelled with England. Even Paris, at last, expelled the

The Erle Richard was att sege of Rov, there set furst betwen the kyng[?]
tents and seynt katryns, And whan seynt katryns was wonne, he
was sette to kepe port Chawkedysle

HENRY V LAYS SIEGE TO ROUEN, July 1418 to January 1419. The city succumbed to hunger; thousands of civilians died between the enemy lines. The king, crowned and wearing a coat of arms, is on the left. On the right is Richard Beauchamp, Count of Warwick, father-in-law of Warwick the Kingmaker. (British Museum. Cotton Ms. Julius E. IV, art. 69, f° 196, known as «The Life and Acts of Richard Beauchamp, Earl of Warwick,» late 15th century). *Mansell Collection.*

JOAN OF ARC CAPTURED AT COMPIEGNE, 24 May 1430. Victim of the warring factions in France, she was captured by the Burgundians and sold to the English who burnt her as a witch after a mock trial before an ecclesiastical court. (Bibliothèque nationale, Paris. «Vigiles de la mort du roi Charles VII» by Martial of Paris. Ms. fr. 5054, f° 70). *Hachette.*

English garrison. Normandy was set free. When Charles VII died in 1461 the English held not an acre of France except the town of Calais, which they were to hold for a century longer, a Gibraltar of the Channel.

It is remarkable that modern English historians, just as they regard Bouvines, a French victory, as a fortunate battle, now agree in admiration of Joan of Arc, and in believing that she saved England from despotism. Had it not been for her, the King of England would have lived in Paris; and there, supported by a French army and enriched by taxes levied in France, he would have refused to submit to the control of his own subjects. Thanks to her, an end was made of the parlous dream of Continental empire which so long enticed the English sovereigns. These long years of struggle had given other lasting results. In both countries the sense of nationality, a new and powerful emotion, was born of contact with strangers. The people of Rouen and Orleans, Bourges and Bordeaux, with all their differences and old enmities, nevertheless felt that between them was something which

marked them off from the 'goddams', as the English were termed. And the English, on their side, notwithstanding their ultimate defeat, had now the memory of great deeds done in common.

The French wars over, England was flooded by troops of soldiery used to profitable pillaging, and quite ready to espouse any cause, good or bad. In 1450 the men of Kent rose under the leadership of an adventurer named Jack Cade, who styled himself Mortimer and claimed descent from Edward III. This leader reached London and, before being killed himself, beheaded the King's Treasurer and a sheriff of Kent. The nobles were at this time ready enough to follow such usurpers because the King himself was merely the son or grandson of a usurper. These Lancastrian Kings knew this well enough. When Henry V, at his father's death-bed, thought him gone and laid his hand on the crown, Henry IV raised himself from lethargy to murmur: 'It is not yet yours, nor was it ever mine...' Against the weak Henry VI there rose Edward, Duke of York, a nearer heir of Edward III through his maternal descent from the Duke of

THE CHILD-KING HENRY VI OF ENGLAND CROWNED
KING OF FRANCE. The ceremony took place
at Notre Dame, Paris, on 16 December 1431
on the instance of the king's uncle, the Duke
of Bedford, Regent of France. Joan of Arc,
however, had already had the French Dauphin
crowned Charles VII at Rheims two years earlier.
(*Bibliothèque nationale*, Paris. Ms. fr. 83, fº 205).

THE COURT OF THE KING'S BENCH IN THE REIGN OF HENRY VI. In the foreground the prisoners await the sentence. From a 15th century Ms. in the library of the Inner Temple, London. *The Bench of the Inner Temple.*

HENRY V, King of England, 1413-1422. A remarkable portrait in profile, by an unknown English artist. This king is chiefly remembered for his expedition to France and victory over Charles VI at Agincourt, 1415. (National Portrait Gallery). *Hachette.*

K. Henry. v

Clarence, whereas the Lancastrians sprang only from the younger son, John of Gaunt. And round the Red Rose of Lancaster and the White Rose of York there gathered groups of warrior lords whose sole political aim was to win fortune by the triumph of their faction.

These struggles of private ambition and greed roused scant interest in the country at large. Life went on, tilth and harvest. London's trade developed. The Hanseatic League met a formidable rival. These battles were waged only by a score or so of great barons, their friends and vassals, and above all by their mercenaries. They had to be prudent and respect the neutrality of towns and villages in their conflicts, as armed men were numerous, and if vexed would rally against one Rose or the other. The battles which determined the possession of the throne were fought out by a few thousands of men. But despite the small numbers of combatants, these battles drew vast quantities of blood from the one class involved in them, and after the Wars of the Roses the English noble families were gravely reduced in number.

The hapless Henry VI was born out of time. He was no fool, but certainly no king: a saint, rather, and in worldly matters a child. In the great wars of his reign he was only an onlooker, leaving Somerset or Warwick to act, and himself appearing on the stage only to take his place in a procession or ceremony. His only pleasures were in hearing daily Mass, and the study of history and theology. Hating pomp, he dressed as an ordinary burgess, and when he donned his royal robe, it was over a hairshirt. He said his prayers like a monk at every meal, and on the table before him there always stood an image showing the five wounds of Christ. These pious, weakling monarchs, as Chesterton remarked, were those who left the noblest and most enduring memorials. Edward the Confessor had built Westminster Abbey; Henry VI founded Eton College (1440), and built the wonderful chapel of King's College, Cambridge. These great foundations ruined him. At a time when everybody, nobles and merchants alike, grew richer, the King alone was overwhelmed with debts. This naïve, insubstantial sovereign was to become an easy prey to brutal and unscrupulous knights.

In 1453 Henry VI, who was a grandson of the mad King Charles VI of France, showed unmistakable signs of insanity. He had lost his memory and reasoning power, and could not walk or stand upright. He did not even understand that a son had been born to him. His cousin the Duke of York, supported by Warwick, a powerful lord who won the twofold designation of the Last of the

EDWARD IV ENTHRONED. Kneeling at his feet are Sir William Herbert and his wife. Head of the House of York in the Wars of the Roses, he won the crown with the aid of Warwick the Kingmaker and proved an autocratic monarch. From a mid-15th century manuscript. (*British Museum*. Royal Ms. 18 D. II, f° 6).

Barons and the Kingmaker, had himself crowned at Westminster under the title of Edward IV. After years of fugitive existence, the gentle Henry was shut up in the Tower. Then a quarrel between Edward IV and the Kingmaker suddenly restored the throne to Henry and the Red Rose. Finally, Edward of York defeated Warwick, who was killed at Barnet in 1471; he also slew the Prince of Wales and caused the King himself to be murdered in the Tower. After which systematic massacre Edward IV reigned almost unopposed until 1483.

The accession of the House of York dealt a rather heavy blow to the prestige of Parliament. Whereas the usurping Lancastrian kings had requested their investiture at the hands of Parliament, the Yorkists claimed to rule by sole right of inheritance. Edward IV left two young sons, the elder of whom succeeded under the regency of Richard, Duke of Gloucester, who, however, had his nephews confined in the Tower and murdered, whereupon he became king himself as Richard III in 1483. When the twofold murder in the Tower became generally known, a definite outlet was given to the sense of revolt which had long been fermenting in the hearts of Englishmen weary of

civil wars and the snatching of crowns. There seemed to be a chance of reconciling the two Roses. There remained one Lancaster, Henry Tudor, Duke of Richmond, who had cautiously fled into Brittany, and was directly descended through his mother from John of Gaunt. If this Henry could marry Elizabeth of York, the daughter of Edward IV, the two houses would be merged. Richard saw the danger, and tried to conciliate the burgesses by summoning a Parliament. He thought of marrying his niece himself. But Henry Tudor landed in Milford Haven with two thousand soldiers, English refugees and Breton adventurers. Wales rallied to him because the Tudors were Welsh. In 1485 he met Richard on Bosworth Field, the battle's outcome being decided by the Stanleys, great lords in Lancashire, who sided with Henry because Lord Stanley had been the second husband of Henry's mother. Richard bravely rushed into the swirl of the fight, laid low several warriors, but was himself slain. The crown which he wore during the battle fell into a bush, and was recovered afterwards, to be placed by Stanley on the head of his stepson, who thus became Henry VII. The Wars of the Roses were over.

IV

The Triumph of the Monarchy Under the Tudors

Henry VII to Elizabeth I, 1485-1603

FOR FIFTEEN years longer pretenders would arise, but at no moment would they endanger the throne of Henry VII, now united in marriage with Elizabeth of York. This stability was the more surprising as Henry was no warrior. Round this sad, grave, thoughtful man two legends took shape. One, the creation of Henry himself in his own lifetime, evoked the image of someone distant and enigmatic, a sovereign who was no longer the foremost amongst his noble peers, but a being set apart — in fact, the *monarch*. The second, the legend of the historians, depicted a distrustful, avaricious king who drained vast treasures from the coffers of the nobility into his own. The truth seems to have been that this first King of the Tudor line loved money because, with the collapse of feudal society, money had become the new token of strength. In the sixteenth century a king in poverty would have been a king in chains, subject to his nobles and his Parliament. Henry VII and his children were to be dependent on neither. With no standing army beyond a bodyguard of a few score men, their sovereignty became more than respected: it was revered.

The Wars of the Roses had not annihilated the great lords, but it had certainly attenuated them. Only twenty-nine lords temporal were summoned to Henry VII's Parliament, and their influence in the country seemed to be trifling. After the fall of the Empire and the anarchy of the invasions, the feudal lords, in the absence of a strong central power, had provided fairly well for the defence of the soil and the administration of justice. The success of the Norman and Angevin kings had then robbed that warrior aristocracy of its essential functions. Then, at the end of the fifteenth century, Spain and France formed States greater and stronger than England, and this left the warrior

nobles no opportunities for Continental adventuring. They could only fight amongst themselves, and the Wars of the Roses had the twofold result of making citizens and peasantry weary of all feudal anarchy, and of enfeebling the relics of the Anglo-Norman baronage. Who could inherit their power? There was the Parliament, but after a brilliant start Parliament also had lost much of its prestige. The House of Commons made itself felt only by joining hands with one faction or the other. In any case, it could be freely elected only if a strong central power protected the electors against interference from local magnates. Only the king could bridge the gap between feudal and parliamentary rule. With nobility and the Commons in abeyance, the path lay open to monarchy.

In disarming the surviving nobles and their partisan bands, the Tudor kings made use of three newer classes — the gentry, the yeomen, and the merchants. The gentry consisted in the mass of country gentlemen. A ' gentleman ' need not be of noble rank, need not even own feudal lands. The gentry comprised the descendants of the knight as well as the rich merchant, the former mayor of his borough, who had bought an estate to retire to, and likewise the successful lawyer who had become a landed proprietor. Then as now, doubtless, there was a probationary period before the county families proper accepted the new squire. The gentry's minimum line in property qualification was the twenty pounds of revenue which in the old days constitued the knight, and by now entitled a landowner to be a justice of the peace. In fact, wealth succeeded birth as the basis of a small aristocracy.

The yeomen also were a rural class, coming below the gentry, and above the old-time villein. Roughly speaking the yeomanry included persons

HENRY VII. He was a Lancaster on his mother's side. By marrying Elizabeth of York, daughter of Edward IV, he reconciled the Red Rose with the White. (*National Portrait Gallery*).

having at least forty shillings of revenue requisite for jury service or a county electoral qualification, but not attaining the twenty pounds which would make them, in this sense, gentlemen. These yeomen were the famous bowmen of the Hundred Years War. They feared neither fighting nor manual toil; they formed a staunch and solid body, economically, politically and socially; and having everything to lose by public disorder, they sided with the king.

In the early sixteenth century the English merchants did not yet hold their later pre-eminence in the wider world. A few, half pirates, half ship-owners, pushed as far as Russia to sell their cloth, or competed with Venetians or Genoese in the Mediterranean; but, in the conquest of new worlds which was then beginning, England took no part. There was, however, one man in those days who caught a glimpse of his country's future lying on the seas; and that man was Henry VII. He encouraged navigation as far as lay in his power. He built great ships, like the *Mary Fortune* and the *Sweepstake*, which he hired out to merchants, and he fitted out expeditions such as Cabot's which,

seeking the spices of the Orient, discovered the cod of Newfoundland. His Navigation Act (1489) forbade the importation of Bordeaux wines in foreign ships. Henry VII apparently realized that the struggle for external markets would become a dominating political issue; his fostering of the fleet and of sea-borne trade won him the loyalty of the large towns, and of London in particular.

Supported by this triple power of gentry, yeomen and merchants, the king could checkmate the surviving power of the baronage. Knowing how provincial juries could be intimidated by the prestige of their former masters, he brought any dangerous charges before a prerogative court, formed from his own Council, which was called the court of Star Chamber from the decoration of the room where it sat. Sentence of death was rare under Henry VII. 'He drew more gold than blood', being rightly persuaded that an extraction of money would be quite soon forgotten by the victim, whilst it would certainly fill the royal coffers. But he compelled respect for his will. Once, when visiting the Earl of Oxford, he was received by a whole company of uniformed servants. A recent law strictly forbade noblemen to maintain such body-guards, who could too readily be transformed into soldiers. As he left, King Henry said to his host: 'I thank you for your good cheer, my Lord, but I may not endure to have my laws broken in my sight. My attorney must speak with you.' And the Earl was glad to be free of the matter with a fine of £10,000. These methods of combating the old feudal machine were harsh but salutary, and the Star Chamber itself performed much useful work. But the principle of the prerogative courts, inasmuch as they deprived the accused of the benefit of jury trial, was reprehensible, and contrary to the liberties of the realm. This was clearly seen when, under the Stuarts, they became instruments of tyranny.

In politics as in justice, Henry VII gave legality a holiday. He summoned Parliament only seven times during his reign. But who could grumble? The confusion of the civil wars had resolved any political conflict in favour of the Crown. True, the king ruled only with the help of his Council, but the Council did not, like that of the Norman kings, represent only magnates and prelates. The new councillors were the sons of burgesses, trained in the universities. Noble lines were founded, not now by the warrior, but by the high functionary. The personal servant of the king was succeeded by the Secretary of State.

An important contrast between French and English history is found in the development in France of a hierarchy of officials dependent on, and paid by, the central government, as against the growth in England of local institutions voluntarily administered. The natural tendency of the Tudor sovereign was to use whatever was ready to hand, and to solve new problems by referring them to the established mechanism. What survived of the old Saxon *folkmoot* in the countryside, after several centuries of feudalism? The parish meeting seemed to bear the nearest resemblance; and the parish revenue, administered by representatives of the parishioners, came from its land, or from herds belonging to the parish, and from the church rate, as fixed by the vestrymen in proportion to every man's goods.

With the sixteenth century the problem of the poor assumed new and grave aspects, and the Tudor kings adopted the parish as the basis of a system of relief. Every Eastertide the parish had to appoint four guardians of the poor, who collected alms with the churchwardens. Every parishioner was asked for such charity as he could give weekly to the poor. The amount of alms was at first left to each man's discretion; those who refused to give were summoned before the bishop, and occasionally imprisoned. But with the spread of poverty in the land, the charge had to be made compulsory. In principle every parish had sole responsibility for its poor, and it was strictly forbidden for any person without means of subsistence to wander from village to village. To give alms to a vagabond was an offence. If a vagabond were caught, he was liable to a whipping, and if habitually offending branded with a 'V' on the shoulder to mark him out. The rogue, or dangerous vagabond, was marked with an 'R'. Custom being thus, no parish could tolerate the settlement within its bounds of an indigent family whose children might one day be a charge upon its resources. A man might become, in effect, a prisoner in his parish.

But in the sixteenth century it was coming to be recognized that society has a duty to keep alive, after a fashion at least, its aged and infirm, its blind and crazed. A law of 1597 ordered the building of hospitals for the infirm on waste lands, and the provision by the guardians of stocks of raw material to enable them to give work to the workless, and also that poor children should be put out as apprentices. This led to the building by wealthy men of free houses for the poor, almshouses, buildings which often strike us nowadays as full of charm, for it was an age of many graces. The law required that every cottage be surrounded by about four acres, to enable the occupant, by cultivating his plot of land, to produce his own livelihood. To the penniless aged, the parish had to pay a weekly pittance of a groat, or a shilling. If the burden of the poor of one parish became excessive, a richer parish might be ordered to help its neighbour. But the principle of local help was maintained, and the central government never took part in such relief.

In every parish one man was charged with arresting and whipping vagabonds, pacifying brawlers, stopping illegal games, and in general compelling respect for the King's Peace. This non-professional police officer was elected for one year and was called the petty constable. The office had been created by Edward I, to inspect weapons,

SIR THOMAS MORE AND HIS FAMILY. This family portrait was painted by an unknown artist c. 1593; the left side is based on a sketch made by Holbein in 1527. Thomas More, wearing his chain of office as Lord Chancellor, sits next to his father. He went to the block for refusing to acknowledge Henry VIII as head of the Church in England. (National Portrait Gallery). *Hachette.*

ensure the protection of villages, and pursue malefactors. This unfortunate citizen had a troublesome year before him, as he was entirely responsible for the tranquillity of his parish. If a vagabond was arrested by someone else, the constable instantly found himself sentenced to a fine for neglect of his duties. If he himself made an arrest, he must keep the malefactor in his own house (there being frequently no prison), and then conduct him to the county court. It was he, too, who had to place petty offenders in the village stocks.

Just as the yeoman was called upon to act as constable or sit on the jury, so it was the squire's duty to accept the function of justice of the peace. This post was not an elected one; he was chosen by the king, and the commission could be revoked at the royal pleasure. He was the link between parish and county. In the parish wherein he was the big landowner, living in the manor-house, he was respected as the leading personality in the community. Four times a year he sat with his colleagues in a county-town at the quarter sessions, where he dealt with the most diverse business, some judicial, some administrative. Thus all the parish life passed under the eye of a justice of the peace, before whom delinquents were brought by the constable. The village horizon was narrow. The communal fields still survived, in regions where they had been customary, providing plenty of trouble for the constable as they facilitated theft and bickering. On week-days everybody worked, not to work being an offence. Church attendance on Sunday was obligatory, and those who failed to go were fined for the benefit of the poor. All activities were under surveillance. It was a grave offence to accuse a woman of witchcraft, as the consequences for her might be terrible. Sometimes old women were suspected of casting spells on cattle or men, but fortunately the justices shrugged their shoulders and refrained from burning all the witches brought before them. No man dared leave his village without valid and lawful reason. Strolling players could move about only with a warrant granted by a justice of the peace, in default of which they were treated as rogues and vagabonds, and whipped and branded accordingly. University students wishing to travel had to carry passes from their colleges. Tilling the fields and performing the numerous public duties of the village left men little leisure to think of other matters. But they could catch glimpses of the function of a central government. New edicts were proclaimed in the king's name, from the pulpit or at the market cross. The yeomen went to the town for the quarter sessions; the justices received their commissions from the king himself; the Lord Lieutenant occasionally went to London and was acquainted with the king's ministers. Slowly, in every village, there was forming the living cell of a great body, the State.

Side by side with the transformation of the medieval political structure, there came about in Tudor times a corresponding change in the spiritual and intellectual structure of England. The consequences there of the Italian Renaissance and the German Reformation were very remarkable. The sensuousness of the great Italians, their passionate love of statues and pictures, their awakening to pagan antiquity, the sermons exalting the Christian virtues by lines from Horace or apophthegms of Seneca, the humanist and all-too-human Popes, were all very disturbing to many young Englishmen who came to sit at the feet of Savonarola or Marsilio Ficino. Italy welcomed rebels or artists, and inspired Chaucer; but she startled the average Englishman. ' Englishman italianate, devil incarnate, ' said a sixteenth-century proverb. And yet the Englishman felt himself as remote from Germanic violence as from Italian sensuality. The brutality of Luther's genius alarmed the scholars of Oxford, and at first attracted only the Cambridge youth or the Lollard ' poor priests '. The early Oxford reformers desired to rectify the errors of the Roman Church, but did not imagine that a Christian could leave its fold. Some of those who first spread the new learning, men like Thomas More and John Fisher, were later to die for the old Church.

John Colet, at once a great Latinist and a rich burgess, is the most representative figure of this generation. He was the son of a Lord Mayor of London and pursued his studies at Oxford, reading Plato and Plotinus. About 1493 he travelled in France and Italy, where he acquired a deeper knowledge of the Church Fathers, whose philosophy he preferred to the scholastic doctrines still taught at Oxford. On returning to his own university, this young man drew crowds of enthusiastic students to his lectures on the Epistles of St. Paul by the stimulating character of his understanding; and he

JOHN COLET was an Oxford scholar in the van of ecclesiastical reform and became Dean of St. Paul's. He was a friend of More and Erasmus. The portrait is by Hans Holbein. (Collection of H. M. the Queen). *Crown Copyright reserved.*

sprang into sudden fame. Priests came to consult him, and were reassured; he cannot have been regarded as dangerous, since he was appointed Dean of St. Paul's at an early age. When his father left him a large fortune, he devoted it to founding St. Paul's School in London, where Greek and Latin should be taught to one hundred and fifty-three boys.

Of Colet's friends and followers, the most remarkable was Thomas More, who was at once a great administrator and a great writer, his *Utopia* being the best book of its age. In it More proclaimed a communistic mode of society, disdainful of gold, making work obligatory upon all, although limited to nine hours a day. Monkish asceticism he condemned, and believed in the excellence of human nature. And in his pictured utopia all religions were permitted, Christianity being given no peculiar privilege. The true aim of John Colet, of Thomas More, and of their friend Erasmus, was the reformation of the Church, not by violence or persecution but by reason and enlightenment. No error could be greater than to view these early English Reformers as precursors of an anti-Catholic movement. They simply wished to improve the spirit and morality of the clergy. But they encountered strong currents of opinion which carried their disciples infinitely further away than they would themselves have desired. Sixteenth-century England was not anti-religious, but anti-clerical. All the old grievances were still alive — ecclesiastical

courts, monastic wealth, episcopal luxury. English monarchs and statesmen were pained to see their sovereignty partially delegated to the foreign power of a Papacy which knew so little about their country. And since the days of Wycliffe, Lollardry was an underground force. In merchants' lofts, in the taverns of Oxford and Cambridge, the English version of the Bible was read and commented upon by fervent voices. In the middle classes, under Wycliffite influence, centres of ascetic, individualist morality had come into being, which in years to come would be rekindled and fanned into living flames. Here the doctrines of Luther would find a ready welcome, the ascetic teachings of Calvin still more.

The reign of Henry VII (1485-1509) favoured the development of the studies and ponderings of such Reformers, as it was a reign of comparative peacefulness. If the Tudors contrived to strike solid roots, if local institutions became strong enough to supplant the machinery of feudalism, this was due to the twenty-five years of peace at home and abroad which this cautious, mysterious progenitor gave to his country before the dramatic reigns of his son and grandchildren.

Fashion moulds kings just as it imposes costume and custom. A great medieval king had to be courteous, chivalrous, stern and devout; a great prince of the Renaissance was a cultured libertine, spectacular, and often cruel. Henry VIII had all those qualities, but they were translated into Eng-

HENRY VIII JOUSTING BEFORE HIS WIFE, CATHERINE OF ARAGON. The king has just broken a lance. His saddle-cloth is adorned with the letter K (Katherine) and with hearts. The box in which the queen and courtiers sit is adorned with Tudor roses and Henry's portcullis emblem. From the « Westminster Tournament Roll » in the *Victoria and Albert Museum.*

lish: that is, his libertine life was conjugal, his culture was theological and sporting, his splendour was in good taste, his cruelty was legally correct. So he remained in his subjects' eyes, despite his crimes, a popular sovereign. Even to-day he is defended by English historians. The grave Bishop Stubbs opines that the portraits of his wives explain, if they do not perhaps justify, his haste to eliminate them. Professor Pollard wonders why it is particularly blameworthy to have had six wives, when Catherine Parr had had four husbands and her brother-in-law the Duke of Suffolk four wives without anyone blaming them. Henry, he says, might have had many more than six mistresses without damaging his reputation. True enough; but Henry IV of France never had the necks of the fair Corisande or Gabrielle d'Estrées laid on the block.

When Henry VIII succeeded his father in 1509, he was eighteen years of age, a fine athlete, proud of his person (immensely gratified when the Venetian ambassador told him that his calf was more shapely than Francis I's), a capital bowman and tennis player, a great horseman who could wear out ten horses in a day's hunting. He had literary tastes, being well grounded at once in theology and the romances, composed poems, set his own hymns to music, and played the lute 'divinely'. Erasmus knew him as a child, and was struck by his precocious intelligence. The new humanists found in

him a friend. He brought Colet to London and appointed him a court preacher; he made the reluctant Thomas More a courtier, and then his Chancellor; he asked Erasmus to accept a chair at Cambridge. It should be added that he was very devout, and that his Oxford friends, Reformers though they were, had strengthened his respect for the Catholic faith. Surprising as it may seem, he sought throughout his life to satisfy the scruples and fears of 'a completely medieval conscience'.

Shortly after his accession the King married Catherine of Aragon, widow of his brother Arthur and a daughter of Ferdinand of Spain. She was neither his choice nor his love: it was a political marriage. To contemporary England, a secondary power, this Spanish alliance was both an honour and a safeguard, and when it was broken by the early death of Prince Arthur, the Council, in their anxiety to have Catherine as Queen, begged Henry to take her as his wife. But a text in Leviticus forbade the union of brother-in-law with sister-in-law, and a Papal bull had to be obtained in 1503; it had to be proved that Catherine's first marriage had not been consummated. Witnesses were found to swear this, and on the day of the wedding with Henry she wore the hanging tresses of maidenhood. These facts assumed significance later, when the King sought to repudiate her.

Henry at first took little part in governing, and left all authority to the minister of his choice —

Thomas Wolsey, the son of a wealthy butcher in Ipswich, whom the Pope at Henry's request appointed a Cardinal. Vanity and ambition ruled Wolsey's character. His household was regal, with its four hundred servants, its sixteen chaplains, its own choirboys. To found the great college at Oxford, now known as Christ Church, and to compel admiration of his liberality, this archbishop did not scruple to rob the monasteries. When Pope Leo X made him not only Cardinal, but Papal Legate in England as well, Wolsey held in his own hands the whole civil and ecclesiastical power in England. He thus inured the English to the new idea of spiritual and temporal authority being both in one man's hands. Intoxicated with power, Wolsey treated Rome with scorn; he had schemes for bribing the Sacred College and having himself elected Pope, threatening the Church with schism if he were not chosen. Such gestures of violence prepared the English Catholics for rupture with Rome, but neither the Cardinal nor his royal master then supposed the break to be near. When Luther's declaration was made public, the King himself wrote a refutation which earned him the Papal title of Defender of the Faith (1521).

Foreign affairs were Wolsey's favourite concern. Abroad as in England, strong monarchies were then emerging from the feudal struggles. The Kings of France and Spain were by now the heads of great states: if one gained mastery and dominated Europe, where would England stand? The natural role of England was to maintain the balance of power on the Continent. This involved a shifting and apparently treacherous policy, which at first succeeded. Francis I and Charles V of Austria were rivals for the alliance of Henry VIII. On the Field of the Cloth of Gold, in 1520, the Kings of France and England staged a contest in magnificence which was never to be equalled again. But to follow that meeting speedily, Wolsey had already prepared another — between his master and the Emperor Charles. After a long show of favour for the French alliance, Wolsey at last chose that of the Emperor, because the English merchants so insisted. An interruption of trade with Spain and the Low Countries would have ruined the wool-merchants and drapers. But trade is a bad counsellor in diplomacy. By sacrificing Francis I, England upset the balance of power in favour of Charles V. After the battle of Pavia in 1525, the Emperor, sovereign of Spain, Italy, Germany and the Low Countries, was the master of all Europe. In particular, he had the Pope within his grip; and this, by indirect ways, was to prove the undoing of Cardinal Wolsey.

It is unjust towards Henry VIII to explain his divorce and the breach with Rome by his passion for the dark eyes of Anne Boleyn. If England was to be spared a new War of the Roses (and dire memories of anarchy were still fresh in many minds), it seemed essential that the royal spouses should have a son. But Catherine, after frequent miscarriages, had produced only one daughter, Mary, born in 1516; and her health left small hope of her bearing other children. The King, eager to have a son, began to wonder whether some evil star did not overhang his marriage. Had the Papal dispensation been valid? Henry was superstitiously ready to doubt it, after so many disappointments. But he still hesitated to divorce. Catherine was the aunt of Charles V, who would certainly side with her, and it was Henry's cherished hope that the Emperor would marry Mary, to crown a great alliance. When Charles went back on his promises and chose as his consort an Infanta of Portugal, the King of England felt that he need not trouble further about the Emperor's feelings.

In love with the charming, merry, young Anne Boleyn, Henry VIII wished to marry her in order to have a lawful heir, and sought means of getting rid of Catherine of Aragon. Civil divorce was unknown, and the King had to petition Rome for the annulment of his marriage. This seemed easy enough, as the Pope had previously shown extreme latitude in such matters where crowned heads were concerned. The rumour spread that Henry doubted the lawfulness of his marriage, and had grave scruples of conscience about remaining illegally wedded. Wolsey was instructed to negotiate with the Papal court, and immediately met with an opposition of a quite secular kind: Charles V, with Rome in his grasp, refused to let his aunt Catherine and his cousin Mary be sacrificed. The Pope, for his part, would have been ready enough to satisfy Henry, and sent as Legate to England the Cardinal Campeggio, who was to hear the case along with Wolsey. The King supposed that the matter was settled, but Catherine appealed to Rome and induced the Pope to have the case heard in his own

ANNE BOLEYN (1507-1536). A lady-in-waiting to Catherine of Aragon, she caught Henry's fancy and might have remained nothing more than his mistress had he not been anxious for a legitimate male heir. For failing to produce one — she bore Queen Elizabeth instead — and for other misdemeanours she was decapitated. *National Portrait Gallery.*

court. Henry's annoyance this time was extreme, and Wolsey's position became dangerous. Like all men with ambition, the Cardinal had enemies. A charge of *praemunire*, tantamount to treason, was made against him because, being an English subject, he had consented to be a Papal Legate and deal with matters pertaining to the King's court before a foreign tribunal. The charge was absurd, as the King himself had authorized and favoured the nomination. But the Cardinal found no defenders; he had to give up all his wealth, and only mortal illness saved him from the scaffold.

With anxiety in his heart, Sir Thomas More took Wolsey's place as Lord Chancellor. But the two men who at the moment had most authority with the King himself were chosen because, in this matter of the divorce, they brought a gleam of hope. The other was Thomas Cranmer, an ecclesiastic with whom Henry's secretary Gardiner had once had conversation, in the course of which he had said that the King need not pursue his case at Rome: all he needed was that some eminent theologians should certify the nullity of his first marriage, and he could then take the moral responsibility of a fresh marriage with neither scruples nor danger. The King was delighted, and began to follow his advice by consulting the universities. Theologians, like lawyers, can make texts square with facts. From Oxford and Cambridge the desired opinions were produced by a little cajoling and intimidation; the University of Paris was favourable because it hated Charles V; and the universities of northern Italy followed Paris. Before long the King was able to lay before Parliament the opinion of eight learned societies, agreeing that a marriage with a deceased brother's widow was null and void, and that not even the Pope could in such a case grant dispensation. Members of Parliament were requested to report these facts to their constituencies and to describe generally the scruples of the King. Henry, indeed, felt that the country was opposed to the divorce. But time was going by. Anne was expecting a child, who ought to be the desired heir and must therefore be born in wedlock. The gentle, malleable Cranmer was appointed Archbishop of Canterbury, and secretly married the King and Anne in January 1533. At Easter the marriage was made public; Anne was crowned, Henry excommunicated. The breach with Rome had come.

The rupture would have been less crude if Henry VIII had not had other counsellors besides More and Cranmer. The former, a man of fine conscience, would have accepted only wise and temperate reform; Cranmer, too weak to be harmful, would have talked and temporized. It was Thomas Cromwell who played the Iago to this Othello. Cromwell began life at Putney as a wool-merchant and fuller; travel in Flanders and Italy taught him the arts of trading, the new political ideas, and made him a fervent reader of Italian books on statecraft. On his return he became a moneylender, and a favoured servant of Cardinal Wolsey. Cromwell was highly intelligent, vulgar but witty, and had in him neither scruples nor religion. Rival theologies were of no account to him, but he was conquered by the theory of State supremacy. When he met the King he advised him to follow the example of the German princes who had broken with Rome. England should no longer have two masters or twofold systems of justice and taxation. As the Pope refused to confirm the repudiation of Catherine, the King should not bow, but must make the Church his servant. Henry VIII despised Cromwell; he

always called him 'the wool-carder', and ill-treated him. But he made use of his skill, his servility, and his strength. The wool-carder became within a few years Master of the Rolls, Lord Privy Seal, Vicar-General of the Church, Lord Great Chamberlain, a Knight of the Garter, and Earl of Essex.

The spoliation of the Church was according to law, and Henry VIII respected parliamentary forms. The Parliament of 1529, which sat for seven years, voted all the special measures put before it by the Crown. To begin with, the clergy were informed that, like Wolsey, they had violated the Statute of Praemunire, in agreeing to recognize the authority of the Cardinal as Legate. As amends for this offence they had to pay a fine of two million pounds, grant the King the title of Protector and Supreme Head of the Church, and abolish the annates, or first fruits of ecclesiastical benefices and posts, which had previously been paid to the Pope. (They were in fact appropriated to Henry's use.) The Parliament then voted successively the Statute of Appeals, forbidding appeals to Rome; the Act of Supremacy, making the King the sole and supreme head of the Church of England, giving him spiritual as well as lay jurisdiction, as also the right to reform and suppress error and heresy; and lastly the Act of Succession, which annulled the first marriage, deprived children born thereof of their rights to the throne in favour of the offspring of Anne Boleyn, and obliged all the King's subjects to swear that they accepted the religious validity of the divorce. It may be wondered how a Catholic Parliament voted these measures confirming the schism, in which the Pope was referred to merely as 'Bishop of Rome'. But it should be borne in mind that there was the deepest respect for the King's person and will; that the nascent nationalism of England had long been intolerant of foreign jurisdiction; that the Papacy was regarded as an ally of Spain and France; that, apart from the national sentiment, a strong anti-clerical prejudice demanded, not the ruination of the Church, but the abolition of Church tribunals and the seizure of monastic wealth; and lastly, that new social classes had learned to read printed books, and that many men desired an English Prayer Book and an English Bible. The Reformation in England was not only a sovereign's caprice, but also the religious mani-

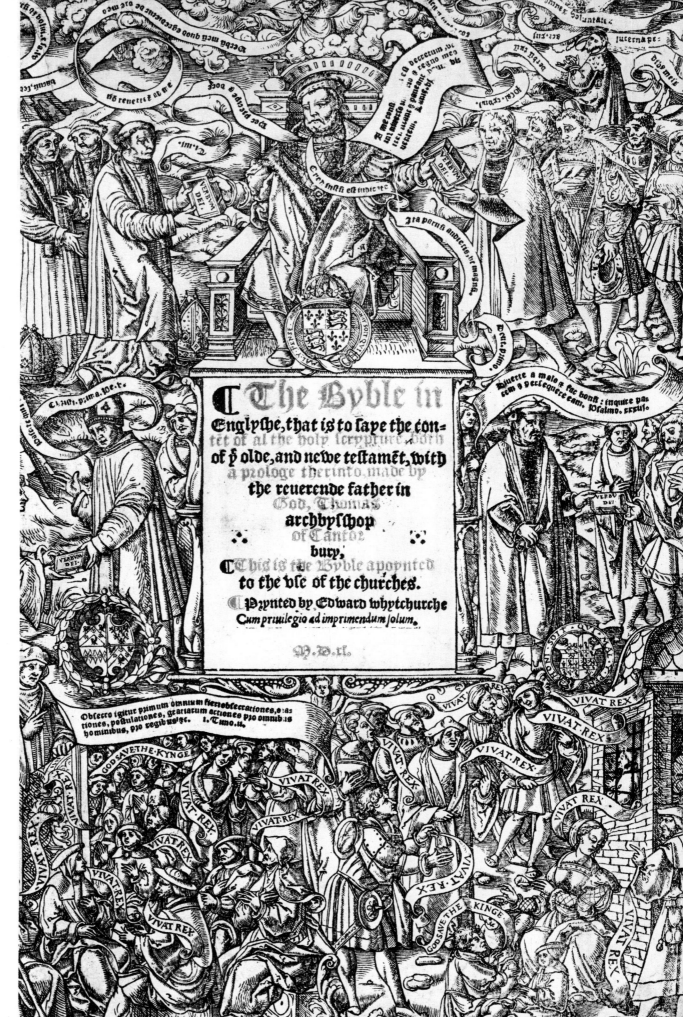

FRONTISPIECE OF THE «CRAN-
MER BIBLE» (1540). King
Henry VIII is seen present-
ing a copy of «the byble in
Englyshe» to Thomas Cran-
mer, the reformed (and
married) Archbishop of Canterbury, author of the pro-
logue, and to Thomas
Cromwell, Earl of Essex,
Henry's Lord Great Cham-
berlain. These two, in
their turn, distribute the
book among the common
people. *British Museum.*

festation of an insular and linguistic nationalism which had long been germinating.

A Church with ten or twelve centuries behind it has deep roots, and the most powerful of monarchs could not wrench them up without a struggle. Yet, with a few exceptions, bishops and priests showed remarkable pliability. They had long been affected by the growing strength of national sentiment, and the English prelates were on the whole statesmen rather than churchmen. The higher clergy were pervaded by a sort of pre-Anglicanism. The lesser clergy were poor, and felt some measure of security in becoming a body of State officials; they had been influenced by Lollard teachings, and had never gladly accepted the celibacy of their order. When the oath was submitted to all, and it became treasonable to deny the chastity and sanctity of the marriage between Henry and Anne, and to acknowledge the supremacy of ' the Bishop of Rome who usurps the title of Pope ', nearly all the priesthood swore to it. But the Lord Chancellor, Sir Thomas More, and Bishop John Fisher refused to recant the articles of Catholic faith, and both were beheaded. This divorce comedy was becoming a hideous tragedy, and a reign of terror set in. Numerous monks were hanged, drawn and quartered. In some counties the Catholics were inflamed with just horror when they heard of these human butcheries, and rose in revolt. But they were crushed.

The refusal of the monks to accept the oath rejoiced the heart of Thomas Cromwell, who had long been pondering their undoing. England contained about twelve hundred monastic houses, owning vast domains. Confiscation of their property would enrich the King and the liquidators. The popular wave of feeling against the monks, and widespread legends of their vices, would silence their defenders. These legends were exaggerated, but Cromwell, appointed as Vicar-General with the right of visitation, compiled huge records of the monks' misdeeds, and by revealing these ' atrocities ' to Parliament procured the dissolution, first, of the smaller monasteries, and then of all religious houses. In five years' time the liquidation of monastic property was completed, bringing much to the royal treasury, and enriching those to whom the King handed over the abbeys, or those who bought them cheap. The political outcome of these measures was analogous with those seen in France when the national properties were sold after the Revolution of 1789. The purchasers became accomplices. Fear of a return of the former owners gave the new religious regime the support of a rich and powerful class. Henceforward self-interest and doctrine would conspire against a counter-attack from Roman Catholicism.

The Credo of this new Church was for a long time vague. If the hands of Cromwell, Crammer and Latimer had been free, they would have linked it to the Lutheran body. But Henry VIII, like his people, had instinct, and knew that although Englishmen had often been hostile to monks and eccle-

ANNE OF CLEVES (1515-1557), Henry's fourth wife. Thomas Cromwell, seeing a politically advantageous match, brought her over from Germany but the king found her unappealing and divorced her. He also had Cromwell executed. The portrait is by Holbein. (Copyright *Victoria and Albert Museum*).

HENRY VIII BESTOWS THE SUCCESSION ON EDWARD VI. A satirical painting (c. 1548) which shows the young king who, in Roman eyes, is illegitimate, triumphing over the Pope. Through the window reformers can be seen overthrowing religious statues. (National Portrait Gallery). *Hachette.*

siastical courts, they were in general unlikely to
welcome the innovations of the Protestants. Henry
himself clung to his title of Defender of the Faith,
and to his claim to be the head of a 'Catholic'
Church; but he wanted this, contradictory though
it seemed, to be a national Catholicism. His persecution of the loyalists of the ancient faith was
followed by one, no less vigorous, of the Protestants. The first printer of an English Bible, William
Tyndale, was sent to the stake, and others perished
likewise for denying Transubstantiation. After
several attempts at formulating an Anglican creed,
Henry brought the House of Lords to pass the
Six Articles, which affirmed the truth of Transubstantiation, the needlessness of communion in both
kinds, the validity of vows of chastity, the excellence
of clerical celibacy, and approved confession and
private Masses. Flagrant contravention was pun-
ishable by the stake, and not even recantation would
save the guilty. The Protestant bishops, such as
Latimer, had to resign.

It had required a schism to rupture Henry's first
marriage; an axe sufficed to sunder the second.
Poor Anne Boleyn made two mistakes; instead of
the expected heir, she produced a daughter, Elizabeth, then a stillborn son; and she deceived the
King. For these crimes her pretty head was slashed
off. Within a few days, clad in white, Henry
married Jane Seymour. The obsequious Cranmer
had annulled the second marriage, and the Princess
Elizabeth, like Mary before her, became a bastard.
Jane Seymour had a son, who was to reign as
Edward VI, but she died in childbed. Cromwell,
ever anxious to bring the King closer to the Lu-
therans, suggested a fresh matrimonial alliance, this
time with a German princess, Anne of Cleves. The
man of affairs sought to play the role of match-
maker; but the wife proved distasteful and the
experiment cost Cromwell his life. Henry's fifth
wife, Catherine Howard, also went to the block for
infidelity to her lord. His sixth, Catherine Parr,
survived him. The reign ended in blood.

A strange trio, the children of Henry VIII. The
heir to the throne, Edward VI, son of Jane Seymour, was a solemn, precocious little boy, who
read ten chapters of the Bible every day and was
styled by the Reformers 'a new Josiah'. Mary,
daughter of Catherine of Aragon, was already
thirty-one. She was beginning to look faded, with
the pallor of her round face accentuated by the red
hair, and she seemed sickly and gloomy. More
proud of being the descendant of the Kings of
Spain than of being the King of England's daughter, she remained a fervent Catholic, surrounded

by priests and spending her life in the chapel. Anne Boleyn's daughter, Elizabeth, was a slight girl of fourteen, quite pretty, well built, very vivacious, and showing the traditional Tudor fondness for classical culture. Being a Protestant like her half-brother Edward, though with less conviction, she was on terms of real understanding with the boy-King, and they both stood together in opposition to Mary.

The religious problem had not been solved by the schism. Whilst some counties were regretting Catholicism, London was stirred up by Protestant preachers like Latimer and desired a more complete Reformation. Most Englishmen were ready to accept a compromise which, while maintaining the essential rites familiar to them, would have loosed all ties with Rome. The Archbishop of Canterbury, Cranmer, continued to waver nervously between Lutheran and Roman views. But it was he who gave the Church of England its Book of Common Prayer, written in truly admirable prose, to which he himself contributed litanies and collects, and so enabled that Church to acquire in succession to the Church of Rome that aesthetic potency without which a religion has little hold over the souls of men. Anti-Catholic persecutions continued. In the churches walls were whitewashed, stained glass broken, the crucifix replaced by the royal escutch-

eon. All symbolic ceremonies were abolished. The Act of Uniformity, voted by Parliament, obliged all churches to use the Book of Common Prayer and observe the same ritual. But even this uniformity had a variety of forms.

These far-reaching changes were painful to simple souls, who clung to the rites which for a thousand years had been woven into the pattern of their ancestors' and their own lives. It was a time of deep popular discontent. Unemployment, almost unknown in the medieval economy, was becoming a grave evil. Its causes were manifold. The enforced disbanding of the lords' armed men in the opening years of the century had sent thousands of soldiers tramping the roads with no craft or trade. Agricultural labourers found work scarce. At the time of the Black Death some of the great landowners began to breed and graze sheep instead of growing grain, and this needed fewer hands. During the sixteenth century many squires made bold to enclose parts of the common meadows and heaths, in order to keep their flocks. This process of 'enclosures' deprived peasants of their land, workers of their work. By the time of King Henry's death the peasants were murmuring.

During the minority of Edward VI, the regency was in the hands of his uncle, Edward Seymour,

on page 125:

THE EXECUTION OF LATIMER AND RIDLEY, at Oxford, October 1555. An illustration from Foxe's *Book of Martyrs*. They were leading Oxford reformers, who, like Cranmer, suffered death for their convictions under Mary. The cause of Anglicanism was immeasurably advanced. *British Museum*.

MARY TUDOR AT THE AGE OF 28. The daughter of Henry VIII by Catherine of Aragon, she was the first queen of England to reign in her own right. Her marriage to Philip of Spain did not make her popular in England; nor did her ruthless attempt to restore Catholicism in the country. She died after a five-year reign. This portrait is by Joannes Corvus. (National Portrait Gallery). *Walker and Boutall*, London.

Duke of Somerset, the brother of Jane Seymour. The most conspicuous of his qualities was his tolerance. But he was held responsible for these agrarian disturbances, his pride offended the courtiers, and the landed aristocracy, led by the Earl of Warwick, took forfeit of his head. Warwick, later Duke of Northumberland, became chief of the council of regency, and undertook the persecution of the Catholics with a vigour that Somerset had lacked. Edward VI then fell ill, and when it was clear that his sickness was mortal, Northumberland, in apprehension of the Crown coming to the Spanish and Romanist Mary, put forward the claims of Lady Jane Grey, a great-grand-daughter of Henry VII, and married her to his own son. He made the dying King sign a testament in favour of Lady Jane.

This hapless young woman, an unwilling usurper, was proclaimed Queen by Northumberland, who marched on London. But Mary was not the woman to be brushed aside unprotesting. A true Spaniard, she had a soldier's courage and a fanatical devoutness. She had only to show herself to conquer, and the glamour of her father's name was a shield. The Catholics, still vigorous, welcomed their deliverance at her hands; she promised impartiality to the Protestants; and the numerous masses of indifferent men were weary of a regime which confiscated their property for the benefit of private exploiters on the pretext of reforming Church ritual. Bonfires blazed when Mary appeared in London, and the counties sent troops to her. The Council sent a herald and four trumpeters to proclaim her Queen in the City, where she made a triumphal entry, her sister Elizabeth riding alongside her. Northumberland was imprisoned in the Tower and beheaded. The girl who had been his toy, poor Lady Jane Grey, had to wait six months before the same axe fell.

Mary Tudor is a lamentable example of the ravages that may be wrought in a woman's soul by the conjunction of love, bigotry and absolute power. She was a Catholic in a country where the generation now attaining manhood had been born out of the Roman allegiance, and where the capital city, the centre of gravity, had very strong Protestant leanings. During the long and painful years of her youth religion had been her one consolation. Now she was ready to undergo martyrdom to bring her people back to Rome. Through her first Parliament she re-established the Latin Mass and expelled married priests from the Church. The abrupt return to Papacy was the Queen's first rash step; her marriage completed her alienation from

the people. Parliament had good reason for dreading the influence of a foreign king, and respectfully prayed Mary to marry an Englishman. The Council and the nation had chosen for her young Edward Courtenay, a great-grandson of Edward IV. She denied their right to limit her matrimonial choice. The Spanish ambassador Renard, who had great influence with her, thereupon broached a plan of Charles V, who offered Mary the hand of his son Philip. Although these negotiations were kept secret, their purport was guessed by the Queen's ministers, to their perturbation. If an alliance were made between England, a weak and lately schismatic nation, and Spain, orthodox and all-powerful, what would be the fate of England? The English heretics already feared the courts of the Inquisition and the *auto-da-fé*, as frequent in Madrid as bull-fights. But alas, as soon as this virgin of thirty-six beheld a portrait of the handsome Spanish prince, she fell passionately in love. Everything conspired to heighten her passion for him: by marrying Philip she would satisfy at once her pride in being a Spanish princess, her Catholic beliefs, and her strong and unsatisfied desires.

The Spanish ambassador melted down four thousand gold coins, and had chains forged of this gold for distribution to members of the Council. Was

his action symbolic? The councillors were converted to the idea of the marriage by gifts, arguments and promises, but nevertheless they advised prudence in action. Philip must respect the laws of England; if Mary died, he could have no claim to the crown; a son born of the marriage would inherit the thrones of England, Burgundy, and the Low Countries; and Philip must pledge himself never to draw England into his wars against France. It was a sound treaty, but what real safeguards did it offer against a woman in love? The English people, hostile to foreigners and very hostile to Spaniards, showed their displeasure at once. And in several counties revolt broke out. Sir Thomas Wyatt marched on London, but her faith and her love seemed to make Mary invincible. Her ministers sought to make her take refuge in the Tower; but she remained at Whitehall, smiling, and thanks to the spell of the Tudors gained so ample a victory that nobody again ventured to raise a voice against the Spanish marriage. Rebels were hanged by the dozen. After which came the arrival of the Spanish prince. His father had described the pride of Englishmen, and bade him doff his Castilian arrogance. Philip did his best to be ingratiating, not without success, and the London merchants were impressed by the procession through the city of twenty carts of bullion from the gold-mines of America. On one point Philip remained intractable: there must be a reconciliation with Rome. He would rather not reign at all than reign over heretics. The Pope was advised of this, and sent over Cardinal Pole as his Legate to receive the submission of England. The gold bars in the Tower helped to prepare the minds of the noble families for this great event.

The Papal Legate landed. Philip and Mary declared that he had been created by Providence for this mission, which he certainly accomplished with the utmost tact. At Dover he was enthusiastically welcomed. It was known that the Pope had undertaken that the holders of ecclesiastical property should remain in possession. Parliament assembled at Whitehall to receive the Legate, and there in a lengthy speech he reviewed the history of the schism, and a few days later granted plenary absolution for the past. Both Houses received this kneeling. England was made whole.

The Queen believed herself pregnant. But when the day of confinement came and the bells were already pealing, the doctors realized that the pregnancy had been a manifestation of nervous imagination. This was a painful blow to Mary, and her mental state caused anxiety. In fact, the cruelty of her persecution of the Protestants, which gave her the name of 'Bloody' Mary, is doubtless partly explicable by a mental disorder which came very near to madness. Such rigorous action did not come from Philip's counsel. The burning of heretics, he thought, was excellent in Spain and the Netherlands; but in England prudence called for patience. Mary had none. On January 20, 1555, the law against heresy was restored; two days later the commissions began their sessions; on February 3 the first married priest was burned at Smithfield. About three hundred Protestants were martyred at the stake.

The accounts of these sacrifices were collected by a Protestant writer, John Foxe, in his *Book of Martyrs*, which long held a place beside the Bible in English homes. Mary's persecution gave the Protestants something which hitherto they had lacked — a sentimental and heroic tradition. Hatred of the Queen and the Spaniards rose higher. Despite his pledges, Philip drew his Queen into a war against France, and the campaign cost England

the stronghold of Calais. 'May God preserve Mistress Elizabeth!' murmured the subjects of Mary Tudor. And Mary meanwhile was a dying woman, abandoned by all. Even Pope Paul IV had sided against her and against Spain. On November 17, 1558, Queen Mary left this world. For a whole month she had been almost alone, while the whole court had gathered round Princess Elizabeth.

The accession of Elizabeth was greeted by the English people with almost unanimous joy. After their dread of Spanish tyranny, it was a relief to hail a Queen free of any foreign link. Not since the Norman Conquest had England had a sovereign so purely English in blood. Through her father Elizabeth was descended from the traditional kings; through her mother, from native gentry. Throughout her reign she flirted with her people. It has been said that the Tudor monarchy was as fully absolute as that of Louis XIV or the Empire of the Caesars; it has been recalled that Elizabeth led her Parliaments on a halter, that her warrants were like *lettres de cachet*, that her judges tortured accused parties in defiance of the law of the land. But Louis XIV and Tiberius had armies at their bidding to compel their will. Elizabeth, like her father and grandfather before her, had only a guard which the City militia could easily have put to rout. She was strong only because she was loved, or at least was preferred to others. At a time when nearly every kingdom in Europe was torn by religious strife, or stifled by terrors, she enjoyed showing the foreign ambassadors how she trusted her subjects. She forced her coach into the heart of the crowd, stood up, and talked with those surrounding it. 'God save your Majesty!' they cried. 'And God save my people!' she answered.

Her strength had many secrets; the most effective was a swift intuition of what could please her people. There was also a sense of economy worthy of King Henry VII. The people asked few liberties of Elizabeth, because she asked them for little money. Being poor, and also because she was a woman and not cruel, she disliked war. Occasionally she engaged in war, successfully, but she never ran to meet danger. To avoid it she was ready to lie, to swear to an ambassador that she was totally ignorant of a matter which had really been engaging all her attention, or, in the last resort,

ELIZABETH I. A portrait by an unknown artist showing the queen decked out in jewels and rich apparel. Spread out at her feet is southern England. (National Portrait Gallery). *Hachette*.

to shift the discussion on to a sentimental plane where her sex helped her to win her way. Her strength lay in withholding herself from force. Expedition or conquest, whichever it might be, she preferred to leave the responsibility for any bloodshed to others, and if in doubt, to stand aside. Her reign was far from being unstained by injustice; but probably she did as little harm as possible in a difficult time.

On one point, and one only, she always opposed her people's will. The Commons pressed her to marry in order to ensure the succession. So long as the Queen had no heir, her life and the national religion were imperilled. The murder of Elizabeth would suffice to give the throne to the Catholic Mary Stuart, Queen of Scots, the great-granddaughter of Henry VII and wife of the French Dauphin. It was a temptation to fanatics. But Elizabeth refused to consider marriage. Kings and princes paid their court in vain. With one and all she played the same game of coquetry, agreeable messages, poetic and sometimes bold flirtation, but every time she ended matters by slipping out of the long-drawn game. In this way she tantalized Philip II, Prince Eric of Sweden, the Archdukes Ferdinand and Charles of Austria, the Duke of Alençon, not to mention those handsome Englishmen whom she liked so well — Leicester, Essex and Raleigh, courtiers, soldiers and poets, to whom she granted great freedom and incomplete caresses, until the moment came when the woman became again the Queen, and sent them to the Tower. It has been said that she had a physical horror of marriage, and that a definite incapacity for motherhood made her decision final. A childless marriage would have subjected her to a husband and deprived her of her exceptional prestige as the Virgin Queen.

Some of the handsome youths who courted her certainly touched her heart; but she was always able to keep her mind free from the bewilderments of her senses. Her chosen counsellors were men of different stamp. Like her grandfather, she chose them from the ' new ' men, sons of yeomen or merchants, conspicuous for intelligence rather than high birth. In the Middle Ages, chivalrous virtues or ecclesiastical dignities had made men ministers; but Elizabeth required that hers should be men with administrative talents, and gifted with two newer sentiments — patriotism, and a feeling for State interests. Her chief counsellor, William Cecil (later Lord Burleigh), came of a yeoman family enriched by the distribution of monastic property, and was the founder of a family which, like the Russells and Cavendishes, was to be closely linked with the governance of the country until the present day. A middle-class man, he knew the middle classes accurately, and his ideas were congenial to them. On Elizabeth's accession he showed himself distrustful, having little fancy for the rule of women, and even ventured to reproach the ambassadors who addressed themselves to the Queen. Gradually he came to realize her strange, profound wisdom, and in the end they formed a wonderfully matched team, in conjunction with men like the grave Secretary of State Walsingham, more rigorously Protestant than Cecil, who desired ' first the glory of God, and then the safety of the Queen '. So close did the union of Queen and minister become, that it might be said of Elizabeth that she was at once female and male — herself and Cecil.

Was she Catholic or Protestant at heart? Many think she was pagan, or at least a sceptic. After a Protestant upbringing she had not hesitated, like Cecil, to save her life in the Marian persecution by a simulated conversion. She was perhaps philosophically religious, in the manner of Erasmus. On her accession she prayed God to grant her grace to rule without shedding blood. In that she failed, but she did her best. In religion as in politics she temporized, seeking an average in belief and cultivating compromise. Early in her reign Cecil obliged her to revert to the religious position of Henry VIII. In 1559 Parliament voted for a second time an Act of Supremacy, which abolished the Papal power in England, and the Act of Uniformity, which made the Book of Common Prayer obligatory in all parishes, as also the holding of services in the common tongue. By virtue of these Acts anyone upholding the spiritual power of the Pope was liable to confiscation of property. A refractory offender was guilty of high treason.

In 1563 came the adoption of the Thirty-Nine Articles, which were to remain the basis of Anglican belief. Their moderate Protestantism approximated to the feelings of the nation and, when Anglicanism was re-introduced by Crown and Parliament, 7000 out of 8000 priests accepted the change,

although 2000 of the most Protestant had been driven out under the rule of Mary. This submission was proof, not that the English were irreligious, but that many of them desired to retain Catholic rites while suppressing the use of Latin and refusing obedience to the Pope. Except in a few families, devotion to the sovereign was stronger than religious feeling. In the early years of the reign the crypto-Catholics were hardly disturbed. They were asked only to attend the Anglican service, and if they failed to do so had to pay a fine of twelve pence. If Elizabeth had been all-powerful, some degree of toleration would have been established. She wanted neither a Protestant inquisition nor a torture-chamber to test consciences. But her ministers, many more sectarian than herself, sent the refractory to prison; and three factors enabled Cecil, and Walsingham more particularly, to force Elizabeth's hand. The first was the Massacre of St. Bartholomew in Paris; the second, a bull of excommunication against the Queen, delivered at a very inopportune moment by Pope Pius V; and the third, the establishment of seminaries abroad, as at Douai, with the intention of pre-

paring the Catholic reconquest of England. Excommunication of the sovereign implied the freeing of the Catholic subjects from their bonds of loyalty, and it was even alleged that the Pope would willingly grant absolution for the murder of Elizabeth. After 1570, Catholic priests and laymen were executed in England, not for heresy but for high treason. Many of the men thus hanged, with hideous ceremonial and mutilation, were actually innocent, or saints. This was so in the case of the noble Jesuit, Edmund Campion, of whom even Burleigh had to admit that he was ' one of the jewels of England ', whose only crime had been that of going from house to house in disguise, preaching and celebrating the Mass. As he died, he said that he prayed for the Queen. Thus, although Elizabeth inclined to clemency, the victims of fanaticism during her reign were as numerous as under Mary.

Geneva suffered as well as Rome, and Calvinism, then spreading in England, was equally suspect with Catholicism. The Puritans would gladly have obliterated the last traces of Roman ceremonial and suppressed every hierarchy smack-

ing of the 'Scarlet Woman'. They had little respect for the Anglican bishops, parading their detestation of vice and their wondrous zeal for religion. They desired to reorganize the State on biblically inspired lines, and to administer England through the Church elders. Such fanatic Puritan-ism was disquieting to the Queen, the bishops, and the most reasonable among the faithful; but the moderate Puritanism gained adherents. In the Parliament of 1593 the bishops put forward stern measures against Puritanism; but in vain: the bill was rejected. The Puritans were deemed to be truly men of God, His true and wholehearted prophets. The prestige of Elizabeth, however, was such that not even these prophets could pre-vail against her. But this pious demagogy was to prove more dangerous to her successors.

When the European navigators discovered the lands beyond the Atlantic, Spain and Portugal were the only claimants to the new continents, and these two Catholic powers had accepted the arbitration of Pope Alexander VI to devise a just frontier between these unknown lands. The Pope drew a line from one pole to the other on the map of the world: all lands discovered to the West of this line would be Spain's, and to its East, Portu-gal's. This gave Africa and India to Portugal; and to Spain, all of South America except Brazil. His Italian provinces made the King of Spain master of the Mediterranean; through Burgundy he con-trolled the trade of Flanders and the mouth of the Rhine; in his American colonies he had the richest mines of gold and silver in the world. His financial and commercial power seemed invincible. The English merchants, doomed to sniff from afar the prodigious banquet of the Catholic kings, had one last hope. If Spain had found a South-west Passage, and Portugal a South-east Passage to the Indies, perhaps there might be a North-east or a North-west Passage. For years the English seamen sought them. Chancellor went North-east, and found only the route to Muscovy; Frobisher, head-ing North-west, was stopped by the polar ice.

But although the English sovereigns did not dare a breach with the formidable Spaniards, and even if Elizabeth insisted that there must be no

official act of hostility to the Spanish colonies, the English merchants had no grounds for respecting agreements which closed the richest regions in the world against them. 'English piracy in the Channel was notorious in the fifteenth century, and in the sixteenth it attained patriotic proportions.' Only a vague line separated commerce from piracy. Certain forms of the latter, indeed, were lawful. A captain who had been robbed by a foreign ship was given 'letters of marque', which entitled him to reimburse himself at the cost of any other vessel of the same nationality as his aggressor. English seamen, owners of a ship armed with a few guns, would openly ply a trade of robbing Portuguese vessels returning from the Indies. Others would organize profitable raids on the Spanish settlements, where they found themselves in competition with the French corsairs, men of great experience in such enterprises.

John Hawkins, son of a Plymouth shipbuilder, was the first to substitute for piracy a regular commerce with the Spanish colonies. Trader as well as seaman, he had taken part in youth in expeditions to the Guinea Coast, where he learned the arts of abducting negroes to be sold later at a good price to the Canary Islands. In 1562, now on his own account, he carried off a number of slaves and bartered them in the Spanish colonies for ginger and sugar. These voyages were immensely profitable, and on one such he anchored to take in supplies in the Spanish haven of San Juan de Ulloa. Whilst he lay there the Spanish fleet sailed in. Hawkins was not strong enough to offer fight; he tried to come to terms, but was treated as an enemy by the Spanish viceroy. Returning home, he laid a plaint before the Queen. Elizabeth, in Council, solemnly declared that Hawkins was in the wrong, that the Spanish possessions must be respected, and that mariners who violated the treaties would do so at their own peril. After which she took the offender into her service, and made him Treasurer of the Navy. To this he contributed his experience. But Spain would doubtless have long held the mastery of the sea if Francis Drake had not now challenged it.

Francis Drake was a story-book sailor, bold to the pitch of temerity. Worshipped by his crews despite his severity, he was soon the idol of England. Hawkins had tried unavailingly to carry on legal trade with the Spanish colonies; Drake jumped headlong into illegality. With two ships and fifty men he attacked the strongest Spanish fortresses, bringing back his small vessel to Plymouth, laden with gold. Drake had landed on the isthmus of Darien, attacked the mule convoy bringing gold from Peru, routed the escort, captured the treasure. The venture delighted Elizabeth's secret heart. In 1577 Drake set off again in the *Golden Hind* for a long voyage, in the course of which he proposed to circumnavigate the globe, by the Magellan Straits and the East Indies. The expedition was backed by several associates; one of them was the Queen, who still officially castigated these peaceful attacks on a friendly power, but was as eager as any in claiming her share of the booty on its reaching England.

This time Drake's little fleet carried cannon and some hundreds of men. He reckoned it large enough to attack islands and ports where Spain had only one stronghold, and from whose governors he could demand ransom money. But these were only accessory profits; Drake's real aim was to find the fleet which brought the gold and silver every year from Eldorado. Between Lima and Panama, an Indian paddling across a bay, quite incapable of distinguishing between Spaniards and English, mistook Drake for one of his masters and piloted him to a creek where the leading galley lay at anchor with her cargo of gold. Drake had only to transfer the cases. Then, crossing the Indian Ocean and rounding the Cape of Good Hope, he returned to England in 1580 with a cargo valued at £326,580, or, as some say, £600,000. Of this booty Elizabeth had a large proportion.

To the Spanish ambassador's protest Elizabeth replied that she knew nothing of the matter, and would certainly be the last to tolerate shameless attacks on the possessions of her well-beloved brother. Meanwhile, however, Hawkins was putting the fleet on a fighting basis, Sir Thomas Gresham, her best financier, was purchasing arms, and the Queen herself had knighted Drake. War between England and Spain was becoming inevitable. In Spain the Inquisition was ordered to deal with captured English seamen as heretics. Sir Francis Drake, at the head of a royal fleet, harried the Spanish colonies, affirming the right of English seamen to the freedom of the seas, and

DEPARTURE OF A BRITISH EAST INDIA COMPANY SHIP, a mid-17th century painting by Adam Willaerts. The company received its charter in 1600. Its ships traded with Africa and the Orient, and skirmished with its foreign competitors. (*National Maritime Museum*, Greenwich).

of worship. Philip ordered a great Armada to be fitted out at Cadiz to attack England. With unmatched boldness Drake sailed round the Spanish coast, entered this fortified harbour, and there destroyed by gunfire the finest fighting galleys. Within a few minutes, the type of craft which had dominated the Mediterranean for thousands of years, the galley — an oared cruiser — was seen to be doomed, in favour of the sailing ship.

Philip II was tenacious, and despite the damage wrought by Drake at Cadiz, his Armada was ready in 1588. The Spanish plan was grandiose and ingenious. The Duke of Parma, commanding the Spanish troops in the Netherlands, was to prepare a landing by 30,000 men, and barges for their transport to England. But infantry loaded into barges would be defenceless, and the warships from Spain were to line the course of their crossing, ready to stop any enemy vessel. At the head of the Armada, bringing another 30,000 soldiers, was placed the Duke of Medina-Sidonia, a great gentleman and soldier, but ignorant of maritime matters. The English fleet was commanded by Lord Howard of Effingham, who had Hawkins, Drake and Frobisher under his orders, and consisted of thirty-four warships built for Elizabeth by Hawkins, and one hundred and fifty merchant vessels furnished by the ports. The great Spanish fleet arrived off Plymouth in a formation like that of a land army. The Duke of Medina-Sidonia, as was then customary, counted on transforming the naval battle into a contest of foot-soldiers. The grappling-irons were already prepared for boarding, the invincible Spanish infantry were massed on the raised decks, when the English fleet was seen to be assuming an unexpected formation. The vessels of Drake and Hawkins came on in Indian file, out of range of any armament. Then the tragedy began. The English opened fire and Medina-Sidonia, in impotent despair, saw that the English guns out-ranged his own. He could do nothing but break off the action, which he did as best he could by laying a course for the Low Countries and the Duke of Parma. He succeeded in making off without excessive losses, after a battle which was indecisive because the English fleet was short of munitions.

SHIPS OF THE SPANISH ARMADA, 1588. Philip II's fleet left Lisbon under the command of the Duke of Medina-Sidonia, with 150 ships, 2000 cannon and 30,000 soldiers. Storms at sea and Drake's fireships prevented it from completing its mission of landing an army in England. (Cartoon for a tapestry. *National Maritime Museum*, Greenwich).

SIR WALTER RALEIGH AND HIS 8-YEAR-OLD SON (1602). Sailor, explorer, poet and eventually victim of political expediency, he was executed under James I for having exacerbated the Spaniards. The more fortunate Drake had been knighted by Elizabeth for committing the identical sin. *National Portrait Gallery.*

Parma was not ready and asked Medina-Sidonia for another fortnight. But the English admirals espied the Spanish fleet at anchor off Calais and attacked it with fire-ships filled with powder and tar. The Spaniards had to cut their cables to escape this new danger and headed towards the North Sea, where the English cannon accounted for numerous vessels. A storm joined in the battle. The Duke decided to head for Ireland, a Catholic country, where he hoped to be able to land if need be, and accordingly tried to round the north of Scotland. But disorder soon became disaster: scattered by gales, pillaged by coastal dwellers, the fleet which a week before had been the glorious Armada found itself at the mercy of waves and rocks. Out of a hundred and fifty ships about fifty returned to Spain. Out of 30,000 soldiers, 10,000 were drowned, without counting the victims of cannon-balls or sickness. Spain had lost the mastery of the seas.

It can hardly be said that Elizabeth's reign saw the first foundations of the British Empire laid. Newfoundland, where English fishermen had long been going, was occupied, though precariously, in 1583. One of Elizabeth's favourites, who was also one of her most cultivated subjects, Sir Walter Raleigh, spent a great part of his fortune in trying to establish a colony on the coast of North America, to which the Queen herself gave the name of Virginia. But the colonists whom he left there in the course of his expedition of 1587, numbering eighty-nine men and seventeen women, were not to be found when an expedition with fresh stores was sent there two years later. One of Raleigh's followers is credited with introducing the potato and tobacco into England. The great Companies, owned by shareholders and holding monopolies of trading in special countries, developed during the sixteenth century. The Merchant Adventurers controlled in particular the trade with the German rivers, the Rhine and Elbe. Another Company was concerned with the Baltic trade. The Muscovy Company held a monopoly for Russia, Armenia, Persia and the Caspian. The Levant Company dealt with Turkey and the Adriatic ports. And at the very close of the reign, in 1600, the East India Company was founded, having the sole right of trading with the islands and ports of Asia, Africa and America, from the Cape of Good Hope to the Magellan Straits. This system of Companies, which incited at once to aggression and to commercial greed, was the most dangerous of all colonizing methods to the natives of the lands concerned, and the most difficult for the national government to control.

Ever since the repulse of Edward I, Scotland had succeeded in maintaining independence from the English kings. The rude, undisciplined Scottish nobility remained quite feudal. The ruling dynasty was that of the Stuarts, who were descended from a daughter of Robert the Bruce. This dynasty had the twofold support of the Catholic Church and the Franco-Scottish alliance, a circumstance which was disturbing to England. James IV of Scotland had married Margaret, the daughter of Henry VII of England. The son of Margaret Tudor was James V; and from his marriage with the French princess, Mary of Guise, was born Mary Stuart, whose birth took place only a short time before her father died, so that from her cradle she was Queen of a wild, restless people. Her mother, Mary of Guise, acted as Regent of Scotland, and had her brought up in France. She grew up a pale, long-faced girl, whose loveliness captivated the Dauphin Francis. Scarcely had she married him when her father-in-law, Henry II of France, died, and the Queen of Scots found herself also Queen of France. In 1560 her tuberculous husband died of an aural infection; the Guise faction lost its power in France; Mary Stuart had to return to Scotland.

She came back to rule a country little suited to her. The new Reformed religion had instantly attracted a thoughtful and poverty-stricken people, who had cared little for the feudal splendour of the Catholic bishops; and the Scottish nobles, their appetite whetted by the example of England, coveted the spoils of the monasteries. The real master of Scotland at the time of Queen Mary's return in 1561 was John Knox, a man formidable in the strength and narrowness of his faith, and whose rugged biblical eloquence delighted his compatriots. In the time of Mary Tudor he lived at Geneva, where he was completely won over to the Calvinist doctrines. Like Calvin, Knox believed in predestination; he held that religious truth must be sought only in the Scriptures, without recourse to any dogma introduced by men; that worship should be austere, with neither pomp nor

MARY, QUEEN OF SCOTS, AND HER HUSBAND LORD DARNLEY, whose murderer she married, thus arousing Scotland to fury. She escaped to England where Elizabeth held her prisoner for nineteen years before deciding to execute her. Her son, James VI of Scotland became James I of England. *Mansell Collection.*

images; that the Calvinistic institution of the Elders of the Church should supplant bishops and archbishops; and that John Knox himself was one of the elect and directly inspired by God. Having convinced the Scots of all this, he made the Scottish Kirk into a Presbyterian body, completely democratic, with no hierarchy. The church-members of every parish appointed their ministers, and in the General Assemblies of the Church these ministers and the leading laymen sat side by side. The union of squires and burgesses to control the Crown, which in England took a parliamentary form, appeared in Scotland as an ecclesiastic assembly. There, the Church was the State.

Mary Stuart returned to Scotland and landed at Leith in a dense wet fog. 'The very face of Heaven,' said Knox, 'did manifestly speak what comfort was brought into this country with her — to wit, sorrow, dolour, darkness and all impiety.' She came with youth and grace and poetry about her; and she met violence, fanaticism, hate. Her subjects welcomed her at first with great demonstrations, but their uncouthness startled the young woman. They sang psalms under her windows at Holyrood all night. On the route of her procession platforms had been put up, on which there were cheerful pictures of idolaters burned for their sins. The denizens of one district proposed to display also the effigy of a priest slain before the altar at the Elevation of the Host, but were persuaded that this was tactless. Yet, with patience surprising in a girl of eighteen, Mary slowly gained a foothold. She spoke little, plied her embroidery needle at meetings of her Council, and even won over some of the Protestant nobles by her charm.

Few women, indeed, have better claim to indulgence than Mary Stuart, thrown so young and uncounselled among the unscrupulous nobles and inhuman preachers of a fierce and troublous age. Her courage won the first game. But when she allowed her womanhood to come before her sovereignty, troubles came thick and fast. It was natural that she should refuse the handsome Leicester, recommended by Elizabeth, as husband; she had no mind to take her cousin's leavings, and in any case Leicester would have made a poor king. But Lord Darnley, her own choice, was worse, and Mary tired of him as quickly as she had fallen in love with him. She was then foolish enough to make a favoured counsellor of a young Italian musician, David Rizzio, who had come to Scotland in the train of the Duke of Savoy. The court

EXECUTION OF MARY, QUEEN OF SCOTS:
Francis Delaram. In the eyes of the Roman
Church, which did not accept Elizabeth's
legitimacy, Mary Stuart was the rightful
heir to the English Throne. When she
was discovered to be accessory to a plot,
Elizabeth had to sign her death warrant.
(Bibliothèque nationale, Paris). *Hachette*.

lords, outraged at an upstart's eminence, swore
revenge, and plotted with Darnley to get rid of
Rizzio. They killed him clinging to Mary's skirts
when he was at supper with her. Three months
later she gave birth to a son, who was to become
James VI of Scotland and James I of England,
and was at the time reputed to be the son of
Rizzio. Mary's position became untenable. She
hated her husband, Darnley, and was wildly in
love with the most redoubtable of the Scottish
lords, the Earl of Bothwell, who had first violated,
then conquered her, and was distrusted by all
Scotland. Bothwell prepared the murder of Darnley. Was Mary Stuart privy to the plot? It is certain that the Queen installed her husband, when
he was ill, in an isolated house outside the city
walls of Edinburgh; there, in Kirk o' Field, she
left him one evening; during the night the house
blew up and he was found dead in the garden. No

one doubted Bothwell's guilt. But, three months
later, the Queen married the murderer, and this
was more than public opinion, even in the sixteenth
century, could stand. Mary was abandoned by the
Pope, by Spain and France, by all her friends.
There was a rising in Scotland. After a short
struggle Bothwell fled, in cowardly style, and
Mary was brought captive to Edinburgh by
soldiers who cried out, 'Burn the whore!' She
was deposed in favour of her son, James VI.

She would certainly have been executed if Elizabeth had not shielded her, greatly to the distress
of Cecil and Walsingham, who could explain their
mistress's policy only by her horror of the Scottish
rebels and her wish not to offer her own subjects
the spectacle and example of a queen's head on the
block. At last, after ten months in captivity on
Loch Leven, Mary escaped on horseback and reached England in May 1568. What was Elizabeth to

THE ENGLISH IN VIRGINIA. An engraving by Theodore de Bry after a drawing by John White who took part in this expedition to Virginia led by Raleigh, 1585-1586. (Thomas Hariot, «Admiranda narratio, fida tamen, de commodis et incolarum ritibus Virginiae...». Frankfurt 1590, Plate I. Bibliothèque nationale, Paris). *Hachette*.

BALL AT THE ENGLISH COURT. The dancers are identified as Queen Elizabeth and Robert Dudley, Earl of Leicester, her enduring favourite, whose earnest, but frustrated, ambition was to marry her. (Collection of Lord de l'Isle and Dudley, Penshurst Place, Kent). *National Portrait Gallery*. ▶

do? Must she tolerate the presence within her realm of so dangerous a claimant? Mary asked for an investigation to be made by Elizabeth into the actions of the Scottish rebels. Elizabeth agreed to this, but ordered the inquiry to be extended to the murder of Darnley, in order, she said, that 'her sister' might be cleared of any suspicion. The court found the charges not proven. But Elizabeth still held her prisoner — and can hardly be blamed for so doing, as the hapless Queen of Scots had been, and still was, connected with all conspiracies. The number of plots hinging on Mary makes one marvel at Elizabeth's patience. It was for Mary that the Catholic north rose in 1569, and for her that the Duke of Norfolk died. She encouraged Spain as well as France, the Duke of Alençon as well as Don John of Austria. She conspired against Elizabeth with the Pope, through certain Florentine bankers. There can be no doubt that Elizabeth might have had a round score of sound reasons for executing her fair cousin. But she refused.

Nineteen years went past for Mary in her English captivity, from 1568 until 1587, while she embroidered small objects for Elizabeth, and plotted, plotted incorrigibly. Elizabeth was growing old; it was certain now that she would die childless; the question of the succession became more and more grave. After this prolonged incarceration, the Pope and the Church were forgetting that Mary had been an adulteress, perhaps a murderess, and again built high hopes on her. Good Protestants grew anxious at the day of reckoning drawing near. Walsingham, charged with her supervision, contrived to intercept her correspondence regularly. Now, in 1587, a war with Spain seemed a likelihood, and Walsingham deemed it essential to stifle any risks of internal danger before engaging on war abroad. A spy was sent to lay a trap for Mary, into which she fell completely. A band of young men had planned to kill Elizabeth, and their leader, Anthony Babington, wrote a letter to Mary, which of course was intercepted, in which he announced the murder and asked her advice. Mary's enemies anxiously awaited her reply. It did not disappoint them. She approved, and even gave advice to the murderers. This time Walsingham had her head in his hands. Mary was tried at Fotheringhay, and unanimously found guilty. The Commons demanded immediate execution. Elizabeth still hesitated. In obedience

to real clemency? To horror of her action? To fear for her safety? At last she signed the death warrant. It needed three strokes of the executioner's sword to sever that head, on the morning of February 8, 1587. The calamities of Mary's youth had been forgotten, and in the eyes of the Catholics she became as a saint.

Elizabeth lived to be seventy, a very advanced age for the time; and almost to the last she shone, she flirted, she danced. Burleigh had died before her, and she had replaced him by his second son, Robert Cecil, a great minister like his father before him. Leicester had been succeeded in the old woman's favour by the Earl of Essex. Emboldened by the queen's feeling for him, a vague sentiment compounded at once of maternal fondness, tenderness and sensuality, and having been further encouraged by a successful expedition to Cadiz which made him a popular idol, he became insufferable. But he played his last card when he asked for command of the army sent by Elizabeth to crush the Irish revolt instigated by the Spaniards in 1594. He behaved like a spoilt child and, as a traitor, had thoughts of bringing his troops back to London to dethrone his sovereign, and at the same time was writing her angry, passionate letters. Elizabeth now viewed him sanely, and when he came home after deserting his post, and tried to organize a plot to seize her, she handed him over to his fate. The handsome Essex was beheaded at the Tower, and met his fate with humility and devoutness.

His death cast a shadow of sorrow over the Queen's last years. She still dyed her hair an unnatural hue, still bedecked herself with pearls and diamonds and cloth of silver and gold; she still received the homage of her Parliaments. But the end was near, and she knew it. Only at the last would she name her successor. She knew it must be James VI of Scotland, and that her ministers were already in correspondence with Edinburgh. She never spoke of it. In January 1603 she felt more stricken, went to bed, refused to see a doctor, and turning her face to the wall sank into a lethargy from which she never emerged.

To many historians, the Elizabethans have seemed as monsters, astonishing men by the contrast between the delicacy of their poems and the cruelty of their public shows, between the splendour of their dress and the filth of their living. Because

VIEW OF LONDON IN THE EARLY 17TH CENTURY.
Detail of an etching by W. Hollar. The river,
which was crossed only by London Bridge,
constituted London's main thoroughfare. In
the foreground is Southwark, with the Globe
Theatre of Shakespearian fame, pulled down
by the Puritans c. 1650. (*Bibliothèque nationale*,
Paris).

the Queen loved luxury, and as the country was growing richer, fashion exercised a ruthless and capricious tyranny over the Elizabethans. The richest materials — velvet, damask, and cloth of gold or silver — were needed for the gowns of ladies or the doublets of men. Luxury and comfort pervaded their houses, and all over the countryside rose new mansions, mingling Italian styles with the traditional Gothic. In gardens as in houses men sought symmetrical plans and variegated ornament. Yews and box trees were clipped in spheres and spirals. And the speech of the lords and ladies was no less fantastically turned than the topiary in their gardens. The joy of inventing words and phrases, the mental intoxication of a reborn language, engendered a preciosity which was manifested both in poems and speech. It was under Elizabeth that the theatre took an outstanding place in the life of London. Since the days of Henry VII there had been troupes of players, but few permanent playhouses. These mummers played in the yards of taverns or in manor halls. When the City authorities turned Puritan and expelled the actors, they took refuge across the river, beyond the Lord Mayor's jurisdiction. Several playhouses were then built, the most famous being the Globe, a share in which was owned by Shakespeare. The builders of these early theatres nearly all tried to reproduce the courtyard of an inn, with its open-air gallery running along the doors of the rooms. This gallery was useful for representing, as it might be, the parapets of a fortress, the balcony of a lady's room, or the summit of a tower. The spectators paid a penny for admission, and from sixpence to a shilling for a seat, either on the stage itself or in the galleries, which, with a reminiscence of the ancestral inn, preserved their separate rooms — whence, probably, the modern boxes. The opening of the play

was announced, as may still be seen in country fairs, by a flourish of trumpets. The public, a throng of apprentices, law students, soldiers and gentlemen, was intelligent and serious. They relished the bloodthirsty melodramas, but could equally well appreciate the most poetic plays of Marlowe, or Ben Jonson, or Shakespeare.

Was Shakespeare superior to all other dramatists of his day? Remarkable as these were, it yet seems certain that he was. No other touched so immeasurable a range of themes and kinds, or gave expression to such profound thoughts on human nature and human passions in language so compelling. Was his superiority recognized by his contemporaries? Not with the unanimity of modern opinion. When this actor-playwright began about 1590 to offer his manuscripts to the theatrical companies, he excited the jealousy of his competitors, the erudite university poets. But the public applauded him. Friendly with persons at court, and sharing their life in the last years of Queen Elizabeth, he could present the fierceness of ambition and the torments of power as well as he could the passions of love.

The England of Shakespeare's time seems to us to be burgeoning with songs and poems, and we are tempted to imagine the humblest apprentice or the simplest villager playing the viol or tossing off a madrigal. But the poetry and blitheness of Elizabethan England need not be exaggerated. Life for the common folk was as hard then as to-day, and harder. In Shakespeare we can catch glimpses of the hard-pressed farm-wench, clattering her pail of frozen milk in the dead of winter, her nose red with the cold, her hands chapped with scrubbing dirty clothes. Although the price of wheat had risen as a result of the falling value of gold, rural unemployment must have been severe, as it proved necessary to frame two important Poor Laws in 1597 and 1601. The squires, whose power was waxing, often proved harsh, and religious persecution was formidable for any who ventured on independent ways of thinking. But there were also Christian landowners who cultivated hospitality and courtesy. The manors, like the villages, were still self-sufficing. A good housewife, be she lady or farmer's wife, did all the work of her house, making everything from jellies to candles. There was grace in the village festivities, and villagers

could play diverting comedies, as Shakespeare showed in *A Midsummer Night's Dream*, and foreigners noted that the English were the most musical people in the world. Not only did they produce composers as admirable as William Byrd, but nearly every house had its lute, viol or virginal, and songbooks in plenty. All visitors, and many menials, could read the score of a song at sight and take their part in a glee for three or four voices.

This taste for poetry and music called for a fairly advanced education. And this the Elizabethans did not lack. After Winchester and Eton, new schools were founded by rich patrons — Rugby in 1567, Harrow in 1590. In principle these schools were free and intended for the children of the neighbourhood, the founder paying the masters' salaries and the pupils' board. Only those from other parts paid fees, and these were nearly always sons of the well-to-do in the country. Gradually these outsiders gained a majority, and for them the schools came chiefly to exist, Harrow, for instance, retaining only forty free scholars. Elementary education was provided in the 'petty schools', often by women who taught the alphabet and the rudiments of writing from a stock of knowledge hardly extending any further. Later a boy might go to the 'grammar school', there to be taught often by a teacher of real learning, even in the country. Even the small towns had their men of culture at this time. The literary historians used to be astonished by the wide knowledge that Shakespeare, an actor of humble origins, possessed. But it was a knowledge shared by a wide public.

The rule of the Tudor monarchs was a strong one, but its force did not depend on soldiery or police. Based on public opinion, on the yeomen and farmers and merchants, it acquired possession of the spiritual power. The Kings of France and Spain made common cause with the Church of Rome to create absolute monarchies; the Kings of England made alliance with Parliament to oppose Rome, and themselves to head a national Church. Their espousal of the Reformation might have ruined England if the two great Catholic powers had joined forces to crush this lesser kingdom. The Tudors were saved by the rivalries of Habsburg and Valois. Thanks to a European cleavage, England was able to engage in that policy of the balance of power which is forced upon her by her situation: confronting the dominant power on the Continent with coalitions supported by English wealth and an English fleet.

The English monarchy, however, was soon to be weakened by the very services which it rendered. The immense respect which invested the Tudors was born as much from memory of the disasters previous to their advent as from the inherent merits of this family. Encouraged by the internal order restored by the monarchy, and by the external security arising from England's new maritime power and the divided state of Europe, the squires and burgesses were soon seeking to impose their will on the King, as expressed through Parliament. Crown and Commons were to play a great match, the stake being the supreme power; and the rashness of a new dynasty gave Parliament the victory.

V

The Triumph of Parliament

James I to James II, 1603-1688

ON THE day of Elizabeth's death (March 24, 1603), a deep disquiet began to move across the country. Patrols were out in the London streets. Protestant seamen left their ports to ward off a possible Papist invasion from the Low Countries. Calm was restored when it was learned that the Calvinist James VI was to come south from his Scottish kingdom as James I of England, uniting the two crowns. From the border, all the way to London, the new King's progress was a prolonged triumph.

James was thirty-seven, a rather ludicrous figure of a man, devoid of any dignity; a chatterbox impeded by a tongue too large for his mouth. But the buffoonery of his conversation disguised its substance, which was never savourless. It has been remarked that the succession of James I to Elizabeth Tudor was the supplanting of a masculine by a feminine nature. And certainly a childhood and youth spent in a maze of murders and plots had left King James with a terror of armed men. His clothes were padded to withstand stabbing, and the sight of a sword made him queasy. He was fairly cultured, but intellectual rather than intelligent. In a precocious youth he wrote verses, theological treatises, and works on political doctrine wherein he demonstrated that Kings are intended by God to rule, and subjects intended likewise to give obedience. The King, therefore, was above the Law, but, except in exceptional cases of which he alone could be judge, he ought to submit to the Law in order to set an example.

This was proud teaching, but it had served well in Scotland to compel the respect of an overweening and formidable clergy. James I arrived in England with a dangerous conviction of his intellectual superiority. In all good faith he believed himself a theologian of genius who would bring the truth to the bemused English. He knew virtually nothing of the character of his new subjects, and did not try to understand them. He expected his eloquence and erudition to be praised to the skies. But he was dealing with a race who were in no temper to lend ear to an argumentative intruder.

In spite of a Calvinist upbringing, the new King settled down quite comfortably with the Anglican Church. He had suffered from the democratic freedom of the Presbyterians in Scotland, and was not displeased at finding in England a Church which acknowledged a hierarchy having the King at its summit. Elizabeth had imposed a conformity as rigorous as the old one of the Roman Church. To the true Anglican the Reformation did not appear as a break with the past; his Church seemed to him ' Catholic ', that is, universal. The Anglican doctrine, which was the State religion, found itself attacked on both flanks, by the Catholics and the Puritans. The Catholics in England, during the latter part of Queen Elizabeth's reign, had suffered persecutions the severity of which was intensified by the war with Spain and the Jesuit conspiracies. Excluded from all local or national official posts, they were not even allowed to leave their own properties without the signed permission of a justice of the peace. They were liable to heavy fines for non-attendance at the Anglican service. A priest who said Mass, and any who harboured him, could be sentenced to a traitor's hideous death, but the threat was comparatively rarely carried out, and in many country-houses the Catholic chaplain was secreted in a hidden loft. By the early years of James I's reign the adherents of the old faith numbered barely one in twenty of the population. They cherished high hopes when a son of Mary Stuart ascended the throne. He was known to have corresponded with the Pope and to favour toleration. He did, in fact, offer to abolish fines

for religious offences, but only on condition that the Catholics declared their loyalty to the King and not to the Pope, and that they should refrain from proselytizing. These terms were incompatible with genuine faith, and it was not long before the Catholics became so disappointed that a number of them began plotting against the King.

The most dangerous of these conspiracies was the famous Gunpowder Plot. Its aim was the simultaneous slaying of the King, the Lords and the Commons, by blowing up the House of Lords when all were there assembled. With the Protestants thus left leaderless, a Catholic rising would have a chance of success, as the plotters counted on the inertia of the masses. The conspirators were men of good birth. The most famous of them, Guy Fawkes, a Catholic soldier, had learned the arts of sapping and tunnelling during the wars in Flanders. He and his friends began by renting a cellar opposite the Houses of Parliament, but soon discovered accidentally a site lying immediately beneath the House of Lords, which would free them from the need for digging a mine themselves. Renting this, they filled the place with barrels of powder concealed under faggots; and their attempt would doubtless have succeeded if the plotters had not deemed it necessary to warn some of their partisans in order to organize the rising which was to follow the explosion. One of their confidants felt it his duty to warn the authorities. Guy Fawkes stayed on alone, with great courage, to light the fuse at the proper moment. He was found and arrested on the night of November 4-5, 1605, and put to a cruel death. With him died also his

JAMES I LISTENS TO A SERMON PREACHED AT ST PAUL'S CATHEDRAL.
The Gothic cathedral was destroyed in the Great Fire of 1666 and
Christopher Wren built the present Renaissance edifice on the site.
From a painting on wood. (*Society of Antiquaries, London*).

accomplices, and Henry Garnet, the Provincial of
the English Jesuits, accused of instigating the crime.
This charge seems to have been untrue: Garnet
sinned only by his silence, but the indignation
roused by the disclosure of an attempt so grave
and so nearly successful, made all Catholics still
more suspect. They were deprived of civic rights,
banned form the Bar and from the practice of
medicine, and even from managing the property
of their children under age. The Gunpowder Plot
achieved the ruin of Catholicism in England for
many years to come.

On its other flank the Anglican Church had to
suffer the attacks of the Puritans, those who wished
to purify the Church, not only from all contact
with Rome, but from any Romanist practice as
well. It was not so much a doctrine as a mental
attitude. On James I's accession a petition was
presented to him by the Puritan clergy, who asked
that every clergyman should be entitled to decide
for himself whether he should wear a surplice, that
the sign of the cross be suppressed in baptism, as
also the bowing of the head on uttering the name
of Jesus, genuflexion before the altar and the ring in
the marriage ceremony; and they called for strict
Sabbath observance. Others, more radical in temper, wanted to abolish bishops and set up a Presbyterian Church on the Scottish model. A third
group, the Independents, claimed for every man
the right to choose his beliefs. But all three shared
a deep dislike of gaiety and an intense love of civic
liberties, a fondness for simplicity of living and
austerity in worship. Constant reading of the Bible
made them live in a collective dream, gloomy

if often exalted. They hated all who did not share their beliefs, seeing these as the children of darkness and themselves as the children of light. They deplored the theatre, were horrified by sin, especially by the sins of the flesh, dressed with wilfully outmoded modesty, and cut their hair short to show their scorn for the courtiers with their curled wigs.

At the beginning of James's reign the Puritans formed part of the national Church and hoped to imbue it with their teachings. A conference was held at Hampton Court, under the King's presidency, to consider their petition. James took pleasure in this theological debate until the words ' presbytery ' and ' synod ' were introduced. They had painful associations for him. ' A Scottish Presbytery ', he said, ' agreeth as well with a monarchy as God with the Devil...' And taking up his hat to close the sitting, he exclaimed: ' ... No Bishop, no King !... I shall make them conform themselves or I will harry them out of the land. ' With that one sentence he turned the religious quarrel into a political one. The Bible had taught these Puritans that the faith must be militant, and that it is the duty of every man who has seen the truth to make the truth prevail. And they would try to make it prevail against the King himself, since he so constrained them. In 1604 James had to expel from the Church three hundred Puritan clergy who refused to observe the Anglican rite.

From now onwards three parties must be distinguished in the English clergy: a High Church party, the nearest to the Church of Rome and accepting the ritual imposed by the Tudor kings; a Presbyterian, non-conforming party, remaining within the Church but anxious for its reform; and an independent or congregationalist party, disapproving equally of Anglican episcopacy and Presbyterian synods. The Independents held that there should be no such thing as a State Church, whether of the English or the Scottish pattern.

It is important to realize that the independent Protestants, if they remained in England, could not hope to practise their faith in peace. Within the official Church a clergyman could be more or less ritualistic; outside it, there was no safety. Many chose exile, and after 1608 emigrated to Holland; and even there many of the extremists were perturbed by the heresies in the air. In 1620 some of them returned from Holland to Southampton, but only to embark at once on the ship *Mayflower*, which was to convey them to America. They planned to settle within the northern limits of the Virginia Company's claims, but winds and tides took them to a still more northern landing-place, on the coast of what is now called New England. During the next few years, which were not favourable to the Puritans in England, they were joined over there by thousands of emigrants, and in their new country these men who had preferred exile to heresy established, as the logical outcome, a theocracy.

King James I and his Parliament had nothing in common. A frivolous and vicious court seethed with scandals, of which adultery was the most trifling. The King, a fond and feeble man, could not dispense with favourites, chosen for their looks rather than for statesmanlike gifts. On his accession he was wise enough to keep by his side Robert Cecil, whom he created Earl of Salisbury in 1605, and a few others of Elizabeth's ablest counsellors. But gradually power slipped into the hands of his favourite, Robert Carr, who became Earl of Somerset, and then to George Villiers, a superbly handsome youth in his early twenties, poor but well-born, who was cynically pushed forward by the Archbishop and his allies to supplant Somerset. Groom of the Chamber, Knight of the Garter, Baron, Viscount, Marquess, Lord High Admiral, Warden of the Cinque Ports, Duke of Buckingham, the favourite minister of James I, then of his son, Charles I — ' Never ', said Clarendon, ' any man in any age, nor, I believe, in any country, rose in so short a time to so much greatness of honour, power, or fortune upon no other advantages or recommendation than of the beauty and graciousness of his person. ' It is easy to picture how this merrymaking and dissolute court horrified the sober knights who represented the English yeomen and burgesses in Parliament. They were, it has been well said, the heirs of long generations of a healthy country life, formed by the Elizabethan culture and inspired by the Puritan religion. The court had no grip on them. They were not covetous of preferment, and they knew that the King's only armed force was the trained bands or country militia, who thought as Parliament thought. Impervious to fear or favour, they proudly exercised the privilege of attacking the royal administration.

Such was the Parliament, conscious of its duties

JAMES VI OF SCOTLAND, who in 1603 became James I of England. He wanted to be an autocratic ruler but lacked the personality; moreover he had underestimated English parliamentary tradition. (National Portrait Gallery). *Hachette*.

Jacob der 6. Königk
inn Schottland

and its strength, upon which James I ingenuously wished to impose the doctrine of the divine and hereditary rights of kings. According to the royal theologian, not only did the King, crowned and anointed, become a sacred personage, but, as God had in advance chosen and consecrated all future Kings, Parliament could merely record the divine ordinances. The King was responsible to God, but not to his subjects. He was not subject to law, because he was the law. This doctrine, with which James I had successfully confronted the claims of the Scottish Church, could only offend the House of Commons.

Against the King's abstract system, Parliament set up English custom. It did not yet claim control of the executive's action. Save for treason, ministers had never been responsible to Parliament, on which their administrative acts were not dependent. But the general principles for the governance of the nation — that is to say, the laws — should be laid down only by 'the Crown in Parliament', and such laws were obligatory on the King himself, on his ministers, and on his Council. When the Stuarts came upon the scene, the conflict began between Royal absolutism and the legislative power of Parliament. Considering only the theoretic right, a case could be made for both positions, that of absolute monarchy and that of limited monarchy. As a matter of practice, however, the conflict had to be settled.

A government respects the liberty of the citizens in so far as it needs their assent to the imposition of taxes. Elizabeth's power was increased in proportion to her economical spending and to the exceptional sums accruing to her from the exploits of Drake and the pillage of the Spanish treasures. James I, with his ostentatious court and favourites to be loaded with gifts, was bound to be an extravagant sovereign. His very feminine taste for jewellery cost him sometimes as much as £37,000 a year, whereas he devoted only £27,000 to the army. In 1614 he needed £155,000 for his household, whereas Elizabeth spent on this only £27,000 in 1601. Although James I avoided wars, he spent £600,000 a year, while his revenues amounted only to about £400,000, of which £150,000 came from the tunnage and poundage, fixed duties on wool and leather which Parliament customarily voted to the King for life. To fill up the gap James tried various expedients: he solicited freewill offerings;

he forced landowners who declined knighthood on account of its obligations, to pay a substantial sum to release themselves; he sold peerages; he sold the timber of Crown forests. Finally, he proposed to Parliament the Great Compact, whereby the King was to renounce all his former feudal rights in exchange for a life income of £200,000. This compromise was rejected by Parliament, which was dissolved by the King. For ten years on end, between 1611 and 1621, it was not again summoned, except for a few weeks in 1614. Could the Crown live without it? The solution of the problem of sovereignty depended on the answer to that question.

If a king is to live without money, he must live without war. And this was the fervent desire of the pacific James. In 1604 he concluded an inglorious but not shameful peace with Spain. The Spaniards gave England her claim to the freedom of the European seas; the English did not renounce the freedom of the Ocean. Nothing was settled; there was no real compromise. With the death of Cecil in 1612, Elizabethan prudence vanished from the royal Councils. Attempts were made to arrange for the marriage of the heir to the throne with a Spanish Infanta. No scheme could be more unpopular. An Infanta, the Protestants believed, would bring Jesuits, faggots and plots in her wedding-chest. The Prince himself declared that he would not lay two religions in one bed. After the disgrace of Somerset the anti-Spanish party seemed for a few years to have the upper hand. A veteran of the Elizabethan wars, Sir Walter Raleigh, was fetched out of the Tower of London, where James had confined him for supposed conspiracy. Raleigh had always desired an empire for England, and now, after thirteen years of captivity, he passed suddenly from prison to a ship's bridge, and sailed by the King's orders for Guiana, whence, like Drake, he was supposed to bring back fabulous treasure. But he was badly equipped and poorly supported, and was beaten by the Spaniards. Then, after ' that sea-whiff between dungeon and death ', he was beheaded by his King to placate Spanish feeling. George Villiers, Duke of Buckingham, who had taken Somerset's place in the King's affections, was in his turn beguiled by the ambassadors of the Escorial. Prince Henry had died in 1612, and Charles, the new heir-apparent, seemed less staunchly Protestant.

The religious struggles on the Continent at this time roused those violent passions in the English Puritans which are always kindled in a country by foreign happenings which seem to mirror its own internal struggles.

In 1618 there began in Central Europe that great war which was later called the Thirty Years War, whereby the House of Austria, with Spanish support, strove to renew the unity of the Empire and the hegemony of the Roman Church. The oppressed Hussites of Bohemia had entrusted themselves to the young Elector Palatine, who had married the Princess Elizabeth, the attractive daughter of James I. Attacked by the Catholic princes in both of his kingdoms, the Elector appealed to his father-in-law for aid. Public opinion in England backed him. The Puritans would have hesitated to pledge England to a campaign in Bohemia, but they were ready to defend the frontier of the Rhine. To do so it would have been necessary to prevent the Spaniards from landing in the Low Countries, and this meant having a fleet as powerful as England had had in Drake's day. But James had been negligent of his strength. With no Parliament and no money, he had also no ships ready for war. And so at last in 1621, in order to prepare for war against Spain, or at least to give the Spaniards that impression, James had to summon Parliament.

Between a Parliament knowing it was reluctantly summoned, and a King who disbelieved in its rightful claims, a clash was inevitable. Parliament subordinated the voting of subsidies to the redressing of grievances. Abuses were numerous — the sale of monopolies and posts, the corruption of judges. The Lord Chancellor, Francis Bacon, a man of high intellect but weak character, was made a scapegoat, confessed to malpractices, and was condemned to confiscation of property and dismissal. This was the first impeachment of a great public figure since 1459, and a clear sign of the independence of the Commons. They wished also to intervene in foreign affairs. A strongly Protestant House wanted war against Spain and a campaign in the Palatinate. The King's intention had been only to threaten Spain, and it would have horrified him to go on from threats to action. Along with Buckingham, he prepared a scheme for a Spanish marriage for his son Charles, hoping that the restoration of the Palatinate to his son-in-law would be a clause in the contract. Parliament expressed strong dislike of this compromising policy, and the King informed it that high matters of State were not its concern. To which the Parliament's reply was that the liberties and privileges of Parliament were the ancient and undisputed heritage of English subjects, and that difficult and urgent matters concerning the King, the State, the defence of the realm and of the Church of England, were appropriate subjects for debate by Parliament. So deeply did these assertions shock the King that he tore the page that showed them from the records of the House, expelled the members, and arrested seven of their number, amongst them John Pym, one of those responsible for the offending page and a man of high authority in the House of Commons. Then, in February 1621, he sent off Prince Charles and the Duke of Buckingham to achieve the conquest of the Infanta in Spain.

The joint letters of Charles and Buckingham during this journey show how highly personal and rather puerile any policy of favouritism is. These two romantic youths had left in disguise. They addressed the King in their letters as 'Dear Dad and Gossip', and signed them 'your Baby and your Dog' — Charles being the baby and Buckingham the dog. James I was in correspondence with the Pope, to whom he promised lenient treatment of English Catholics if the Holy See would sanction the Spanish marriage without insisting on excessively strict religious terms. The Pope replied by requiring that any children born of the marriage should have Catholic nurses. Meanwhile the Spaniards were being riled by the conceit and behaviour of the English mission. Sir Edmund Verney, who accompanied the Prince, struck a Spanish priest, and the King of Spain sternly requested Buckingham to send back the Protestant members of his retinue to England. Negotiations carried on in this spirit were bound to collapse. In October 1621, James recalled his 'baby and dog'. Londoners were so delighted at this rupture, and at seeing their Prince return still unwed and un-Romanized, that they gave Charles and his mentor an enthusiastic welcome. Their plaudits alone sufficed to fling the vain, flimsy Buckingham into the anti-Spanish camp, and suddenly the detested favourite became the popular leader for a war desired by Englishmen. James, notwithstanding

THE SOMERSET HOUSE CONFERENCE, 1604, at which English, Spanish and Dutch delegates sorted out their differences, particularly with regard to overseas trade. The English are on the right with Robert Cecil, Earl of Salisbury, in the foreground. The painting is attributed to the Dutch artist Gheeraedts. *National Portrait Gallery*.

his pacifism, had to yield. From that time until King James died in 1625, and even during the early years of Charles I's reign, Buckingham had the power, without the prudence, of a king.

To scrutinize in Van Dyck's portraits the sad and beautiful features of King Charles I, is to be the less surprised at his woes. His face showed nobility, honesty, timidity, but also a kind of sombre obstinacy. Charles was pious and chaste. He blushed at hearing an improper word, and fell silent when someone's demeanour displeased him. Devoid of imagination, he never foresaw the reaction of his subjects, and when these were hostile, the surprise set loose the blind violence of a timid man. He was sincerely eager to act well, but had contrived for himself a system of ideas which neither argument nor experience could ever alter.

After the breakdown of negotiations for the projected Spanish marriage, Buckingham suggested and negotiated for the King a marriage with Henrietta Maria, the youngest daughter of King Henry IV of France. To bring a Catholic Queen, with a foreign retinue, into a country still quivering from the shock of the Gunpowder Plot, was a grave error. Admittedly Charles was at pains to declare that the future Queen would have religious freedom only for herself and her attendants, and that there would be no change in the position of the English recusants; but by a secret clause in the marriage contract, the King actually pledged protection for the Catholics.

Buckingham was anxious to secure a French alliance against Spain but, being neither a diplomat nor a general, his foreign policy was as inconsistent as it was rash. When the quarrel with Spain broke out, he had for some time dallied with the role of champion of the Protestant nations; and this won him loud plaudits in London. But to play this part in earnest on the Continent would have needed a powerful army. England, however, was a small country, with no desire to be a military power. The expeditions which tempted Buckingham into Holland and to Cadiz all ended in disaster, through lack of organization. A policy of alliance with Catholic France would have been conceivable, as hatred of the House of Austria might incline Richelieu to seek allies in the Reformers' camp. But to promise Richelieu — as Buckingham was bold enough to do — the support of Protestant

seamen against the Huguenots of La Rochelle, was sheer folly. Having discovered that he could not count on a close alliance between Charles I and Louis XIII, Buckingham avenged himself on the latter by openly making love to his wife, Anne of Austria. And then, having made certain foes of Spain and France, the two great powers of the West, and lacking the money to support such a struggle, he found himself forced to apply to Parliament.

The Parliaments of Charles I had a growing list of grievances and were more skilled in tactics than their predecessors. Their members, nearly all cultivated and devout squires, knew and respected the common law. A new theory was taking shape in their minds, that of ministerial responsibility. The King can do no wrong; if he is in error, the guilt lies only with the minister who ought to have enlightened him; and this minister, even if approved by the King, deserves the impeachment formerly reserved for traitors. Charles I, who had admired the courts of France and Spain and believed, like his father, in the divine right of kings, would not admit this doctrine, or allow the House to discuss his servants, and insisted on his own sovereign responsibility. But how was he to secure obedience? Could the King rule without Parliament, depending on freewill gifts or forced loans? Such devices only produced slender revenues in a time of mounting expenditure. After humiliating defeats at the hands of France, particularly at the Ile de Ré, the King had perforce to recall the House of Commons.

This 1628 Parliament, elected in anger, set about the task of requiring due respect from the King for the law of the realm. It drew up the famous Petition of Right, which was a clarified reiteration of what were supposed to be the principles of Magna Carta. The original feature of the Petition of Right lay in the fact that it sought to fix definite bounds between the royal power and the power of the law. It recalled all the earlier conventions made between the English people and their sovereigns. Men had thought that there would be no more forced loans, that no free man could be imprisoned without lawful reason, but all such principles had been violated. Furthermore, Parliament complained of the conduct of Buckingham's soldiers and sailors, of the obligation laid on citizens to lodge these undisciplined troops, and of

GEORGE VILLIERS, FIRST DUKE OF
BUCKINGHAM, 1592-1628.   He
was the favourite both of James
I and of Charles I, and enriched
himself considerably in high
office.   He posed as Protestant
champion on the Continent,
dragged the country into useless
military expeditions and at the
age of thirty-six was assassinated
by a Puritan fanatic. (National
Portrait Gallery). *Hachette*.

the irregular application of martial law; and His
Most Excellent Majesty was respectfully begged to
remedy these matters. For a long time the King
hesitated. He had a deep dislike of the ideas upheld
in this petition, but the Lords themselves joined
with the Commons in its presentation. In the end
he answered as Parliament wished him: '*Soit droit
fait comme il est désiré*' — 'Let right be done as
is desired' — and the Petition became a fundamental law of the realm. It placed conspicuous
reins on the King's prerogative. In particular, it
checked the right to billet troops and the exercise
of martial law.

After giving way on the Petition of Right, the
King could justifiably hope that tunnage and
poundage would be granted to him for life. But
it was not so. Actually, the desire of the Commons
was not just to revive the old liberties, but to acquire new ones, and to become the sole power in
the realm. Such a defeat and such new ideas the
Crown could not possibly accept without a struggle. The death of Buckingham, who was stabbed
by one Felton in August 1628, did not relieve the
tension. From the windows of his palace the King
witnessed the delight of the London crowd, and

men drinking the murderer's health. Charles was
too dignified to show his feelings, but he never
forgot that flaunting of hatred. In the next session
the conflict with Parliament was resumed. And
this time it wore a mainly religious aspect.

Puritans and Ritualists were still striving for
control of the Church of England. The King
favoured the High Church faction, partly because
of his wife's influence, and partly because the High
Church clergy were absolutist in their political
views and supported the King's intervention in
ecclesiastical matters. Laud, Bishop of London
and later Archbishop of Canterbury, made it his
custom to consult the King on all such matters,
and even on the punishments that should be inflicted on sinners. He prepared for the King a
list of the clergy, marking their names as Orthodox or Puritan, 'O' or 'P', and thereafter only
an 'O' received high preferment. But the mass
of the people and Parliament were of Calvinist
hue. Laud and the court believed in the doctrine
of free will, whereas London and Parliament inclined to predestination, until the free will cause
became confounded, as Trevelyan points out, with
that of despotic government, and that of predes-

tination with the defence of Parliamentary privileges. Theological, political, and fiscal questions became inextricably mingled.

From this situation arose the curious and well-known 'three resolutions' voted by Parliament in 1629. They laid it down, first, that whosoever might seek to introduce Popery into England would be regarded as an enemy of the commonwealth; second, that whosoever might advise the collection of taxes unauthorized by Parliament would be similarly regarded; and third, that any merchant or other person paying such taxes, not voted by Parliament, would be a traitor and a public enemy. Charles retorted by imprisoning nine members of the House contrary to the Petition of Right. The King was now determined to dispense with Parliaments. But there remained the eternal question of how he was to obtain money. On that, ultimately, the stability of any government depends.

So now Charles I was alone in his palace of Whitehall with his young French Queen. Where could he look for support in his rule, now that he was deprived of the contact with public opinion which annual Parliaments might have given him? He found two men who shared his authoritarian

creed and believed that firm wielding of the royal prerogative could ensure the people's happiness: one was William Laud, Archbishop of Canterbury since 1633, who directed ecclesiastical affairs and then had added financial matters to his charge; the other was a former member of that dangerous Parliament of 1628, Thomas Wentworth, created Earl of Strafford in 1640.

Strafford suffered undue calumny. Because he had been a friend of the rebel Parliamentarians, like Pym and Eliot and Hampden, they regarded his rallying to the royal cause as treachery. But where was the treachery? From the start of his career Wentworth had made plain where he stood: his rule, he declared, would be not to 'contend with the prerogative out of Parliament.' He held that popular trust and royal authority were two indispensable elements in any healthy State, the King being the keystone which could not be touched without bringing down the edifice. Charles at once recognized the gulf that separated this Government man from the Opposition. If he had been employed in England from the first, it is possible that Strafford would have raised the standing army without which the Crown's prerogatives were shad-

ows, not substance, and that in this event the destiny of England would have had more affinities with the France of Louis XIV. But Charles made profession of Strafford's doctrines without having either his strength of character or his organizing genius. When at last the King decided to set him in the highest place, the game was lost for both.

Laud too was a stern man, but a man of good faith. This authoritarian prelate was ill-suited to rule Englishmen; he genuinely believed that firmness of Church doctrine was worth more than freedom of opinion. He wanted to impose forcibly a perfect uniformity of beliefs and ritual, and he was disdainful of patient persuasion. He had no cruelty in his nature, and used neither stake nor rack, but administratively he was a tyrant in the Church. Using the ecclesiastical courts, and the Court of High Commission in particular, Laud carried out a purge of the universities and the clergy. He kept an eye on sermons too Protestant in colour, and had them shortened. He forbade the malcontent communities from calling in ' readers ' to supplement Anglican preaching. He closed the private chapels of the Puritans and forbade their pious meetings. In despair, many Puritans there-

upon decided to banish themselves and live in America, remote from Lauds and Popes. Over twenty thousand went forth to join the *Mayflower's* Pilgrim Fathers, forming the nucleus of New England, where they introduced the most characteristic English institutions of their age.

What taxes could actually be raised by a monarch who respected the Law, at least in form? There was tunnage and poundage. But this depended on the volume of trade transactions, and for six months the London merchants protested againt the wrongful imprisonment of Sir John Eliot, an eminent Parliamentarian, by refraining from buying and selling. With the help of lawyers probing into ancient texts for archaic rights, the King produced taxes which had fallen into disuse. He laid claim to ' voluntary ' gifts, to the obligation on those who for centuries had been settled in royal forests to purchase their lands outright from the Crown, to the sale of titles of nobility, to compulsory knighthood, to ' coat and conduct money ', to a tax on hackney coaches, to the sale of monopolies to courtiers, which filled both the Treasury and the pockets of the concessionaires at the expense of the public. Charles sought to impose on his

THE ROYAL EXCHANGE, LONDON, IN 1644.
The building was constructed at the expense
of Sir Thomas Gresham, a rich merchant
and financier who was knighted by Queen
Elizabeth. The City merchants who there
forgathered enjoyed a traditional preponderance in the shaping of national policies.
The engraving is by W. Hollar. (Bibliothèque nationale, Paris). *Hachette*.

THE CUCUMBER SELLER. A 17th century print, one of
many illustrating «The Cries of London». (Bibliothèque nationale, Paris). *Hachette*.

subjects the use of a particular soap, indifferently
manufactured by a corporation of monopolists.
This preparation, which injured both linen and
washerwomen's hands, was called 'the Popish
soap', and London housewives believed that these
injuries were symbolic, and that its use was also
deleterious to the soul.

And so a high wall of prejudice and grievance
and silence arose between the royal couple, secluded in Whitehall amongst the fine Dutch and
Italian paintings which the King purchased from
abroad, surrounded by lace-collared courtiers with
wide-brimmed plumed hats on their long curling
hair, and on the other side, the London merchants
with their short-haired apprentices and staid, grey-
clad Puritan wives. Public opinion was hostile
and had no safety valve. With no Parliament,
there were no public speeches; writings were cen-
sored; sermons were pruned by Laud; public meetings were forbidden. Despite the unpopularity of
these measures, no serious outburst took place for
a long time. The people were deeply respectful
of legality, and a century of Tudor monarchy had
accustomed them to regard the sovereign as a
sacred figure, so that rebellion against the King

still seemed to them a monstrous proceeding. To
break down this fearful awe, the most extreme
errors had to be committed by the Crown.

Amongst the old levies revived by the King's
servants was one known as 'ship money'. It had
always been customary for the maritime towns to
be called upon to participate in coastal defence by
providing ships and ships' crews. Charles I enforced this obligation on the whole country, and
demanded, not ships, but money to build ships.
It was not an unreasonable request. For lack of
an effective fleet, the English merchant marine had
been at the mercy of pirates since the time of James
I. The Barbary corsairs even ventured to attack
vessels in English waters and to make slave-raids
on the Irish coast. But utility was not enough
to secure Englishmen's acceptance of a tax; it had
also to be voted by Parliament. So ran the charter
of English liberties, and such was the thesis upheld
by certain citizens, the most famous of whom was
John Hampden. In 1637 the sheriff of his county
claimed thirty-one shillings and sixpence from him
in respect of one of his properties, and twenty
shillings on another, as ship money. He refused
to pay, not because of the sum (his fortune was

substantial), but on principle. He allowed himself to be brought before successive courts, and although in the end the Court of Exchequer gave judgement against him by seven votes to five, he was acquitted and idolized by public opinion.

Notwithstanding the strict censorship, pamphlets attacking the court were rife. William Prynne, a Puritan pamphleteer, concerned with reforming the morals of his time, had written one for which he was put in the pillory, and his ears were cut off by the common hangman. The London crowd viewed with just horror this barbarous treatment of a respectable citizen. The wrath of the English people was waxing greater, a grave situation in a State wherein the sovereign's sole mainstay was the affection of his subjects. The crowning folly was an attempt to impose Anglican prayers and ritual on the Scots, the ardent defenders of their Presbyterian Kirk. Charles, King of both kingdoms, was even more ignorant of Scotland than of England. Although his father, James I, had given bishops to the Scots, the Kirk remained essentially Presbyterian; and when the bishops, at Laud's bidding, introduced the new ritual to Scotland, the congregations would not allow the service to go on. All classes in the land, nobles, burgesses, peasants, signed a pact, the Solemn Covenant, vowing fidelity to their Kirk as constituted. Charles set about breaking this religious league by armed force. But dragooning without dragoons is a perilous expedient and, when the King put in the field the few Englishmen he had been able to muster against the excellent Scottish army, the troops in both camps came to terms. If this ' Bishops' War' did not end in disaster, it was only because the Scots were halted by negotiation.

The King had one last hope — Strafford. He was the one strong man of the regime. When Charles consulted him, he advised firm action. Parliament should be summoned, and subsidies should be obtained by revealing the intrigues of the Scots with Richelieu. Then war would be waged wholeheartedly. But the Parliament convoked by Charles in 1640, the first for twelve years, had not forgotten old grudges. Far from granting support for a new war, the Commons demanded redressing of their grievances. Pym recounted all Charles's failings, and the Parliamentarians negotiated with the Scots. On Straf-

ford's advice this so-called Short Parliament was dissolved after only eighteen days of session.

With neither money nor loyal troops, beaten by the Scots, who occupied the northern counties and demanded for their evacuation not only religious liberty (which none could refuse them) but an indemnity as well, Charles I had to bow to the will of the most resolute among his subjects. The Lords invited him to summon a new Parliament; a petition signed with ten thousand names obtained by Pym requested likewise; he yielded. The second Parliament of 1640 was not a reforming Parliament; it was a revolutionary Parliament. But it was not a demagogic assembly. The members of the Long Parliament (as it came to be called) were to a great extent gentlemen and landowners, staid, devout, cultivated men, and anxious to return as soon as possible to their family estates. Such men have no liking for turbulence, and only regretfully call in the help of the crowd. Far from being hostile to the institution of monarchy, they envisaged no other. But they felt bound to settle two issues with Charles, one political, the other religious, which had been poisoning the bloodstream of England since the House of Stuart came to the throne.

It was Strafford whom Pym and the Parliamentarians feared, much more than they feared the King. Their hatred of him was all the greater because he had once been in their camp. One of the first acts of the new Parliament was to impeach Strafford for high treason before the Lords. For several weeks Strafford had been aware that if he went to Parliament he was lost. He said so to Charles, who replied that, as he was King of England, he could shield him from any danger, and that Parliament should not touch one hair of his head. Strafford therefore presented himself before the House of Lords just when Pym, leading a deputation of the Commons, came to demand his arrest. Strafford had entered with a bold mien; he had to kneel at the bar of the House to hear the charge against him, and only left it a prisoner. The impeachment had no legal validity. How could a charge of high treason, a crime against the King, be laid against the King's most faithful servant? Attempts were made to compromise Strafford by quoting remarks made by him in Privy Council; he was said to have suggested the idea of using an Irish army to bring England to subjection. But only one witness,

THE EXECUTION OF CHARLES I which took place at Whitehall on
30 January 1649. While absolute monarchy was still to survive
in France for a great many years, in England the king had to
learn the ways of constitutional monarchy or perish. The painting is of the Flemish school, by Gonzales Coques. (Musée de
Picardie, Amiens). *Hachette.*

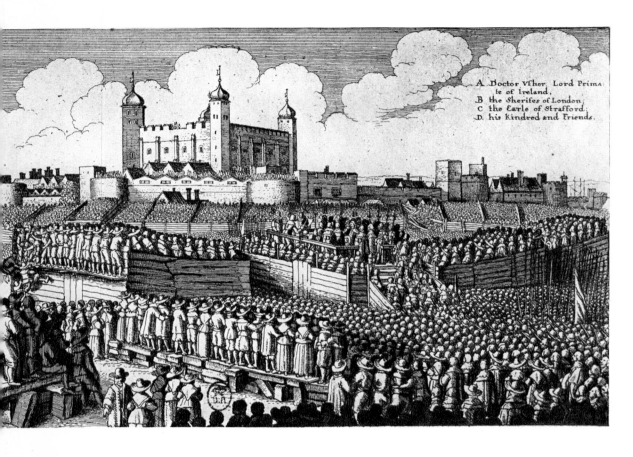

A Doctor Vsher, Lord Prima-
   te of Ireland,
B the Sherifes of London,
C the Earle of Strafford,
D his kindred and friends.

THE EXECUTION OF STRAFFORD, 12
May 1641. Thomas Wentworth,
Earl of Strafford, was executed on
Tower Hill for having too well
served King Charles in his conflict
with Parliament. The king was
forced to abandon him to the vengeance of the Parliamentarians. An
English engraving. *Hachette*.

Sir Harry Vane, could be found; and he was none too sure. The accusers, seeing their prey escaping them, fell back on the simpler and more brutal procedure of a bill of attainder, voted by Parliament and sanctioned by the Crown. This deprived the accused of all the safeguards of a court of justice. Perhaps it would have been wiser for Pym and his associates to admit frankly that a civil war had begun, and to abandon the hypocrisy of legal form. The bill of attainder was passed in the House of Commons by 204 votes to 59, and the names of the minority, which according to the rules of the time should have remained unknown, were posted up in London as those of Strafford's men and enemies of their country. The City shops closed. Masters and apprentices trooped to Westminster to threaten the supporters of Strafford. Under this mob pressure, even the Lords voted the death-penalty by 26 to 19 votes.

The King had vowed that Parliament should not touch one hair of Strafford's head. Would he sanction the act duly passed? The London crowd massed round Whitehall, and became so menacing that the Catholic courtiers made confession and the bravest captains made ready to die in the defence of the staircases and corridors of the old palace. On May 9 the turmoil increased, and about nine o'clock that night the King signed. Strafford was taken aback by the King's desertion, but he had the nobility to write and tell his master that he gave his life gladly. Thus vanished a great man, whose crime it had been to wish for a monarchy aided, not dominated, by Parliament. From the date of this trial, it may be said that the King ceased to be the State, as it was on account of loyalty towards the sovereign that Strafford was deemed a traitor to the country.

By condemning Strafford, Parliament had eliminated the one man capable of transforming the English monarchy into an authoritarian government on the model given to Europe by Spain or France. To make the victory of absolutism forever impossible, it now had to forbid the King to govern, as he and his father had over long periods done, without a Parliament. Pym and his friends obliged the King to approve certain measures accordingly. Firstly there was an act ensuring the regular summoning of Parliament, at least once in three years; if after three years the King still refrained from so doing, the meeting of Parliament could take place without reference to him; and no Parliament could be dissolved before it had lasted for fifty days, or be prorogued beyond three years. Secondly, an act withdrew the King's power to raise taxes without Parliamentary sanction which meant the end of tunnage and poundage, and of ship money — in a word, of any taxes not agreed to by the Crown's subjects. Thirdly, the powers of the King and his Council were greatly diminished, and the courts of prerogatives (the Star Chamber and the like) yielded to the common law. The ecclesiastical Court of High Commission, which Laud had used against the Puritans, was abolished. The Crown was being made subservient to the Law.

The religious problem was more complex than the political. On one point alone, most of the Parliamentarians were agreed: as Protestants, they feared Popery. But many of them hated Laud's bishops, who had tried to lead Englishmen back to ritualism, whilst others were attached to the old hierarchies. Amongst the enemies of episcopacy, distinctions should be made between the Erastians, followers of the German theologian,

Thomas Erastus (1524-83), who subordinated Church to State in temporal matters, and made lay commissioners take the place of bishops; the Presbyterians, supporters of a religious democracy in the Scottish or Genevan style, with elders and synods; and the Sectarians, or Congregationalists, or Independents, who maintained that God was present with every group of true believers, and who thus, despite their extreme narrow-mindedness, became unwitting precursors of freedom of conscience. These religious and political disputes went on from morning to night, in a city seething with theological passion. All day long the Parliamentarians debated, and often at night, by candlelight. Any rumour might make the merchants and apprentices put up the shutters and hurry to Westminster or Whitehall. There was no armed force to hold this throng in check. Indeed, it was the crowd which actually protected Parliament. The King, for his part, retained a few long-haired officers, captains on half-pay whom the City youths jeered at as 'Cavaliers'; they accepted the nickname with pride, whilst the Queen, looking down from a window on the Protestants with their cropped hair, asked who were these 'Roundheads'? And both names stuck.

Charles meekly confirmed the measures voted by Parliament, and secretly conspired against both

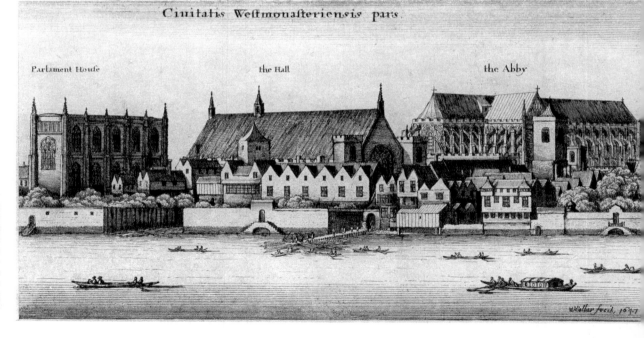

WESTMINSTER IN 1641. An engraving by W. Hollar. The abbey was founded by Edward the Confessor in the 11th century but it was not until the 18th century that its towers were built. Adjacent to it and overlooking the river stood the House of Parliament which was burnt down in 1834. The present Houses of Parliament are built on the old site. *British Museum.*

laws and Parliament. But he regarded himself as being in a state of war, in which everything is permissible. He had one momentary glimpse of deliverance. The Parliamentarians, united in opposition against him, were split on the religious issue. Thanks to this rift, an Anglican and royalist party took shape again.

On January 3, 1642, the Attorney-General suddenly demanded of the Lords the impeachment for high treason of five members of the House of Commons, including Pym and Hampden. It was an unlawful step, as the right of impeachment pertained to the Lower House. The Lords showed hesitancy. The King proceeded in person to the Commons to arrest the five members. They had been warned, and the City had undertaken their concealment. It was a painful scene. The King entered the House followed by Cavaliers and took the Speaker's chair. Members were standing bareheaded. One glance showed the King that 'the birds were flown'. He left amid an excited and hostile crowd, who cried out 'Privilege!' as he passed. The City militia was mustered and assumed the protection of Parliament. A clash between the two forces was becoming inevitable. The King deemed it wiser to leave London.

The time had come for Englishmen, one and all, to choose their side. But most of them would gladly not have chosen. This revolution was not one of those tidal waves which uplift the great masses. It cut across the classes rather than opposing some against others. Thirty peers were left at Westminster: eighty had followed the King; twenty stood neutral. Like the peers, the squires and yeomen were also divided between both camps. London, a Protestant and censorious city, sided with Parliament, but the cathedral towns stood behind their bishops, and therefore behind the King. The rural population was to a great extent indifferent. It was not until later that they grudgingly took one side or the other. Sometimes it was one single, determined squire whose lead was followed by all the gentry of his neighbourhood. The farmers followed their landlords. Pleasure-loving men sided with the King because the Puritans stood for austerity; the sectarians championed Parliament because they hoped, mistakenly, for religious freedom. Nobody in the Parliamentary camp, at the start of the war, wished to strike down Charles Stuart. Nobody supposed that he could be dispensed with. Parliament only wished to be sure of the King's person, to separate him from his evil counsellors, to persuade him not to link his cause with that of the bishops. The idea of the sacred character of royalty, imprinted on men's minds by two centuries of respect, remained intact. When the King raised his standard near Nottingham at the beginning of the war, the symbolic ceremony deeply affected many men whom reason inclined to the Parliamentary side. In point of fact, the issue was not primarily one of a real revolution, which is nearly always provoked by some great economic disorder; it was rather, in this rich and relatively happy country, something which to-day would be termed a party struggle. Through a lack of constitutional machinery, this Parliamentary debate took the form of a pitched battle. It needed the evils of civil war to give birth to political tolerance, just as in other countries it took the horrors of persecution to compel tolerance in religion.

The first moves favoured the King, who was able to concentrate three armies against London, after a drawn battle at Edgehill. Finding his way barred, he withdrew to Oxford, which he made his capital, and the Gothic colleges were thronged with fair ladies and long-haired Cavaliers. In the Royal army the plots of love were interwoven with plots of party and, in reaction against Puritan austerity, gallantry became a point of honour. If Charles had had money, and a more open policy, he might have triumphed. But he tried to negotiate at once with the Scots, with France (through his Queen, who had fled abroad), and with Parliament. In the end his contradictory offers convinced all three of his bad faith. And yet the ball was at his feet, since his adversaries themselves were at cross-purposes. Parliament was trying, as the King had tried, to obtain support from the Scots, but they insisted that in return England must become Presbyterian. The King's sincere convictions had prevented him from agreeing to this; and now Parliament likewise hesitated, because the best of Roundhead soldiers were Independents, who wanted freedom of worship. But in 1643 Parliament finally signed the Solemn League and Covenant, for the sake of hastening victory, and accepted the risk of seeing a Presbyterian army camped outside

London. The Scottish alliance enabled the Parliamentarians to score a victory at Marston Moor, in Yorkshire, in 1644.

The best leadership at Marston Moor was shown by a newcomer — Oliver Cromwell. Distantly connected with Henry VIII's notorious minister of that name, he was a Huntingdonshire squire, a cousin of John Hampden, and like him a Puritan from early youth. But if Cromwell's religion had all the gravity of Hampden's, it was less healthy. A melancholy man, a victim of nightmares, he spent part of his life in states of mystical communion. On several occasions before a great battle or an important decision, he was seen to shut himself away from men, closeted with his Bible and engaged in lengthy prayer. Scriptural language became his natural style. He had lived in the Fens, a countryside then almost as desert as that where Mahomet shaped himself. He shared the Moslem prophet's monotheism, his doctrinal simplicity, and his ruthless will. A member of the 1628 Parliament, and impassioned in his Puritan zeal, he raised a small troop of horse among his neighbours when the Civil War began. His realistic military sense told him that the royal cavalry would hold the upper hand, and that if the Parliamentary army was to win, it must be made up of soldiers devoted to its cause, not of mercenaries or the indifferent. Following his idea of creating a model army, he raised fourteen squadrons, in all about eleven hundred men after his own heart, disciplined, united, responsive to his will. Cromwell did not require them to be Presbyterians, nor even Puritans. He considered that the State need not be concerned with the opinions of men whom it chose for its service: if they were ready to serve it loyally, that was enough. In choosing officers he took no account of birth, but he imposed the strictest discipline on all, in camp as well as on the battlefield. Cromwell's Ironsides neither gambled nor drank, and the villages knew no fears on their approach.

The longer the war dragged on, the more the country suffered and chafed. Shortly before his death, the once-popular Pym was hooted at by the women of London. The execution of Laud, legally murdered after Strafford, separated Charles more drastically than ever from Parliament. But if Parliament was to win a speedy success, it would require an army as strong in all its parts as Cromwell's Ironsides. Cromwell, indeed, made so bold as to tell the Parliamentarians bluntly that their army could not be victorious until members of Parliament ceased to command troops. Cromwell's insistence was met by the passing of the Self-Denying Ordinance, and the New Model army was established under the command of Sir Thomas Fairfax. Henceforth the pay of the troops would be regular, their arms of consistent quality, their uniforms of compulsory type. Cromwell himself was deprived of his command by his own Ordinance, but by special legislation he was authorized to remain Fairfax's lieutenant, with command of the cavalry.

In June 1645, the New Model army defeated the Royalist forces decisively at Naseby, in which victory Cromwell clearly discerned the hand of God. In the following year Fairfax marched on Oxford, and Charles had to flee. This was the end of royal resistance. When he left Oxford on April 27, 1646, he first thought of going to London, but at the eleventh hour he changed his mind and chose to deliver himself to the Scots.

With Oxford taken and Charles in flight, Parliament was the victor. But in a civil war, problems are not all solved by military victory. The country was still monarchist, longing for the time when the villages were not invaded by soldiery, and having no love of the harsh religion of Cromwell's men. Many of the King's partisans, notwithstanding their defeat, looked forward confidently to the time when England would return to her older, kindlier ways. Nevertheless, in the eyes even of the Cavaliers and neutrals, the New Model army stood for order. And if in its hour of victory it had shown some moderation, it would have met with an almost unanimous acceptance. Unfortunately it expected the victory to be the dawn of a new era. The army consisted mainly of Independents and other sectarians, passionate enthusiasts, every one of them a preacher and a prophet, democrats who had scuffled in battle with Royalist Cavaliers and now had no respect for the hierarchy of birth.

Caught up between a conservative populace and a radical soldiery, Parliament understood neither people nor army. Like any assembly left too long in power, it tended to become a collective autocracy. In the folly of pride, Parliament felt strong enough to persecute both Anglicans and Independ-

ents. Against the new Presbyterian Church, with clumsy stupidity, it arrayed the Cavalier gentry by theatening their property, and the Roundhead soldiers by threatening their pay. Bereft of Pym and Hampden, the Long Parliament had lost that sense of possibilities which is indispensable to governance. It first of all tried to make fresh terms with King Charles, whom the Scots, tired of this English quarrel, had now surrendered. Held captive by the Parliamentarians, he was presented with nineteen proposals as terms of peace: he had, for instance, to accept the Covenant, to abolish episcopacy, to hand over to Parliament for twenty years the supreme authority over army and navy, to allow Parliament to appoint the chief officers of State, and to consent to the proscription of numerous Royalists. Charles did not believe that it was his duty to play a straightforward game with the rebels. So, neither refusing nor accepting, he continued to negotiate with France, with Scotland, with Presbyterians against Independents, and with Independents against Presbyterians.

To be able to conclude a valid treaty, Parliament would have had to wield the essential power. But this was in the hands of the army. Thirty thousand men under Fairfax and Cromwell were anxiously waiting to learn their destiny. It was Parliament's desire, firstly, to disband them as soon as possible, retaining only the troops necessary for garrison-duty, and for a campaign in Ireland rendered more and more urgent by disorder in that country; secondly, to keep the Presbyterian officers and retire the Independents, whom it viewed as suspect; thirdly, to refrain from paying arrears of pay. Cromwell, Parliamentarian as well as soldier, but predominantly a soldier, was seriously perturbed by the rising tide of feeling against the army which he saw at Westminster. He was baffled by Parliament's refusal to allow the right of being Christians according to their own light, to victorious soldiers who had fought only to win that right. Still, the idea of ranging the army against Parliament had not yet entered Cromwell's mind, and he had a genuine horror of civil war and of any military dictatorship.

But the army's discontent grew more and more serious. Soldiers' councils were set up in certain

WORD AT · THE LORD OF HOSTS SEP:ÏM
DVNBAR · 3 · 1650

regiments. Parliament sent four members from Westminster, Cromwell and Ireton among them, to negotiate with the malcontents. Cromwell might possibly have restored discipline among them if he had not learned, during the discussions, that the Parliamentarians, whilst feigning interest in the grievances of the army, were making plans to attack it. They were arming the citizens of London and forming Presbyterian train-bands; they were calling in the Scots to the rescue; and they were now offering the King a full restoration if he would accept Presbyterianism for three years. The soldiers resolved not to leave the trump card in the hands of Parliament — possession of the King's person. Cornet Joyce set off with his horsemen to Holdenby near Northampton, where the King then was, and invited Charles to follow him. When Parliament proposed to disband the army with one week's pay, which was simply mockery, Cromwell decided to leave London and join the soldiers. Under his leadership twenty thousand men marched on London: twenty thousand men who prayed long to the Lord God before they started, twenty thousand men who saw eye to eye with their officers in their demand for justice. A letter drawn up by Cromwell was addressed to the Lord Mayor, who might have put up some resistance. In this he voiced his soldiers' claim to profess their own religion. Read before the House of Commons, it was listened to with respect and apprehension. The army moved nearer to London. The military agitators wished to advance on Westminster, but Cromwell preferred to negotiate, arguing that they would thus avoid the reproach of having used force to obtain the assent of Parliament. The army received Parliamentary sanction to enter the City and Fairfax was appointed Constable of the Tower. A few days later the clash between Parliament and soldiers broke out again, sharper than ever.

Cromwell's mind was slow-moving, vigorous, and straightforward. Parliament had been the faith of his youth; he had lost that faith; he made a move towards the King. After all, was not Charles, like the army, apparently demanding tolerance for all Christian men? And would not the fixing of limits to his power suffice to leave it innocuous for the future? But Charles was blind to realities, and in no humour to reach an understanding. He persisted in regarding himself as indispensable and in intriguing with all parties. These balancing feats were dangerous, and disheartened the King's friends. A new faction was forming in the army, styling themselves the Levellers; inspired by a Puritan pamphleteer, they were advancing republican doctrines. Interlaced with plentiful texts from the Bible, their argument was that natural power came only from the people, that the Crown and the House of Lords were vain excrescences, and that government should reside only in one Chamber, elected by universal suffrage.

Cromwell's straightforward, muscular mind could not be affected by such abstractions as the natural rights of man. To believe and to understand, he needed tangible, actual institutions: whence his attempts to treat with the King. But Charles forfeited Cromwell's sympathy, just as he had nullified the hopes of all who espoused his cause. On November 11, 1647, he disappeared, and it was shortly learned that he was in the Isle of Wight. But Charles had fled his captors only to fall into the hands of another. In Carisbrooke Castle he had hoped to find a refuge. He found a prison. He still corresponded with the King of France, with the Scots, but no longer with Oliver Cromwell who had learned to mistrust Charles. An intercepted letter to the Queen revealed that he was again trying to bring a Scottish army into England. Faced by the danger of a Royalist rising with Scottish support, Parliament and the army joined hands. And in the second Civil War (1646), Cromwell's victory was swift and complete. Released from all fears by this victory, Parliament started negotiations with Charles, whom it regarded as henceforth harmless. The King accepted most of the Presbyterian conditions with the firm resolve not to put them into force.

The position of the Independents and the army was becoming dangerous. The mass of the nation, critical in temper, only awaited a sign of weakness to turn against them: London, the chief source of State revenue, and Parliament, the only lawful power, were hostile to them; and the Levellers were still snarling. Many a Puritan officer was beginning to say that no real peace could be secured so long as Charles Stuart, 'that bloody man', remained on the stage of action. But Fairfax was still a loyalist, and Cromwell himself hesitated, with prayer and weeping. What was the Lord's will? Whatever was to be done, it was necessary to act, or to perish. The army marched against Parliament. On December 6, 1648, Colonel Pride and his musketeers posted themselves at the doors of the House of Commons, with lists in their hands, stopping suspects, and sent the forty most dangerous members to a tavern popularly known as 'Hell'. They left at Westminster only about fifty men of their own. It would now be certain that this Rump Parliament would vote whatever the army leaders bade them vote. There remained the King. Cromwell saw clearly that to sacrifice the life of Charles Stuart would lead to a deep cleavage between the army and the nation, but he felt convinced that no peace was possible so long as this mischief-maker lived.

His decision was sudden, and he attributed it, as ever, to divine inspiration. On January 20, 1649, the trial of the King was opened. The charge laid against him was that, having been trusted 'with a limited power to govern by and according to the laws of the land, and not otherwise', he had sought 'to erect an unlimited and tyrannical power to rule according to his will, and in pursuance of this design had levied war against the present Parliament, and the people therein represented.' It was further alleged that he was to be held responsible for all the bloodshed and rapine issuing from that war. Charles was condemned to death, but right up to his last moments he stood fast by the political ideas for which he was dying. He desired the liberty of his people as much as any man, he urged; but that liberty consisted in having a government and laws whereby their life and property could be called their own. It did not consist in the self-government of the people. Government did not pertain to them. That, indeed, was the whole issue in the trial.

Cromwell, the Rump, and the army were now left at the head of England. The country was hostile and outraged, but it had to be governed. By condemning Charles I, Parliament had declared that the Commons of England assembled in Parliament were the supreme power, and that anything willed by them had the force of law, even without the assent of the Lords and the King. But this fiction deceived nobody. How far was the nation represented by these fragments, chosen not by the people but by the military, of a Parliament already over eight years old? These men were at West-minster because the army had kept them there; the people hated the army; and the army despised Parliament.

In March 1649, the Rump Parliament abolished the House of Lords and the office of king, the latter as being 'unnecessary, burdensome, and dangerous to the liberty, safety and public interest of the people.' Henceforth England was to be a Commonwealth, or Republic. But if the word were to have a real meaning, an election would be necessary, which the Independents could not venture upon. Royalists and Presbyterians would have joined hands to oust them. These Republicans were forced to maintain a military dictatorship in flat contradiction to their principles, and justified themselves by quoting from the Bible. The Commons set up a Council of State, comprising squires, lawyers and soldiers, which proved competent in its administration of finance, the army, and the navy.

A military dictatorship presupposes that the dictator can count on the army's favour. But here the army, who had supposed they were making a democratic revolution, soon grew vexed at having set up an oligarchy in power, and it was not long before hostility to the Government became almost unanimous. Cromwell was bound to be intolerant of this agitation. He believed in the necessity of an aristocracy, which he would have defined in terms of faith rather than of birth. He hated all disorder. But conscience pricked him. In the days of Pym and Hampden, he himself had trusted to law and Parliament; and although nowadays he might impose the rule of the sword, reassuring himself by calling it the sword of the Lord God, he could not always convince himself. His remedy for moral perturbation had always been — action. The battlefield revived his common sense and his practical virtues. And opportunities for action were still at hand. In Ireland a Catholic party had been in control of the country for several years, and English Protestants had been murdered there. And to Ireland Cromwell proceeded, at the head of a New Model army, in almost regal state. He annihilated the forces on the spot, and avenged massacre with massacre; a soldier of Jehovah, he rigorously and wholeheartedly applied all the warlike methods of the Old Testament. He settled Protestant soldiers in the eastern parts of the country, and with the same instinct as the old invaders he pushed the Irish

back towards Connaught, in the West. Then began the long martyrdom of Ireland. The land was handed over to foreign and often absentee landlords.

In Scotland things looked more dangerous. The execution of Charles I, a King of Scottish blood, had reconciled the Kirk and the Scottish nobility in a common hatred of the regicides. The Prince of Wales, at the age of nineteen, was proclaimed King under the title of Charles II, and signed the Covenant. An invasion of England by a Royalist army became probable, and Cromwell advocated a preventive war. The loyal Fairfax refused to take part, declaring that it would be a violation of the solemn league previously formed, and Cromwell became commander-in-chief. His moves against the Scots were bold. He allowed them to enter England, moved between them and Scotland, and defeated them heavily at Worcester in 1651. The young Charles II, who had fought courageously, had to flee. Scotland, like Ireland, seemed to be mastered, but her old Parliament was revived at the Restoration. The unity of Great Britain was now complete, and for some weeks the victory made Cromwell popular. Nevertheless, Cromwell knew all too well that this country which he would have wished to see governed by Saints was being exploited by the unscrupulous, that the army of 50,000 men, useless after having defeated the foes without, was ruining the country, that debtors filled the prisons and beggars the roads.

CROMWELL DISSOLVES PARLIAMENT. A satirical Dutch print showing the scene in 1653 when Cromwell decided he had no further use for Parliament. «This House is to let» is the legend on the wall to the right. *Mansell Collection.*

JOHN MILTON (1608-1674) who wrote his epic poem, *Paradise Lost*, in an attempt «to justify the ways of God to men». In this portrait by the Dutch painter Pieter van der Plaas, the blind poet is seen contemplating the Risen Christ. (National Portrait Gallery). *Mansell Collection.*

He realized that this was the moment to revert from military to civil law, from force to justice. But by what means? Prayer and meditation notwithstanding, Cromwell could not discern a remedy. Bereft of action, his mind became confused. He had no money. His soldiers now were costing the nation a hundred times what it had paid for King Charles's ships, the cost of which had been a prime cause of the revolution. What could he do? Order an election? But did he not know that if he allowed *all* the citizens to vote freely, they might recall the Stuarts? Cromwell was weary of the intolerance of his friends, and was beginning to have some shadowy picture of a Protestant England, united and imperial. What other solution was there? To disband the army? It would mutiny. Or to set up a monarchy again? Whatever happened, the Rump must be dismissed; the army was tired of it. On April 20, 1653, the Lord General Cromwell entered the House of Commons and took his seat on one of the benches. He listened, grew restive, and rose. 'Come, come,' he said, 'I will put an end to your prating.' Then he lifted up the Mace, the sacred emblem of Parliament's power. 'What shall we do with this bauble?' he said; and cried to an officer, 'Here, take it away!' And having driven all the members out, he set padlocks on the doors.

After the Crown, the Mace; after the sovereign, the Parliament: no trace was left of this country's long history of freedom. But, once again, how was

Non est potestas Super Terram quæ Comparetur ei Iob. 41. 24

FRONTISPIECE TO HOBBES' LEVIATHAN, 1651. The book promotes
the advantages of the totalitarian State, compared to Leviathan,
the «great sea beast» of the bible. The head of the State is the
prince, who holds exclusive civil power — the sword — and
religious authority — the crozier. *Hachette*.

government to be carried on? Cromwell's choice was for the Saints. He dared not trust to an election, but called upon the Independent churches to select good men, and thus set up a Parliament of one hundred and fifty members. It was called the Barebones Parliament, from the name of one of its members, Praisegod Barebones, a leather-merchant of Fleet Street. Cromwell himself soon tired of these men whom he had drawn forth from obscurity, and would doubtless have sent them packing in their turn if they had not dissolved themselves.

A new constitution was drawn up by the army leaders. This Instrument of Government, as it was called, is conspicuous for the boldness of its ideas, so novel that they could not then be put into practice. More fully even than modern England, this document was a foreshadowing of the United States as we know them to-day. Supreme authority was to be vested in a Lord Protector, a Council and a Parliament, shortly completed by a House of Lords. Any measure voted by Parliament became law, even after the Protector's veto, provided that it was not contrary to the fundamental ideas of the Republic. For the first time England, Scotland and Ireland found themselves united under the same laws. English judges sat in Scotland, and order was maintained there by English soldiers under General Monk; the Westminster Parliament would legislate for Scotland. Ireland, too, was represented in the common Parliament, and across St. George's Channel the English settlers were expropriating the native population. But this forcible 'union' remained precarious, and with the Restoration the old Parliaments of Scotland and Ireland reappeared. Most of the measures passed at this time were likewise ephemeral, because they were premature; but many of them (such as free education, a public postal service, the freedom of the press, female suffrage, secrecy of the ballot, a national bank) were to be revived in time, and to triumph after long eclipse.

The conflicts of Cromwell with his Commons were as grave as those between Charles and his Parliament had been; but the Protector had something which Charles had lacked — a good army. Every intelligent rebel who attains power becomes a government man. Cromwell was one by instinct. This country, he told himself, had suffered enough. What was now needed was the binding up of wounds and the revival of traditional England.

This too was very much what Parliament felt. But the Commons urged that, above all things, the constitution should not be imposed on Parliament by a military leader, and Cromwell was refusing to allow them to discuss the essential features of the Instrument of Government — as drawn up by the army. The Parliamentarians demanded control of the armed forces, and it was Cromwell's belief that to place these in the service of factions would have meant the revival of civil war. Finally, Cromwell desired some measure of religious toleration (in 1655 he even tacitly authorized the return of the Jews, banned from England since the time of Edward I); Parliament was opposed at once to toleration and to military despotism. The sword won the day. England was divided into military regions, each set under the authority of a Major-General. The austere discipline of the Puritans was imposed by stages over the whole country. They had closed the London playhouses, and now they imprisoned strolling players, forbade the village sports, and closed ale-houses. Shakespeare's England became virtuous by compulsion, and sighed for the old Cavalier justice of the peace, who had at least been jovial.

Englishmen had no love of their army, but abroad their army and fleet made the name of England respected. The chief foe for many years was Holland. These two countries were rivals in trade and in mercantile traffic. The Navigation Act of 1651 forbade the importation of goods into England except in English ships. The Dutch refuse to salute the English flag in English waters. A conflict ensued in which two great admirals, the Dutchman Van Tromp and the English Robert Blake, were confronted. Their fighting fleets were evenly matched, but Holland's trade was the more vulnerable and she suffered more than her rival. After peace with the Dutch was concluded in 1654, Cromwell's chief enemy abroad was Spain. Against her he made alliance with France, who, although a Catholic power, was carrying on a Protestant foreign policy on account of her hatred of the House of Austria. Cromwell seized Jamaica from Spain, and his 'plantation' there of English settlers created a prosperous colony. He was the first English statesman to have the idea of maintaining an English fleet in the Mediterranean, and to ensure its safe passage he fortified Gibraltar. Maritime and Medi-

terranean power enabled Cromwell to intervene effectively in Continental broils; he shielded the Vaudois Protestants against the Duke of Savoy, bombarded Tunis, and was able to demand indemnities from Tuscany and the Pope. Cardinal Mazarin sought his alliance and the Ironsides garrisoned Dunkirk. But these wars were costly, and notwithstanding all his successes on land and sea, Cromwell's foreign policy was unpopular.

When he died in 1658, still only fifty-eight years old, the victim of melancholy and fever, the whole edifice which he had hastily erected in an attempt to make a substitute for traditional England, was shaken to its foundations. As his successor Cromwell had named his son Richard, a harmless but uninspired man, who proved powerless to resolve the latent conflict between the army and the civil power, and incapable of smoothing out the even graver discords between the rival army leaders. There followed eighteen months of anarchy, during which Parliament and officers were at grips. At

last only two generals were left in the lists — the Republican Lambert, and Monk, a secret Royalist. Monk came to London, and John Milton was among those who urged him to restore the Long Parliament for the saving of the Commonwealth. But the aspect of the streets showed clearly enough how Englishmen felt. The citizens and apprentices were burning the Rump in effigy in bonfires. The energetic and reasonable Monk acted with cautious deliberation. Although the return of the King was desired by Cavaliers and Presbyterians alike, that is to say the great mass of the nation, it was difficult to prepare this lawfully since only a Parliament could recall the King, and only a King could summon Parliament. Monk convoked as many of the Lords as he could, and called on the electors to return a House of Commons. The King later confirmed this summons, the jurists maintaining the legal fiction that the monarchy had never ceased to exist. The Restoration was achieved without civil strife, because Monk took the precaution of promising the troops their pay. Within two years of Cromwell's death his whole edifice, like himself, was dust.

The new sovereign whom England had so long proscribed but now awaited as a saviour, was in no way the seraphic character imagined by the fervent adherents of his father, the Martyr King. Charles II had not the noble, sorrowful face of his father; his heavy, sensuous lips, his sturdy nose and laughing eyes were reminiscent rather of his grandfather, Henry IV of France. From him he inherited his gaiety, his wit, his taste for women. Long exile had not soured him, but had given him an experience of poverty, and a firm determination not to set out again ' on his travels '. In spite of pressure from his mother and his sister, Henrietta, who were both Catholics, he had not renounced his Protestantism. Catholicism had attracted, perhaps convinced him; but remembering the Puritan passions, he was reluctant to compromise his throne. The changeable moods of nations are surprising. London gave the king a warm welcome, though everything in Charles's character ought to have shocked his subjects. In his train he brought back a beautiful mistress, Barbara Palmer, later Lady Castlemaine, and in her company, cynically, he spent his first night in Whitehall. Ere long he lived surrounded by a veritable seraglio, and court morals imitated the King's. But a touch of folly was not displeasing after the constraints of Puritanism. Dissipation seemed to accord with loyalty, as gravity had done with rebellion. The King's wandering youth had induced habits of idling and irresponsibility. All real power he left to the servant of his exile, Edward Hyde, whom he had made Earl of Clarendon, and the beginnings of this administration were cleverly handled. An act of indemnity reassured those who had taken part in the Great Rebellion, and only a few regicides were executed, in repulsive butchery. The bodies of Oliver Cromwell and some others were exhumed, hung up, and then buried at the gibbet's foot. A restoration could abandon a few heads to the avenging executioner, provided that it did not tamper with fortunes acquired. Clarendon was shrewd enough to pay in full all wages due to the Commonwealth soldiery, which enabled him to disband this formidable army without a clash.

To avoid any more of his ' travels ', Charles was resolved upon lawful rule. In 1661 he summoned a Parliament. In the body which had recalled Charles, Presbyterians and Cavaliers shared the seats. This time the country sent to Westminster a Parliament which has been described as more

THE PRINCE OF WALES DANCES WITH ELIZABETH, THE PRINCESS PALATINE, 1650: C. J. Van Ceulen. The prince, later Charles II, led a not unpleasant life in exile before his expedition to Scotland. The princess, daughter of Frederic V of Bavaria and granddaughter of James I of England was a pupil of Descartes and preferred scholarship to marriage. She retired to a Lutheran monastery. (Collection, of H. M. the Queen, Windsor Castle). *Crown Copyright reserved.*

BARBARA, LADY CASTLEMAINE, DUCHESS OF CLEVELAND, Charles II's mistress at the moment of his return to Whitehall. She was appointed lady-in-waiting to Charles' Queen, Catherine of Braganza, despite that lady's protests, and was mother of two bastard dukes. She later became mistress of the Duke of Marlborough. The portrait is by Sir Peter Lely who painted all Charles II's mistresses. (Raby Castle, Durham). *Mansell Collection.*

Multituds flying from London by water in boats & borges.

Flying by land.

Burying the dead with a bell before them. Searchers

Carts full of dead to bury.

THE GREAT PLAGUE OF LONDON, 1665. The population flees by water and land (leaving old St. Paul's in the background). The dead were buried in mass graves. Almost a sixth of the population succumbed. *Clarendon Press*, Oxford.

Royalist than the King and more Anglican than the bishops, entirely devoted to the interests of landed property and the Established Church. The King retained this House for eighteen years, but so deeply ingrained was the jealousy for English liberties that even this House showed its resolve to grant the King no standing army; nor were his revenues sufficient; so he could not dispense with Parliament, or establish any courts of royal prerogative. The King, on his side, remembered the history of his father and was careful not to step across these bounds. No constitutional check had been laid on him, and no responsible Cabinet was interposed between Crown and Parliament. But Charles, when his ministers became unpopular, always managed to dismiss them just in time. Thus Parliament was the ruler *de facto*, if not *de jure*.

If the Puritans expected religious tolerance from the new King, they were disappointed. Parliament and Lord Clarendon both showed a stern front against independent sects, and even against the Presbyterians. A series of enactments known as the Clarendon Code enforced strict conformity. These measures forced all mayors and municipal officials to renounce the Presbyterian Covenant and to receive the Anglican sacraments, obliged all clergymen to be ordained by a bishop, to use the Prayer Book and English liturgy, forbade any religious service except the Anglican whereat more than four adherents were present, and required nonconformist ministers to retire at least five miles from any important town or from any parish where they had preached. These laws deeply influenced English life. They won the final support of the squires for Anglicanism, as the ban against dissenters holding political or civic office forced the submission of anyone having ambitions or important interests. From this time dates the traditional alliance of parson and squire in village life. But many of those who surrendered still had a dissenting temper, and in later years they became politically the supporters of the Whig party, in alliance with the sceptics and rationalists.

Clarendon wore himself out quickly in power. In a youthful and cynical court, he was a pompous, gouty old servant, forever moralizing. Only a pretext was by now needed to get rid of this battered survival; and the course of events produced several. It happened that the King's brother, James, the heir to the throne, had fallen in love during his exile with Clarendon's daughter, Anne Hyde. He married her, secretly at first, and then publicly. From this union sprang two English sovereigns: Mary, who married William of Orange, and Queen Anne. At the time of its celebration the marriage roused popular hostility, and there was strong feeling against Clarendon, who feigned disapproval himself. Furthermore, Clarendon was responsible for the marriage of Charles II with Catherine of Braganza, a Portuguese and Catholic princess, who proved to be sterile. Another charge was laid against him, that he sold Dunkirk to the French for a large sum, and himself pocketed a commission. The public mind was also deeply affected by the terrible plague which ravaged London, with its swarming, dirty streets, during the summer of 1665, and also by the Great Fire which destroyed two-thirds of the City a few months later. And this second disaster (because the people insist that great events must have great causes) was laid at the door of the Papists, the French and Lord Clarendon. A final blow was the arrival in the Thames of a Dutch fleet, which came as far as Chatham and burnt English ships. Panic spread quickly among a people unnerved by plague and fire. It was of no avail that the Treaty of Breda (1667), which ended the Dutch war, gave the English New York, with the whole of the American coast joining Virginia with New England. Englishmen felt they had been betrayed, and in that same year Clarendon, the public enemy, was exiled.

His place was taken not by one minister, but by a group of confidants known as the Cabal — so called from the initial letters of their names: Clifford, Arlington, Buckingham, Ashley, and Lauderdale. With the help of the Cabal, the King not only reigned but ruled. To outward appearance he still idled and fooled with dogs and doxies; but actually, with hidden tenacity, he was pursuing a great project: to secure money and troops by an alliance with Louis XIV, and with this foreign support, perhaps, to re-establish Catholicism. Charles had a sincere admiration for France and her governance. There he found what he would have liked, but did not dare, to be: an absolute monarch. Realizing that such omnipotence was only made possible by harmony between the sovereign and the Church of Rome, he desired to achieve this harmony and to

THE GREAT FIRE OF LONDON, 1666. It broke
out on 2 September at Pudding Lane and
ravaged the city as far as — indeed further
than — Pie Corner, destroying 13,200 houses
and 89 churches. A hundred thousand people
were made homeless; the total death toll,
however, was six persons. The course of
the fire was arrested by pulling down the
timber houses in its path. A graphic descrip-
tion of the disaster was set down by Samuel
Pepys in his Diary. *British Museum.*

imitate his cousin. Notwithstanding Parliament's
desire for alliance with the Protestant powers of
Sweden and Holland against France, who was taking Spain's place as the supreme power on the
Continent, Charles II signed a secret treaty with
France, and against Holland, in 1672. Parliament
refused subsidies for this unpopular war, and the
Dutch defences were effective. In 1674, much
against the grain, Charles had to negotiate with
Holland, and three years later his niece Mary, daughter of James and Anne Hyde, married William of
Orange. That French treaty was the last move
made by Charles personally on the board of foreign
policy, and it was checkmated.

He still had hopes of achieving his great plan in
the religious field. Early in his reign he had tried
to impose on Parliament a Declaration of Indulgence, thinking to make Catholic emancipation
acceptable in return for a corresponding measure
for dissenters. But even the dissenters, Protestants
before all else, opposed the measure, and it was
rejected by Parliament. Later, Charles tried to give
effect to the measure in spite of Parliament, in
virtue of his prerogative. But he chose the wrong
moment, when hatred of Popery and fear of France
had both been quickened by fire and pestilence.
In days gone by, Spain had symbolized persecution
in Protestant eyes; now, France personified absolutism and the loss of the subject's liberties. Parliament stood fast and refused to recognize the
King's right to settle such matters by ordinance.
Charles wavered, remembered the rebellion and his
' travels ' — and yielded. But part of the Cabal
had sided against him, and made him accept the
Test Act, a national and Protestant retort to the
French alliance and the Declaration of Indulgence.
This law excluded from public office any who would
not swear allegiance to the King's supremacy and
to the Anglican faith. Catholic peers under a
further act had to leave the House of Lords.

CHRISTOPHER WREN K.ᵗ
...NT OF THE ROYAL
SOCIETY

The king's reasonable acceptance of defeat gave grounds to suppose for a time that tranquillity would be restored. But within a few days everything was changed by a lie and a mystery. Titus Oates, formerly an Anglican cleric, was a convert to Catholicism more for self-interest than by conviction, a man of base and contemptible character, who had made enemies wherever he went. Expelled from the English Jesuits' college at Saint-Omer, he returned to England penniless, and in 1678 concocted an accusation against the Jesuits, who, he averred, were plotting to set fire to the City, murder the King, set up his brother James, Duke of York, in his place, subdue England with Dutch and French help, and re-establish Catholicism. He sent one copy of this denunciation to the King, another to Sir Edmund Berry Godfrey, a well-known justice of the peace in Westminster. The excitement caused was prodigious, in a London still nervous after the plague and the Great Fire, with memories of the Gunpowder Plot and an unreasoning terror of Jesuits and Popery. A search among the papers of the Duke of York's secretary revealed a compro-mising correspondence with Father La Chaise, the confessor of Louis XIV. Calumny had accidentally come upon an authentic intrigue. And at this point came the dramatic discovery of the murdered body of Godfrey, at the foot of Primrose Hill. Panic ran riot. Armed Jesuits were reported everywere, and a veritable reign of terror began.

Since the Restoration, parties had been forming in embryo, engendered by the passions of the Civil War. Some favoured the King, like the Cavaliers in the past; and their adversaries dubbed them 'Tories', the name of certain Irish freebooters implying that they were merely Papists disguised; but the King's party wore the insult as a cockade. They, in their turn, nicknamed the King's opponents 'Whigs', an abbreviation of 'Whigamores', a Covenanters' faction in the West of Scotland. The Tories represented landed property and the Anglican Church; the Whigs, the dissenters and the mercantile classes. When the King ordered an election in 1679, the first for seventeen years, the two parties invested it with the character which an appeal to the country has to-day, with meetings,

TESTIS OVAT

TITUS OATES, an unbalanced character who invented a false Catholic conspiracy against Charles II which resulted in a new anti-papist scare and further persecution. His imposture was brought to light, however, and James II condemned him to four whippings annually. *Mansell Collection.*

◀ DUTCH WARSHIPS AT THE MOUTH OF THE MEDWAY, 1667. An incident in the Anglo-Dutch war, fought over colonial rivalry, when the Dutch sailed up this Kentish river and set fire to British men-o'-war. The painting is by Cornelis van Soest. (*National Maritime Museum*, Greenwich).

processions, violent speeches. These were noisy methods, but doubtless their infusion of the spectacular and competitive element into politics made for the enduring success of parliamentary rule. In the election of 1679 the Whigs won the day, by taking their stand, in all bad faith, on the calumnies of Titus Oates; and after their success they made the first experiment in constitutional government. A Privy Council of thirty members was to serve as intermediary between King and Parliament, directed by Shaftesbury, Sir William Temple, Lord Russell and Lord Halifax. The 1679 Parliament is best known for the amendment of the law of Habeas Corpus which set up the most stringent precautions against the arbitrary imprisonment of any English subject. No measure shows more clearly the distinction between despotic and free systems of government. Habeas Corpus was never suspended except in times of emergency.

The Whigs' victory had been due to dread of Catholicism, a cause which was associated with that of the Duke of York. As partisans of radical measures, therefore, the Whigs felt that the King's brother ought to be excluded from the royal succession, while the Tories, as good legitimists, held that it would suffice to set limits on his powers. In this matter, however, the Whigs themselves were divided, some favouring the Prince of Orange, the Duke of York's son-in-law, others inclining to the Duke of Monmouth, the natural son of the King. Charles himself supported his brother against his bastard. Very speedily, with their surprising fluidity, the English populace tired of the Whig terror and forgot Titus Oates. In 1681 Charles, having no need of Parliamentary subsidies as he received funds from Louis XIV, was able without undue outcry to dissolve the last Parliament of his reign, which sat at Oxford in order to be at safe distance from the London crowd. The Tories were winning. The triumph of Crown and Tories was followed by a persecution of Whigs. Shaftesbury was prosecuted for high treason, and although acquitted by a jury had to flee to Holland, where he died. The other leading Whigs, Russell and Algernon Sidney, died on the scaffold, Essex cut his throat in the Tower. A wave of mystical devotion to royalty had swept over England. With impunity, during his last years, Charles II lived unblushingly on French subsidies, and regardless of English interests allowed Louis XIV to pursue his aggrandisement in Flanders and the Rhineland. And thus the monarch who had, with so much charm, betrayed England, two Churches, his wife, and all his mistresses, was able to preserve to the last his luxuriant, perilous equilibrium.

Charles II bequeathed to his brother a despotic and almost unquestioned power. The Church of England preached divine right and non-resistance to the tyrant. A Tory Parliament was ready to vote life-taxes to the King. Discreetly Charles had begun to recruit a standing army of ten thousand men, and James was to double the strength — a great novelty for an English sovereign. The country let matters drift, wishing only to be quiet. Even the new King's Catholicism roused no violent opposition. Anglicans and dissenters were agreed that he might practise his religion provided that he did not seek a national conversion. If James II had been a man ready to compromise, like his brother, he might have reigned undisturbed. But he was obstinate, energetic, dutiful, and rather unintelligent. Comparing the two brothers, men reached the conclusion that Charles II could have understood things if he chose, whereas James II would have liked to understand them if he could. He was ingenuous enough to suppose that, because it preached non-resistance, the Church of England would not resist if he should seek to deprive it of its privileges; but the Anglican Church discovered the weakness of the doctrine precisely when this coincided no longer with its interests. James also believed that he could count on the support of dissenters against the Anglicans because he promised tolerance to the former as he did equally to the Catholics; but this was the moment of the revocation of the Edict of Nantes (1685), when the Huguenot fugitives were coming into England with tales that did not provide a heartening example for the English Protestants.

It could be seen at once that repression under the new reign would be merciless. Rebellions, headed in Scotland by the Duke of Argyll, and by the Duke of Monmouth in the West of England, were fairly easily suppressed, and their leaders were put to death. Hundreds of hapless rustics who had followed Monmouth shared his fate, and the 'Bloody Assize' of Judge Jeffreys became notorious. Everywhere the rope, the lash, the dungeon; and even women were sent to their death. The

JUDGE JEFFREYS, who acquired notoriety by the rough justice he meted out at the Bloody Assize held after the Monmouth Rebellion against James II. Once his master had been driven out in the revolution of 1688 Jeffreys was arrested. He escaped but was recaptured and incarcerated in the Tower of London where he died the following year. (Sutherland Collection, Bodleian Library, Oxford). *Mansell Collection.*

days of Mary Tudor seemed to have returned. Having established an armed camp near London, King James felt secure from any rising and had no qualms about violating the law. Unable to obtain from Parliament the abrogation of the Test Act, he declared it inapplicable to Catholics, by virtue of his royal prerogative, and so was able to fill civil and military posts with Catholic officials and officers. Within the Church of England he favoured crypto-Catholic prelates, and amongst the nobility he sought proselytes, for the spirit of resistance showed itself amongst the peers rather than amongst members of the Commons. The great Catholic families themselves, well aware of the national character and foreseeing dangerous reactions to come, refused to accept high appoint-

ments offered them by the King. Pope Innocent XI advised moderation. But James, zealous and blind, hurried boldly on towards the abyss.

To rule, he needed middle-class support. James thought to rally them by a Declaration of Indulgence comprising the dissenters. This was the old, ineradicable fallacy of supposing that Catholicism could be restored by taking advantage of internal conflict among the Protestants. The Anglican clergy were ordered to read this declaration from the pulpit, but the whole Church refused. A petition was addressed to the King by the Archbishop of Canterbury and six bishops. They were sent to the Tower. When they were acquitted by a jury London was illuminated, and seven-branched candlesticks were seen in the windows. The old clash

between the Stuarts and their subjects was starting again, but by now in an emancipated world where rebellion against the King no longer appeared as something incredible and monstrous. People were patient, however, so long as the King had no heir-male. The heiress to the throne was Princess Mary, a good Protestant, and the wife of William of Orange. Such a couple, it was felt, would one day restore order in the realm. But despair fell on the country when James's second wife, Mary of Modena gave birth to a son in 1688. By now, far more than in 1640, the spirit of revolution was rife.

William of Orange, meanwhile, was engaged in mortal strife with Louis XIV of France, and believed that, unless England remained Protestant, liberty in Europe was doomed. Neither he nor his wife had any scruples about declaring against their father or father-in-law; keeping constantly in touch with the English parties, they only awaited a definite invitation before taking action. On the day when the seven bishops were acquitted (June 30, 1688), an invitation to William and Mary was signed by several peers — amongst them Danby, and the wise and attractive Halifax — who risked their lives, and had the support of numerous officers, including Lord Churchill, court favourite

though he was. Louis XIV had recently invaded the Palatinate, thus giving Holland several weeks of respite. William landed in Torbay on November 5, 1688, and advanced towards London. James had an army, but it was untrustworthy. Seized with panic, he made concessions. It was too late. The militia were mustering in the counties, their password 'a free Parliament and a Protestant religion'. The great landlords were siding with William, and James had powerful interests against him. The Church and the universities had everything to fear from this Catholic sovereign. Princess Anne, the King's second daughter, took her stand with the rebels. James felt deserted. If he had fought, William's position would perhaps have become difficult, as the English people in general were in no mind to reopen a civil war. But instead of trying to make James II captive, his adversaries were at pains to open the door to flight for him. He took the chance, and crossed the Channel, casting the Great seal into the Thames in the hope of preventing the transaction of State business. But a seal can be replaced, and so can a king.

To assure the lawful transmission of power was not easy. The Whigs maintained that, as monarchy was a contract between people and sovereign, the

people or its representatives had a right to reject James II and his sons as unworthy of confidence, and to summon William of their own free will. The Tory bishops, true to the doctrine of divine right, could not accept this method and urged a regency. A legal compromise, put forward by Danby, considered the fugitive King as having abdicated, and proclaimed Mary as having inherited the throne. But this plan clashed with the wishes of the royal couple, Mary being unwilling to reign without her spouse, and William not wishing to become a prince-consort. In the end an agreement recognized them both in February, 1689, and the reign was that of William and Mary.

The Stuart adventure brought about the victory of the Common Law, no less than that of Parliament over Crown. After that dynasty, England saw no more of administrative rights and courts of royal prerogative. There was one law for all, as strict for the State as for individuals; Habeas Corpus closed the last gates of the domain of justice against ' reasons of State '. In France the various revolutionary assemblies at the close of the eighteenth century, and later the National Assembly of 1871, having overturned monarchy or empire, were to attempt the immediate creation of a strong State. In contrast, the Revolution of 1688 in England was directed only towards limiting State powers for the benefit of the rights of the subject. Parliament summoned William and Mary, imposing its own terms on them. The truth was that England, shielded from foreign armies by her girdle of sea, and from internal disorder by the law-abiding temper of her people, was not forced primarily to protect her frontiers against invaders nor her counties against anarchy, but simply to defend the religion and freedom and prosperity of her people against the arbitrary interference of their government.

It was good fortune for England that she could achieve the greatest alteration in her history, the transition from despotism to constitutional monarchy, without an unbridgeable gulf being made between Englishmen of opposing views. If Cromwell had remained in power and himself founded a royal dynasty, England would probably have remained for many years divided. The comparative temperateness in political conflict during the eighteenth and nineteenth centuries is largely attributable to the indulgence shown at the Restoration of Charles II, to the fact that both parties were at one in defending Protestantism at the time of James II's flight, and to the circumstance that, after 1788, the last legitimists rallied to the existing monarchy because the legitimate line of kings had come to an end.

THE SHELDONIAN THEATRE, OXFORD. It was built in 1668 at the expense of Archbishop Sheldon, and modelled on the Theatre of Marcellus at Rome. Busts of Roman emperors adorn the wall surrounding it. The print is by David Loggan. (Bibliothèque nationale, Paris). *Hachette.*

VI

Monarchy and Oligarchy

William & Mary to the Fall of Napoleon, 1689-1815

THE FRAIL Dutchman, with his brown hair and penetrating grey eyes, who was crowned King in 1689, was not foreign by blood — being a grandson of Charles I — nor by his marriage — being the husband of the daughter of James II. But to Englishmen, Whigs and Tories alike, he always seemed a foreigner, in character, tastes and ideas. At a time of gay dissipation, they found him, if not impeccable, at least solemn and unamusable; in days of elegant chatter, he was, like the greatest of his Dutch ancestors, a man of silence. Having experienced in the Netherlands the threat of the growing power of Louis XIV, he always retained a Continental point of view, seeing the maintenance of the balance of power in Europe as the main objective.

William and Mary, on ascending the throne, ratified the Declaration of Right of 1688, which became the Bill of Rights later that year. The text of this document, characteristically English in temper, proclaimed no abstract principles. It enumerated the arbitrary acts of King James and declared them illegal; it affirmed that on no pretext can the King violate certain fundamental laws of the realm; and to ensure respect for these laws, Parliament saw to it that subsidies should be voted annually, and that the army's pay should be provided only for one year at a time. Lastly it was decided, in 1694, that Parliaments should be summoned at least every three years, and that no one Parliament could sit for longer than three years. With the Declaration of Right accepted by the King, few grounds for conflict remained between Crown and Parliament. But a method had not yet been found for ensuring co-operation between the executive and the legislature. For several generations England puzzled over this problem of ministerial responsibility without finding its solution.

If William had been able to do so, he would have imposed religious neutrality upon England. But the opposition roused by this new-fangled notion forced him to compromise. A measure granting comparative freedom of worship was passed in 1689, but Catholics and dissenters were still excluded from public office. Some nonconformists consented to become communicants in the Established Church, in order to take municipal posts, and this was termed ' occasional conformity '. It angered the Tories, who regarded the pretence as impious.

Party frontiers became more definite. The Tories were the party of landed proprietors, the Jacobite squires, and adherents of the Anglican Church. The Whig party was made up of three elements: aristocratic families with an anti-Jacobite tradition (such as the Cavendishes, Russells, Pelhams); City merchants, nabobs from the Indies, moneyed men, who at this time were growing rapidly richer and bought themselves seats in Parliament; and dissenters, who had hardly any link with the two former groups beyond a common fear of the Stuarts and of religious intolerance. In the time of James II the Tories had found themselves, to their despair, forced to chose between Church and King. To avoid Rome they chose The Hague. Some regretted it, and dreamed of an impossible restoration. On the other hand, under William, a curious reversal made the Whigs the most staunch upholders of the sovereign, and they supported without reserve his wars against France.

Since the early years of the seventeenth century there had existed at Amsterdam a famous bank, at which all the great merchants of Europe had their accounts, so that transfer payments could be made. England was still content with private bankers having narrower resources. The goldsmiths of the

WILLIAM AND MARY: R. de Hooge and C. Allard. The Declaration of Right of 30 December 1688 and the Bill of Rights of 13 February 1689 maintained that, the erstwhile James II having abdicated, the throne was vacant and that it pleased God to deliver the Kingdom from popery and misrule by the intervention of H. R. H. the Prince of Orange. Although William and Mary were James II's nephew and daughter respectively, their ousting of the Stuarts could only be legally excused by the expedience of installing a Protestant family on the throne of England. *Hachette.*

Stuart period were pioneers of a new banking technique, dealing in gold, lending to the King and to private persons, and accepting deposits of precious metals in return for receipts (goldsmiths' notes), which were the first form of banknote. Even the Exchequer borrowed from the goldsmiths. During the wars against Louis XIV taxation and loans proved inadequate to cover expenses, and it was then that the Whigs invented the National Debt, the Bank of England, and speculation on stocks. The Bank of England was created to enable William to carry on his wars. A number of capitalists raised a sum of £ 1,200,000, all of which was lent to the State at a rate of interest totalling £ 100,000 per annum. The bank established to carry out this operation undertook at the same time to open accounts for private persons, as did the Bank of Amsterdam. It had no reserves, its capital being lent to the Government, but was given the privilege of issuing paper notes up to a sum equivalent to its capital, such notes being payable in gold. The Bank was able to fulfil these obligations by means of its annual interest paid by the government. The State loan of 1694 was the beginning of the National Debt.

It resulted in strengthening the links which united William III with the City and the Whigs. The founding of the Bank, the increase of large-scale business, and the close connection with Amsterdam, all helped to make London the financial and commercial centre of the world.

William was no general, but he waged war all his life. As King of England, he had to defend himself against the dethroned James II, who, with French naval support, effected a landing in Ireland and was aided by the Irish Catholics. With this Catholic army, James tried to occupy the Protestant counties of Ulster, treating their people with cruelty. In 1690, at the head of an Anglo-Dutch army, William won the battle of the Boyne and drove James from the kingdom. Ireland was conquered. William would gladly have granted Ireland some measure of liberty, but here again his desire for tolerance ran counter to old and fierce prejudices. Harsh laws were passed against the religion, and even the trade, of the Irish. The Scottish Highlands, loyal to the Scottish house of Stuart, had likewise sided with James, although the Lowlands had accepted the Revolution after 1690. It was not until 1707, under

Queen Anne, that the Act of Union united the English and Scottish Parliaments. To William III, Continental problems were paramount. It was Louis XIV's ambition to make the Rhine the frontier of France, a trustworthy and neutral boundary. The Dutch and English merchants considered that if Antwerp were held by France, who was already mistress of Europe's resources, they would be ruined. William was determined to oppose this, and accordingly pursued England's traditional policy — the defence of Flanders, mastery at sea, the formation of a league against the strongest Continental power. At first the excellent French fleet scored victories over the combined English and Dutch navies. But France was hard put to it to control both the Mediterranean and the Atlantic, the sea and the Continent, and finally Louis XIV was prepared to negotiate. At the Congress of Ryswick in 1691 he showed wisdom and moderation, agreeing to renounce the Netherlands in favour of Bavaria, and to recognize the house of Orange in England.

The one outstanding danger point was the question of the Spanish succession. The King of Spain, the half-witted Charles II, shortly afterwards died without issue (1700). Who was to succeed him? A son of the Emperor, a French prince, or the Elector of Bavaria? Louis XIV, anxious for peace, proposed to let Spain go to the Elector of Bavaria, to satisfy himself with Naples, the Two Sicilies and Tuscany for the Dauphin, and to yield Milan to Austria. It was a reasonable solution; but ' death had not signed the treaty '. The Elector of Bavaria, a child of five, died. Fresh negotiations opened between Louis XIV and William III, who were both willing to dismember Spain for the preservation of peace. The Spanish ministers were not willing, and secured from their dying King a testament naming the Duke of Anjou and the Duke of Berry as his successors. If these princes refused, the Austrian prince was to be substituted. This forced the hand of Louis XIV. He could no longer refuse the kingdom of Spain for his grandsons without himself restoring the Empire of Charles V. He accepted the perilous honour, sent his grandson to be Philip V to Spain, and manned the strongholds of the lower Rhineland with French garrisons alongside the Dutch (1701). William III was furious. He felt that he had been tricked, and

began negotiations with the Emperor. As a reprisal, and contrary to the Peace of Ryswick, Louis recognized the exiled Stuart Pretender, James III, as the true King of England.

Death checked William just when he was preparing, along with the Empire and Prussia, a new plan of campaign against France (1702). His wife, Mary, had died in 1694, and the Princess Anne, second daughter of James II, had become heir-apparent. She had lost all her children at an early age (the last surviving one died in 1700), and probably would have no more. Accordingly, in the last year of William's reign, the important Act of Settlement had laid down the order of the royal succession. All the heirs-male, being Catholics, were excluded, and it was decided that the crown should pass, after Anne, to the Electress Sophia of Hanover, granddaughter of James I, and to her descendants, provided that they were Protestants. And it is this Act which still orders the succession to the English throne to-day.

Queen Anne had never had the same friends as her brother-in-law, William III. He had upheld the Whigs because they were untainted by Jacobitism, because they supported his policy abroad, and because they showed more tolerance in religious affairs than did their opponents. Anne was insular, narrowly Anglican, fiercely Tory. She was said to be stupid; her letters show, rather, a vein of obstinacy. In the course of her life, Anne had friendships with two women, which had many of the marks of love. The first of these passions was for Sarah Jennings, who became by marriage Lady Churchill, and then Duchess of Marlborough. Sarah Churchill's place was eventually taken by Abigail Hill, who became Mrs. (later Lady) Masham, and ruined the fortunes of the Marlboroughs.

The career of John Churchill (who became Duke of Marlborough in 1702) presents an odd blend of amoral adroitness and genius. The son of a squire, Winston Churchill, he began as a page to the Duke of York, and became a lover of Lady Castlemaine, Duchess of Cleveland, accepting from her a gift of £5000. This ill-gotten money was well invested, and was the foundation of a great fortune. In James II's day John Churchill had reached high military rank. During the Revolution of 1688, he played a double game, till the accession of Queen Anne, who made him the most powerful man in the country. Not only was Marlborough an excellent general, but he was also the wisest and least partisan of politicians. Tory by birth and habit, he consented to work with the Whigs because they were supporting him, as they had upheld William III, against Louis XIV. The two great figures of Anne's reign, Marlborough and Godolphin (or, as they were styled, the General and the Treasurer), were experts set above party divisions.

The Queen's first Parliament was composed of full-blooded Tories. Thereupon the General and the Treasurer found themselves driven towards the Whigs by the demands of their foreign policy. They tried to rule with mixed ministries, but it was 'mixing oil and vinegar'. Political and religious controversy became as violent as they were brilliant. The new-found freedom of the Press allowed the publication of pamphlets from the pens of the foremost writers. This was the time when Steele and Addison, both Whigs, were issuing the *Tatler* and the *Spectator*, when Swift, the friend of the Tories and the High Church, wrote the *Tale of a Tub*, while Daniel Defoe voiced moderate opinion. Spontaneously the country was moving towards that alternation of parties which turns civil strife into a chronically benignant malady.

The War of the Spanish Succession lasted till 1713. The English objective, now as always, was to maintain the balance of power in Europe, pre-vent Louis XIV from uniting the forces of France and Spain, and compel him to quit Flanders and the estuary of the Rhine. France had the advantage of being in occupation of the disputed territories at the start of the war, but she was exhausted by half a century campaigning, and she did not hold the mastery of the sea. Furthermore, England had robbed her of two of her allies — Savoy, and Portugal (after the Methuen Treaty of 1701, which gave England the friendship of the court of Lisbon, a taste for the wine of Oporto, and hereditary gout). The Allied generals, Marlborough and Prince Eugene, shocked conventional ideas by substituting a mobile war for a strategy of sieges. The flintlock and bayonet, in both of the opposing armies, had replaced pike and musket. Losses on both sides were severe; Marlborough overwhelmed the French at Blenheim in 1704, and then reconquered Flanders at Ramillies in 1706. But the Whigs, although they had won the war, were unable to make the peace. To halt a campaign before victory becomes exhaustion is difficult, and demands foresight. In 1709 and after, the English might have been able to obtain a treaty which would have freed them from all fears, so far as Flanders was concerned. But they wanted more, and wished to see the King of Spain expelled from that country by his own grandfather, Louis XIV. This was an insult which rallied Frenchmen to

QUEEN ANNE AND HER PRIVY COUNCIL. A Dutch engraving of 1702, which shows an anti-French slant: the eclipse of the sun (le Roi-Soleil) and the cock being plucked by the queen. The Scottish thistle, possibly representing the Stuarts, lies at the queen's feet. *British Museum.*

PRINCE JAMES AND HIS HALF-BROTHER, THE ▶ DUKE OF BERWICK: Alexis Simon Belle. This James was known as the Old Pretender, being the brother of the queens Mary and Anne and lawful claimant to the throne were it not for the Act of Settlement, 1702, which excluded him. His son, Charles Edward, the Young Pretender, made an armed incursion into England from Scotland in 1745 but was repulsed. James Fitz-James, Duke of Berwick, was a bastard son of James II. The ships symbolise the royal will to return to Great Britain. (Scots College, Paris). *Hachette.*

THE BATTLE OF OUDENARDE. During the War ▶
of the Spanish Succession, pursued by Britain
againt France in an attempt to maintain the
balance of power on the Continent, John
Churchill, Duke of Marlborough, and Prince
Eugene of Savoy defeated the Duke of Ven-
dôme's army on the Scheldt, July 1708. (*Blenheim
Palace*, Oxfordshire).

JONATHAN SWIFT (1667-1745), the satirist, author of *Gulliver's
Travels*, was born in Dublin of English parents. He was for thirty-
two years Dean of St. Patrick's Anglican Cathedral, Dublin. He
exercised considerable influence as a jounalist and pamphleteer. He
died insane. A portrait by Charles Jervas in the *National Portrait Gallery*.

their King. The battle of Malplaquet was not
nearly so fortunate for the Allies as those which
preceded it, costing the victorious side more than
a third of their effectives, and the French retreated
in such good order that pursuit was impossible.
In England, public opinion began to sag. Marlborough was now trying to have himself appointed
by the Queen as generalissimo for life. Such a
claim alarmed Parliament. Would another victorious army produce another Cromwell? The
Tories plucked up courage anew.

The Tory reaction had several causes. Firstly,
there was war-weariness. In his pamphlet, *The
Conduct of the Allies*, Swift wrote that 'after ten
years war with perpetual success, to tell us it is not
yet possible to have a good peace, is very surprising.' Secondly, there was a religious incident which
crystallized the latent discontent of Englishmen.
On November 5, 1709, a violent sermon was
preached at St. Paul's Cathedral by Dr. Sacheverell,
denouncing the tolerance and tepidity of the Whigs,
and all liberal tendencies. Its success was prodigious: forty thousand printed copies were sold.
The Whig ministry made the mistake of demanding
the impeachment of the preacher, and Sacheverell

became a popular hero. In the third place, Tory
sentiments were at one with the Queen's. A bedchamber revolution coincided with the religious
outburst, and Mrs. Masham supplanted the Duchess of Marlborough. The Queen chose Tory ministers to serve her — Harley (later Lord Oxford)
and St. John (later Lord Bolingbroke). Marlborough, just when he thought he had Louis XIV
at his mercy, was recalled. An unforeseen event
strengthened the Tory resolve to treat with France:
the unexpected death of the Emperor of Austria,
which threatened, in the event of Philip V's abdication, to place on the Archduke's head the crown
of Spain as well as that of Austria. The balance of
power was upset; Spain was in Flanders; all that
England had feared for a century was coming to
pass. Cynically adopting the balancing tactics which
were to become the favourite, and perhaps necessary, device of her foreign policy, she abandoned
and betrayed her allies, who were defeated by the
French at Denain in 1712.

The Treaty of Utrecht, concluded in 1713, had
to face severe Whig attacks; but it was not a bad
treaty. The Emperor lost his hope of reconstituting
the Empire of Charles V, and Louis XIV his hope

of uniting the two crowns. In the Mediterranean, England secured two valuable bases in Gibraltar and Port Mahon, Minorca. She further augmented her empire with Newfoundland and Hudson Bay, handed over by France. Unable to wrench from Spain the vast colonial domain on which England's merchants had so long cast envious eyes, she nevertheless obtained privileges therein. England was henceforth entitled to import a certain number of slaves into South America. Moreover, she could send there every year a shipload of her products, which gradually, by shifts and devices, became a whole fleet. Finally, by the Treaty of Utrecht, France bound herself to give asylum no longer to the Pretenders, James III and his son Charles Edward. This treaty marks the beginning of England's preponderance in Europe. She had enfeebled all her Continental rivals, and had acquired, for the time being at least, a mastery of the seas greater even than that of the Dutch. This small island was becoming the arbiter of the world. But Queen Anne was now old, and obviously had not long to live. It would have been prudent to pay court to the future King, George of Hanover, but that was not easy for ministers of Anne. The result was that only the Whigs made advances to Hanover, and it soon became clear that if the Queen died, the Whigs would hold power. What could ministers do? Come to term with James III? But the Tory squires would not have supported a Catholic King, and it was a hopeless position for legitimist ministers to advance the claims of a lawful sovereign whom they knew would not be accepted. The end came with dramatic suddenness when the Queen had an apoplectic stroke and died. It was consequently an unknown sovereign who now arrived from Hanover.

The mediocrity of the first Hanoverian sovereigns gave them historical importance. It completed the transformation of the British monarchy into a constitutional monarchy. On the heads of these foreign Kings, the crown ceased for over a century to be the object of any fervent emotion. It was now ridiculous to speak of the divine right of kings. George I was certainly the great-grandson of James I, but at the time of his accession there were plenty of other princes who, but for the Act of Settlement of 1701, would have had a better title to the throne than he. If George reigned, it

was by the free consent of the nation. There was no trace of English origins in this German princeling. If he had had to choose between the throne of England and the Electorate of Hanover, he would have preferred the latter. He was fond of his small Hanoverian capital, his small Versailles — Herrenhausen by name — and his small army. But a matrimonial tragedy must have spoilt his memories of Hanover. There he had repudiated his wife, Sophia Dorothea, for adultery with the Swede Koenigsmark, who was supposed to have been strangled, and buried beneath the floorboards of the castle. Since this episode, the Princess had been a State prisoner, and George I had consoled himself with mistresses who compensated for the dullness of their wits by the vigour of their charms. Any woman could please him, if she were complaisant and plump, and those who aspired to his favours amplified themselves as best they could. The people of Hanover endured them because they cost the treasury little. The harem which arrived in England with the new King caused more smiles than frowns. In the eyes of George's German retinue, England was merely a country from which riches must be extracted. Of one favourite Walpole said that she would have sold the King's honour for an additional shilling. Nobody in the royal entourage spoke English, and Latin was the only tongue by which the court and ministry could communicate. '*Mentiris impudentissime*,' was a cry heard in the palace corridors. It may seem surprising that the nation consented to this farce. But it was the Whigs who made the miracle possible, because they stood in need of the Hanoverians. Without George, they would have had only a kingdom without a King; without the Whigs, George would have been merely a King without a kingdom. George I was no more than a rather ludicrous convention; but the peace of the lieges depended on the acceptance of that convention.

At the date of his accession, George was already a man of fifty. His habits were set, his ideas fixed. Regarding home affairs in England, he was ready to trust to his English ministers. He was only vaguely acquainted with the laws and constitution of his new kingdom. And as he knew no English, he soon ceased to attend meetings of the Cabinet Council. From this fortuitous circumstance sprang in due course a form of government destined to

GEORGE I by Sir Godfrey Kneller. George, Elector of
Hanover, ascended the throne of England in 1714 on
the death of Queen Anne, knowing not one word of
his subjects' language. He brought in his train an
all-German court, complete with mistresses, and made
little effort to interfere in the domestic policies of his
adoptive country, which he left to his Whig ministers.
Even Kneller, his court painter, was German by birth.
National Portrait Gallery.

enjoy lasting success — that of a Cabinet responsible
to the Commons. Before George I, the idea of
ministerial responsibility remained in the void,
because, with the King present at the Council's
deliberations, its decisions were always deemed to
be his. Frequently, too, ministers had been chosen
by the King from both parties; and this had made
collective responsibility impossible. With the
Hanoverians began a long period of purely Whig
ministries. On the accession of George, the Whigs
rendered the Tory party impotent by exiling
Bolingbroke for some months, and by sending
Oxford to the Tower for a couple of years.
Then they consolidated their position in the
Commons by manipulating the 'rotten' boroughs
and by corruption of the electorate. Being now
sure of the Commons' support, they extended
the duration of the Parliamentary mandate from
three to seven years — a measure modified in
1911, when the period was shortened to five years.

The Cabinet, a body of ministers collectively
responsible to Parliament, was, like nearly all British institutions, not an *a priori* conception, but the
creation of time, chance, compromise and common sense. It was simply a group of Privy Councillors, and ministers had no other official standing.
There was no thought of creating a Prime Minister:
Parliament disliked the name and the idea. But
as the King, through ignorance of the language,
could not preside over the Council, his place had
to be taken by one of the ministers. It happened
that this minister, Walpole, was a master of the
art of governance, and his colleagues came to acknowledge his authority as a matter of course. He
admitted that he derived this authority from his
agreement with the existing majority in the House
of Commons, and when he lost the confidence of
the House, he resigned, contrary to all precedents.

Sir Robert Walpole was one of the greatest of
English ministers, although he fought shy of all
the attributes of greatness. Son of a Norfolk
squire, he had the tastes and manners of a country

ROBERT, FIRST BARON CLIVE (1725-1774), by Nathaniel Dance. He came
from an old Shropshire family, went out to India in the employment
of the East India Company and became embroiled in the struggle with
the French. His victory over Dupleix at Plassey, Bengal, in 1757, marked
the beginning of Britain's effective ascendancy in India. He went on
to consolidate British rule in India but the discovery of scandalous
irregularities in his administration led him to commit suicide. (*National
Portrait Gallery*).

landowner. His cynicism made him suspicious of
exalted ideas, and he laughed aloud when his adversaries spoke of their patriotism. Hating doctrines and crusades, he distrusted anyone who
sought to dictate his conduct to him in accordance
with the history-books, and conducted affairs of
State, like a good business man, from day to day.
If he governed by corruption, as Macaulay said,
it was because in his age there was no possibility
of governing otherwise. Walpole never propounded plans or programmes to the nation, but his
common sense amounted to genius. Throughout
his twenty years of power his political system was
simple; a weak State, he argued, ought to shun
adventures, and in order to consolidate a dynasty
devoid of prestige, it was his duty to play for time.
He therefore sought to lessen taxation, to keep
the Church of England apart from the Jacobites,
to keep the Tories out of power and to maintain
peace by an understanding with France and by
keeping clear of international politics as long as
possible. These may not have been exalted aims,
but by attaining them he gave his country several
years of unmatched prosperity.

During the summer of 1727 George I died of an
apoplectic stroke. It looked as if Walpole might
fall from favour. The Prince of Wales had always
been on bad terms with his father, and now,
as George II, it seemed probable that he would
desire a change of ministry. But very soon the
courtiers were surprised to find Sir Robert more
welcome at court than ever. The new King,
however, was not easy to win over. He was miserly,
malicious, fantastically methodical, and Walpole
put him down as the greatest political coward who
ever wore the crown. Happily for the minister,
and for the country, George II let himself be led
by Queen Caroline, who had intelligence and some
culture and a stoical patience. Tirelessly, for seven
or eight hours a day, she listened to the flood of
words pouring from the poor King, pontificating
about war or genealogy. Her sole compensation
for these trials was the knowledge that she ruled
the country and could uphold her dear Sir Robert.
Thanks to this prop, Walpole survived.

But after twenty years of respite, the great peace-
maker at last found himself forced into war.
Commercial chauvinism was increasing. Under
cover of the treaty entitling England to import
slaves to the Spanish colonies and to send one ship
there annually, a large contraband trade had grown
up. The Spanish coastguards were furious and

searched all English ships. The Opposition exploited these 'atrocities' to attack the inertia of Walpole and, as they said, his passion for negotiating. A certain Captain Jenkins came to the bar of the House of Commons and told how his brig, the *Rebecca*, had been boarded by the Spaniards, who had cut off his ear. To settle this affair Walpole reached an equitable agreement with Spain. It was denounced as dishonourable by a youthful member of Parliament named William Pitt. The truth was that the minister's opponents were anxious for war with Spain, not without thoughts of acquiring some part of her colonies. This would be their war, Walpole told them when, in 1739, he had at last to resign himself to it; and he wished them joy of it.

This war of 'Jenkins's ear', as Walpole foretold, was troublesome. The Opposition, after demanding it, refused the government the wherewithal to win it. Defeated in the Commons, ill and exhausted, the minister at last resigned and went to the House of Lords. His departure gave rise to a curious agitation against the office of Prime Minister. Thirty-one peers drew up a resolution setting forth that this office was not allowed for by the laws of England and was incompatible with the constitution of the country. 'But the wise and excellent' minister had achieved his task. By prolonged tranquillity it had given the dynasty firm roots and enriched the country. This new wealth was throwing up new men. Avid for conquest, England was coveting an Empire. She desired no longer peace, common sense, happiness, but news of victory, lists of captured towns, triumphs, adventures. The age of Walpole was over.

The Whig ministers who succeeded Walpole, contrary to his maxims, proceeded to engage in continental concerns. The Emperor of Austria, Charles VI, by the Pragmatic Sanction, had bequeathed to his daughter Maria Theresa all his dominions (Central Europe, Belgium, Italy): a heritage which was bound to quicken covetousness. On Charles's death Frederick II of Prussia claimed Silesia for himself. By what right? By the right, it has been said, of vigorous troops, full coffers, and a greedy mind. England, unwillingly allied through her dynasty with Hanoverian interests, also plunged into this welter. Before long the seconds were involved. In May 1745 war was declared between France and England; in June the

Young Pretender, Prince Charles Edward, sailed from France and landed in Scotland.

There, once more, a Stuart found the astonishing loyalty of the Highlands to his family; and once more it was proved that the Scots were the best soldiers in Britain. With 6000 men Prince Charles was able to enter England and advance as far as Derby. With the support of an English rising, he could in his own person have restored the Stuart dynasty to the throne of England. But the episode showed the amazing indifference of the mass of the people to this dynastic issue. A few thousand Highlanders had been able to invade Britain; a small army recalled from abroad sufficed to save London, and Charles retreated. In Flanders the war turned in France's favour. Freed from the Austrian menace by the victory of Frederick of Prussia, Marshal Saxe inflicted a resounding defeat on the English at Fontenoy in 1745. If the English had not controlled the seas, if their corsairs had not ruined French trade, and if the Protestants had not driven forth Prince Charles, Louis XV might have hoped for great things indeed. But in April 1746, defeated at Culloden, Charles fled to France, and the Highlands were at last subjugated, not without harshness.

Between 1740 and 1748 England and France were at war not only in Europe, but in Canada and India as well. In North America, the French were anxious to occupy the Ohio and Mississippi valleys, which would have cut off the English coastal colonies from their hinterland. In India, the two rival Companies maintained small armies, which they placed at the service of the native princes whenever they saw an opportunity of extending their territories. There, two great men came into conflict, Clive and Dupleix. The Frenchman held the upper hand at first, and seized the English town of Madras, but had to restore it by the Treaty of Aix-la-Chapelle in 1748. But the peace did not prevent the rival Companies in India from continuing the struggle, under cover of helping local potentates. Clive, despite his youth and a scanty force of soldiers, won conspicuous victories over the native princes. His defence of Arcot in 1751, and his great victory at Plassy in 1757, founded a British Empire in India. His personal fortune, as well as the territory of the East India Company, was enormously aggrandized. The Indian princes,

THE BRISTOL DOCKSIDE IN THE 18TH CEN-
TURY: Peter Monamy. Bristol, on the Avon
a few miles from the sea, was one of
England's busiest ports in the 18th century,
though its commercial prosperity dated
back to the Middle Ages. *Bristol City
Art Gallery.*

to gain the goodwill of their conquerors, lavished
gold and precious stones upon them, and private
fortunes of Indian provenance henceforward played
a leading part in English elections.

The Peace of Aix-la-Chapelle satisfied nobody.
To obtain withdrawal of the French troops occupying Flanders, the English government had to
abandon the island of Cap Breton which commanded Canada. In the Spanish colonies, England
secured a renewal for four years of the right to
import slaves, as also of the annual trading ship;
but Spain reserved the right of search, a source of
future complications. In Canada and in India, the
Anglo-French conflicts were far from being settled.
None of the great European countries accepted
the existing map of the world. All the old systems
of alliance were collapsing. France and Austria
wondered whether their traditional enmity was
justified by any real clash of interests, or whether,
on the contrary, the rise of Prussia did not confront
them both with a formidable threat. France and
England began to realize that, so long as the

question of the mastery of the sea and the colonial
issue remained unsettled, there could be no lasting
peace between them.

Never had England's prestige in Europe been so
extensive. The triumphs of her armies, the foresight
of her Revolution, inspired in other peoples a desire
to study her ideas and institutions. John Locke,
the philosopher of the Whigs, became the master of
his European colleagues. It was his aim to oppose
what he termed natural right against the Stuart
theory of divine right. From Locke's optimism, in
due course, would spring Rousseau's *Social Contract*,
the French declaration of the Rights of Man, and
the American Declaration of Independence.

It may be wondered why the English townsfolk
and peasantry, at a time when philosophers were
teaching that men were born free, submitted so
readily to the authority of a landed aristocracy who
did not even possess, as their feudal predecessors
did, military strength. This was due, firstly, to the
fact that Englishmen regarded concrete realities as
more important than abstract rights. There was

also the fact that England, in Locke's time, had no grave causes of discontent. Englishmen observed that their local institutions, notwithstanding inevitable hardships, were efficient and tolerable. The justice of the peace tempered the measures enacted by Parliament. He was bound to do so: for how could he have enforced them without the assent of the parishes, when his only police consisted of the village constables? His very weakness was a pledge for his relative equity. The penal laws were certainly of archaic severity; vagabonds and poachers were treated as dangerous felons. But the landowners lived on their own lands and respected an honest farmer. Competent agriculturists, the English squires worked in close contact with their cowmen and shepherds. A personal relationship was better than an administrative one.

The squire, with his silver-buttoned coat, his wig, his hunters, his family pew where he dozed in church — the figure was an essential part of the background of English life, in the eyes even of the country folk. Not until after the industrial revolution did the masses transplanted to the towns cease to regard a Parliament of country gentlemen as part of the natural order. In the early eighteenth century they were gratified to see some approximation of the mode of life in the manor to that in the cottage. The squire then was a countryman, using the oaths of his rustics and drinking with them if need be; on polling-day they would insult his son, pelt him with mud, and then acclaim him. Electoral contests at this time have been described as a national sport, as popular as horse-racing. The people of the countryside were not then wretched. Well fed, they lived the lives their fathers had led, and knew no other; the village was still their universe. In the towns, too, the apprentice was still regarded, in many a merchant's or artisan's home, as one of the family.

Stability in the social organism, during the eighteenth century, was matched by stability in literary forms. In the classical mode Alexander Pope, the great poet of the age, wrote his *Dunciad* and epistles and satires, excellent in themselves and traditional in their form. More original, and so more characteristically English, were Swift and Defoe. Steele and Addison fixed the enduring form of the English essay. And art was no less classical than letters.

Grace and simplicity of line are the characteristics of Wedgwood's pottery, the furniture of Chippendale and Sheraton, the architecture of the Adam brothers. Great painters like Gainsborough, Romney and Reynolds, continue for the great noble families the galleries of portraits begun by Holbein and Van Dyck. Handel, coming from Hanover in 1710, where he had been a *Kapellmeister*, became in England a composer of oratorios on Biblical themes, this type of work being fashionable, and *The Messiah* was first performed in Dublin in 1742. In this new Augustan age painters, musicians, writers and politicians formed a real society of their own, foregathering in the coffee-houses, clubs and drawing-rooms. But the age had also its Hogarthian side. 'The commonest pleasures of the English,' wrote a Swiss traveller, 'or at least of Londoners, are wine, women, dicing — in a word, debauchery.' Since the Methuen Treaty with Portugal, the wealthier classes had drunk port to excess. A minister was not ashamed to come drunk into the royal presence, nor a squire to fuddle himself in his daughter's company. The common people drank gin, of which two million gallons were distilled in 1714 and five million in 1735. Violence spread with drunkenness, all the more dangerous in the absence of a police force, and with an army reduced after the Treaty of Utrecht to 8000 men for the whole of Great Britain. People were terrorized in the London streets by a gang of young bloods known as the Mohocks. Mounted highwaymen robbed travellers on the water-logged highways. Gambling was another vice of the age. Play went on in all the clubs, as also amongst women. Those who did not play cards laid wagers or speculated. Rogues preyed upon the lust for lucre, and shady financiers formed companies for the most absurd purposes. Drink, play and gallantry gave rise to quarrels, and these often ended in duels. Meetings took place in all sorts of places, in ballrooms and coffee-houses, even in the corridors of theatres. The custom of killing a man for a chance remark did not completely disappear before the century ended. But after 1730 the duel was tending to vanish, through the influence of a man who left a curious mark on English ways — Richard, or 'Beau', Nash. In 1705 he had become master of ceremonies at Bath, a watering-place which had enjoyed high repute since Roman times, but where visitors suffered prodigiously from ennui. Nash proceeded to enliven it. With unlimited and self-invested authority, he imposed strict and sensible rules. He was the first to make English people of different classes grow used to mixing when they came to take the waters; and it was he who forbade the carrying of swords at Bath. This restriction, at first confined to Bath, later became general, and at least prevented impromptu duelling. Furthermore, Nash set the fashion of silk stockings and open shoes for men. In general the social tone was becoming more refined, and the grossness of Wycherley was being displaced by the wit and frivolity of Sheridan.

THE ELECTION: WILLIAM HOGARTH. The voter is shown equally receptive to the arguments of the opposing canvassers. The peaceful character of the scene suggests that the proceeding was by no means remarkable and contrasts with the animated controversy being disputed in the background. (Sir John Soane's Museum, London). *Hachette*.

◀ LIFE CLASS AT THE ROYAL ACADEMY by John Zoffany. The Royal Academy was founded in 1768 by George III. Around the time this picture was painted it included such luminaries as Thomas Gainsborough, Sir Joshua Reynolds, J. S. Copley, Angelica Kauffmann, and Zoffany himself. (Collection of H. M. the Queen, Windsor Castle). *Crown copyright reserved*.

ALEXANDER POPE (1688-1744) by M. Dahll and J. Simon. «...how wretched
I! / Who can't be silent, and who will not lie.» The author of the
Epistles, *Satires*, *Dunciad* and other devastating writings was a brilliant
and irascible man who made enemies with remarkable facility. His
verse may be cold, polished, precise, but it is a perfect vehicle for his
satirical commentaries. *Giraudon.*

Meanwhile, in the colonies the war went on. How could the governments have resisted it? In bad weather it took two months to reach New York, six to get to Calcutta. Orders from London or Paris arrived when battles were already lost or won. In India, Pondicherry stood in rivalry with Madras, Chandernagore with Calcutta. In America the French governors were striving to join up Louisiana with Canada, the Mississippi with the St. Lawrence, by coming in the rear of the British colonies, which would thus have been encircled between the Alleghanies and the Atlantic. The rivals had come to grips in the Ohio valley in time of peace, and the French, having driven out the English settlers, built Fort Duquesne. Not only were the colonists of both countries, in various quarters of the globe, fighting in defiance of peace treaties, but English squadrons at sea were stopping and attacking French ships. France had a new navy and the English Admiralty was perturbed. Without a declaration of war, they gave chase to French vessels. Actually, since the accession of William III, a new Hundred Years War had begun. The stake was no longer the Angevin or Anglo-French Empire, but the Empire of the world. It would inevitably belong to whichever adversary obtained mastery of the seas. Now, to devote all her strength to the refashioning of a navy, France required peace in Europe; all that England needed, on the contrary, was to have, according to her tradition, a soldier on the Continent. Time and again experience had shown that naval and colonial victories were unavailing if France could occupy Flanders, because it was then necessary, when negotiations began, to restore captured colonies in order to obtain the evacuation of Antwerp. The question remained, to choose the soldier. Up to 1748 England had poured subsidies into the coffers of Austria, but since the last war George had been an admirer of the King of Prussia, Frederick II, who

was less expensive than Maria Theresa, and also a better strategist. England therefore reversed her alliances, and at the same time, partly for this reason, France shifted hers round. The traditional rivalry of the Bourbons and Habsburgs was transformed into an alliance. But during this struggle with France, England produced a statesman who would now view war in Europe as a side-issue and devote the main resources of the country to the colonial struggle.

William Pitt was born in 1708. From being a young cavalry officer, he entered the House of Commons in 1735 as member for Old Sarum, a constituency with virtually no electors, purchased by his wealthy grandfather, a Governor of Madras. He soon made an impression on members by his dramatic, ironic, impassioned eloquence. Adversaries were awed by the gleaming eyes and the long, threatening beak of this young man. They might hate his grandiloquence, but they had to admit his authority. One problem was dominant

in his mind — the formation of an overseas empire for England's benefit. Hanover, Prussia, Austria — the Continental chessboard had little intrinsic importance to Pitt; these matters were only pawns, useful to safeguard the greater pieces, India and America. One fact above all seemed to him inadmissible — Spain's grip on the South American trade. So long as Spain had tolerated English contraband, it had been an endurable evil; but when she tried to apply the treaty terms strictly, the English merchants waxed wroth and Walpole's passivity brought about his downfall. Pitt's first office was a modest one, that of paymaster-general of the army, and for some years it looked as if he would remain in this junior post. King George II disliked the young minister because, in his hostility to Continental engagements, he opposed any Hanoverian policy. His advent to power was made possible, and necessary, only because of grave English reverses in the war which opened in May 1756.

Minorca, the naval base in the Mediterranean, was seized by Marshal de Richelieu; and shortly afterwards Admiral Byng was made the scapegoat and shot, for not having done all that was humanly possible to save the island. In India, Calcutta fell. On the Continent, France, Austria, Russia and Sweden united against Prussia, and imposed the capitulation of Klosterseven on the Anglo-Hanoverian combination. In America the Indian tribes joined the French. And for all these disasters Pitt blamed the ministerial Whigs. The people called for Pitt, and he was ready to take power. He knew, he said, that he could save the country, and that nobody else could. To tighten the moral fibre of the nation, to use unsparingly both men and money to attain the goal, to end party rivalries so long as the outside conflict lasted — such were his methods. The goal was the maintenance and expansion of the Empire by means of the mastery of the sea. For four years Pitt was able to manage the conduct of the war autocratically, because he had public opinion behind him; no man, it was said, left his presence without feeling his courage mount higher. He did not hesitate to pour out all the wealth of England in order to be victorious. In 1758 he had ten millions voted; in 1759, twelve millions; in 1760, fifteen millions. He gave heart and inspiration, zeal and the will to victory to the House of Commons: and equally to the troops dragging their guns up behind Quebec, to the seamen risking their ships off the rocky shores of Brittany. Pitt proceeded simultaneously to blockade the French ports, destroy the French colonial empire, and save Prussia. Wolfe captured Quebec and Clive was victorious in India. In Europe Frederick of Prussia made amends for the defeat of the Anglo-Hanoverian army by the victory of Rossbach. The French minister Choiseul had the sense to realize that in this war France's chief foe was not a Continental one. Having concluded a family pact with Spain, he made preparations for an invasion of England; like the Duke of Parma in days gone by, he could not possibly do this without control of the Channel; but the French fleet was shattered, and after the battle of Quiberon Bay the islands of Brittany themselves were in British hands. Choiseul saw that he must now come to terms. If Pitt had remained in power, he would have imposed a harsh peace indeed upon France. But

George II died in 1760, and his throne was taken (Frederick, Prince of Wales, having died in 1751) by his grandson, George III, a young man of twenty-two. Opposed to foreign adventuring because he wished to push forward a new policy at home, the new King immediately wanted the war to end, and showed scant patience with Pitt's omnipotence. In 1761 Pitt was ready to declare war on Spain, who had just concluded a pact of mutual aid with France; he urged that an end must be made of the House of Bourbon, and that Spain was a harmless adversary because her resources came from her colonies, from which the English fleet would cut her off. With a hundred and fifty ships of the line, in a world where no other great navy existed, Pitt felt prepared to claim a colonial monopoly. But the Council was nervous, the King did not support Pitt, and the country was beginning to think that if England appropriated too much territory, she would soon have a whole Continental coalition against her. Pitt's colleagues declined to collaborate in his new war-plans, and he resigned.

The Peace of Paris, signed in 1763, gave England Canada, Saint Vincent, Dominica, Tobago and Senegal; France undertook to evacuate Hanover and Prussia, and — a painful condition — to dismantle Dunkirk. England restored to France Belle-Isle, Guadaloupe, Martinique, Marie-Galante, Saint Lucia, the French trading stations in India, Saint-Pierre and Miquelon, and likewise the Newfoundland fishing rights. Spain, for ceding Florida to England, was given Louisiana by France as compensation. The King of Prussia, being no longer useful, was thrown over. It was a harsh settlement for France, but less so than Pitt would have desired.

Born and brought up in Britain, George III expected to enjoy a popularity such as his ancestors had never known. In appearance, manners, speech and character he was English. To him, Hanover was only a family memory. But whereas the first two Georges, foreign and rather comical Kings, enjoyed straightforward reigns, the third, a man more worthy of respect, put a severe strain on the monarchy itself. Why, he felt, should he obey the orders of a Cabinet, of a few great families, of a Parliament, none of them representative of the people? No: his duty was to champion his subjects against oligarchies. Such ideas, inciting the King to restore personal power, exposed him to grave

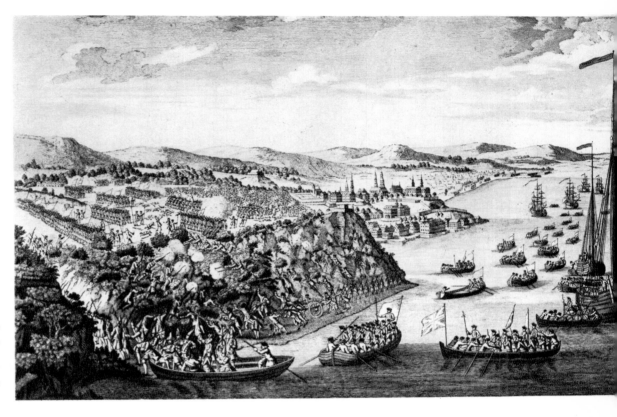

WOLFE CAPTURES QUEBEC, SEPTEMBER 1759. General Wolfe's 50,000 soldiers landed, scaled the cliffs overlooking the St. Lawrence River above Quebec, and defeated the Franco-Indian troops of Montcalm. Wolfe was killed in battle and Montcalm died the following day. The battle was decisive, bringing Canada within the British and out of the French orbit. An engraving of 1797. *National Maritime Museum, Greenwich.*

conflicts with Parliament. The King might advantageously have used Toryism to oppose the Whigs, who were becoming divided after too long a monopoly of power. But his temperament ruined his chances. 'Farmer George' was an honest man, a good husband, thrifty and chaste; but he was both vain and vindictive. At his accession, the war which was heightening the prestige of Pitt was not favoured by George. England had one Patriot King: a William, not a George. And such was George's hatred of William Pitt, that soon he would have accepted defeat abroad if it could have brought him victory at home. Determined to choose his own ministers, George tried to foist on a country which adored Pitt the unpractical Lord Bute. Hooted by the London crowd, who were clearly vexed because their idol was subordinated to a newcomer — and that newcomer a Scotsman — Bute soon lost heart and resigned. His successor, Grenville, was treated no better by the public. One member of the House of Commons, John Wilkes, a brilliant and witty pamphleteer, criticized the speech from the Throne of 1763 in his publication, the *North Briton*. By the King's command he was

arrested, by means of a open warrant against ' any person ' responsible for the publication. This arrest was contrary to Parliamentary privilege. The courts of justice upheld Wilkes, and condemned the Secretary of State to a fine of £800. George III learned, like the Stuarts before him, the necessity for even the most Patriot King to respect the traditional liberties of Englishmen.

Graver events were set in motion in the Colonies through the defence of these liberties. In America the original thirteen ' plantations ' now had a population of three million, a people prosperous and jealous of their independence, who had gradually obliged the royal governors to leave power to the local assemblies. But during the Seven Years War these colonies had had to defend themselves against French Canada. The troops and money necessary for this war had been provided by London; and when it was over, a permanent force had to be maintained in America to guard against a possible rising of French Canadians. Grenville proposed that one-third of the upkeep charges of this small army should be raised in the colonies by a stamp duty. The project did not seem outrageously unjust, but the Americans, like all taxpayers, hated taxes, and found support against this one even in London. ' No taxation without representation ' had been one of England's political maxims since the Middle Ages; and the Colonies were not represented at Westminster. The Colonies' point of view had other arguments in its favour. They had contributed to the prosperity of English commerce; they had been exploited according to mercantile principles, that is to say, in the interests of the mother-country. The doctrine of the mercantile system required, firstly, that a colony should import and export all merchandise in English ships; secondly, that colonial commerce should pass through English ports, even if the colonists themselves should receive better prices in France or Holland; thirdly, that colonies should be forbidden to build factories capable of competing with those of England. To estimate the real contribution of the Colonies to the revenues of England, it was therefore necessary to add, over and above the direct taxes voted by the assemblies, the profits of English manufacturers and merchants, themselves taxable. The mercantile system might be endured, if absolutely necessary, by the Colonies in the South, where the colonists grew tobacco and other products which England would buy from them; they would thus obtain the gold which would enable them, in turn, to acquire the manufactured products sent out from England. But to the colonists in the North, whose products were not adjuncts to, but rivals of, England's, this state of affairs was intolerable. Here lay the direct cause of the War of American Independence. First, a duty imposed on molasses annoyed the distillers who sold rum to the Indians. And then the Stamp Act drew into the fiscal coffers the small stores of gold possessed by the Colonies, and made their commerce almost impossible.

Early in 1766 Pitt intervened. Since his retirement he had lived at Bath, helpless with gout. Although he could not walk without crutches, use a fork at table, or even write legibly, he appeared in the House to advocate the suppression of this taxation. In his opinion, England had no right to tax the Colonies. The Act was annulled, and George III reluctantly had to offer Pitt the ministry. But the crippled statesman was almost out of his mind with physical pain; he left the House of Commons and was made Earl of Chatham. To go

from the Lower House to the Upper was no crime; but for the Great Commoner it was a mistake. An obstinate King, a headless ministry, a paralysed leader — such was the government of England for several months.

Lord North, who in 1770 agreed, as Prime Minister, to mask the personal rule of George III, had the cynicism of Walpole, but not his shrewdness or vigour. In the matter of the Colonies George III made a practical concession by suppressing the Stamp Act; but to safeguard the principle involved, he maintained certain small duties on secondary articles, such as glass and tea. This showed little understanding of the Colonists. Many of them had inherited the strong dissenting spirit of their forefathers, and the principle was precisely what they could not admit. In the end, by a majority of one, Lord North's Cabinet decided to retain one tax only, that on tea. And for the paltry sum of £16,000 Britain lost an empire. When the Americans refused to buy tea on which duty had to be paid, orders were given to the East India Company to ship a cargo of tea to Boston. Warned by sympathizers in London, a number of protesting Americans, disguised as Indians, boarded the ship and pitched the tea-chests into Boston harbour. This act of rebellion led to hostilities. But the Colonists were far from being unanimous. In no battle did George Washington have more than 20,000 men behind him. The aristocracy of Virginia, the common folk, and the middle classes stood out for resistance; but the well-to-do farmers and the more solid men of the liberal professions remained loyalists.

The most experienced heads believed that the Colonists would soon be put down. They had no fortified towns, no trained regiments, no ships of war, no credit. Neither in financial nor in military resources were they a match for England; and besides, if they forfeited the protection of England, they would be exposed to attack by the other maritime powers. And perhaps, in spite of Washington's genius, they would indeed have been defeated if they had not been supported by France, who was delighted to find this opening for revenge and was carried along by a current of public enthusiasm. The French fleets ruled the seas. Their admirals won victory after victory, and the military triumph of the Americans was determined by the naval battle of Chesapeake Bay.

THE RANELAGH ROTUNDA: Attributed to Antonio Canale
(Canaletto). The Rotunda was built as a place for concerts and
festivities by the Earl of Ranelagh in his gardens adjacent to the
grounds of the Chelsea Royal Hospital. The building was closed
in 1803 when it passed out of fashion and its demolition was
undertaken the same year. From 1746 to 1755 Canaletto spent
the greater part of his time in England. (National Gallery, London).
Hachette.

CHARLES JAMES FOX (1749-1806): Michel. The great Whig statesman was an outstanding orator and a man of great influence, who led the Opposition against Pitt and the Tories for a great part of his public life. Although his early life had been dissipated he grew into an idealistic reformer and contributed notably to the abolition of the slave trade. *National Portrait Gallery.*

English public opinion soon suffered a reaction and desired the independence of the Colonies to be recognized. Parliament itself abandoned the king although filled with his servitors. George III's attempt at personal rule was ending in disaster. Ireland was heading for revolt, and in England itself, the growing towns were protesting against the archaic electoral system of the boroughs, and their consequent lack of Parliamentary representation. The collapse of military efforts in America led to a gradual decline of Lord North's majority in the Commons. At length, in March 1782, he felt obliged to resign, though much against the King's inclination. The King had perforce to summon his enemies the Whigs, whose leaders were Rockingham, Edmund Burke, Shelburne, and Charles James Fox, Lord Holland's younger son. Fox, a man of great gifts, widely read, a fine orator, and a delightful and generous friend, had also faults and vices which prevented him from ever holding supreme power. His cynical father deliberately turned him into a libertine and gambler, which made him distasteful to the sober George III. So zealous was his support of the American and Irish insurgents that he virtually desired the defeat of his own country at their hands. Through him and Shelburne was negotiated the peace which ended this disastrous war.

Month after month it had gone on with shifting fortunes. Spain, Holland, and even Russia, had taken a hand against England; but in Rodney England found a great admiral, and notwithstanding a siege by French and Spanish ships in conjunction, she was able to save Gibraltar. The Peace of Versailles in 1783 nevertheless gave France her full revenge for the Treaty of Paris, and inflicted a humiliating peace upon England. She acknowledged the independence of the American Colonies, restored Minorca to Spain, and St. Pierre, Miquelon, St. Lucia, Tobago, and Senegal to France. To many men it looked as if England's day were indeed over. At home things seemed to be breaking up; the Parliamentary system was becoming tyrannical, corrupt, nerveless; personal rule had led to defeat.

Military reverses had brought about the downfall of Lord North, and thereafter England had no other ministries responsible to the King alone. Cabinets were to rise and fall at the will of the majority in the Commons. A Fox-North alliance, with no moral basis, was shortlived. The younger Pitt, second son of the Earl of Chatham, who had shown at the age of twenty-one the full stature of his great father, lent his prestige to Parliamentary government. Moulded from boyhood by his father, he made so brilliant a start in the House of Commons that the highest posts were at once within his reach. When the King, in defiance of the Whigs, made Pitt Prime Minister at the age of twenty-four, the prestige of the head of the Government soon outstripped that of the sovereign. For over twenty years on end, Pitt was to rule England; and into political life he introduced a new and valuable quality — that of purity.

Had it not been for the memory of the elder Pitt, this accession of a stripling to power might have been impossible. But his personal virtues would have sufficed to justify it. At twenty-four he showed the wisdom of maturity. He made the Tories into a genuine party, independent of the Crown, with its own electoral funds, its own boroughs, its own

programme of peace, retrenchment and reform. He restored to the office of Prime Minister the power and status which Walpole had given it. Pitt's opponents believed that they were totally undone when King George III showed clear symptoms of insanity, and a Regent had to be appointed. The Prince of Wales favoured Fox as against Pitt. But happily for the latter, the King's madness was intermittent; and the sovereign was already on the way back to normal health when an event took place which has been described as the most important in the history of eighteenth-century England — the capture of the Bastille.

The French Revolution, in its earlier stages, was hard for Englishmen to understand. They did not anticipate its violence because they knew little or nothing of its nature and causes. England had not herself engendered those intense enmities between the landed gentry and the peasantry, between court circles and the merchant classes, which had been produced in France by the watertight barriers of caste. Inequality there was in plenty, but a career was open to talent, and laws were binding on every class of citizen. Between 1789 and 1792 Englishmen honestly believed that the French were on the way to achieving, with no undue disturbance, institutions roughly analogous to those of Great Britain. When Fox heard of the capture of the Bastille, he greeted the event as the most important and happy event in the world's history; and many thinkers and writers believed likewise. Even Pitt at first refused to side with the crowned heads of Europe against the Revolution. On the contrary, there is a likelihood that he favoured it. His feeling, like that of Tory England in general in 1789, was that a rival power was, fortunately, going to be weakened by internal dissension, and would emerge from the fever regenerated. The execution of Louis XVI and the occupation of the Netherlands by France changed this benevolent optimism into open enmity. When the Terror began, all the sympathies of the ruling classes in England were with the fallen monarchy, and so with the European powers attacking the Revolution. The only sympathizers with Revolutionary France were some radical republicans, such as Tom Paine, and a small body of advanced Whigs grouped round Fox, Sheridan and Grey.

After 1793 the Whig party was cleft asunder and ceased to count; a national coalition took shape round Pitt to combat the plague of subversive ideas and the militant spirit of the French Revolution. The rights of foreigners in the country were limited by law; Habeas Corpus was suspended: the publication of lampoons was severely punished. Every village formed its loyal associations. But Englishmen would still have refrained from declaring a war of principle, as the European monarchies had done, against the French Revolution, if the latter had not been itself so aggressive. As long as it seemed possible, Pitt declared his desire to remain a spectator and ' to enjoy neutrality '. But when France decided to open Antwerp's river, the Scheldt, to navigation, and thus to ruin the Dutch ports, he was forced to act, for Holland was safeguarded against such a threat by solemn treaty. War with France became inevitable. Pitt solaced himself with the idea that, for reasons of finance, the campaign would be brief. It was to last for twenty years.

The general character of this great war is simple

enough. To begin with, England followed her traditional policy and defended her Dutch allies, refusing to allow Antwerp and Belgium to remain in the hands of a major European power. She conquered new colonies and defended the old. In particular she waged a stern campaign in the West Indies, which cost her, through disease rather than battle, some forty thousand men, a price justifiable only by the importance then attached to the sugarcane plantations, a great source of wealth. Then, after the figure of Napoleon began to dominate the stage, England's aim became no longer that of victory over one country or another, but the downfall of this conqueror who threatened to destroy the balance of power in Europe. For the third time in her history she battled against the strongest power on the Continent, and the struggle against Napoleon became the natural sequel to the wars against Philip II and Louis XIV.

England's methods of war were likewise unchanging. Primarily she strove for mastery of the seas. And this she secured because she had a powerful fleet, and a group of first-rate admirals — Hood, Jarvis, and Nelson — to whom the American war had given experience of sea-fighting. Mastery of the seas enabled Britain to repulse any invasion, to transport her troops wherever their presence seemed useful, and also to prevent any supplies from reaching hostile ports. At the same time England was making full use of her other favourite weapon — subsidies to Continental coalitions. She helped the allied States in two ways: direct gifts, and agreed loans. Pitt tripled all taxes, appealed for voluntary contributions, and finally established an income tax, on a very wide basis of incidence, the rate of which was about ten per cent. For this war, then, the country had once again to strain every muscle, and only its vast riches enabled it to sustain an effort in which, at certain moments, England found herself confronting the whole Continent of Europe.

The war opened badly for her. At sea the French were joined by the Spaniards, and then by the Dutch; England found herself barred from the Mediterranean, and this deprived her of much of her potential pressure on the Continental powers. Permeated by the notions of equality then preached in Europe, English sailors mutinied. This happened just when the Continent, after four years of war,

was making peace with France. England was isolated, Ireland in revolt, the Navy mutinous. But the situation was saved by a truly English combination of sternness and indulgence. The mutineers became victors, and in the same year the battle of Cape St. Vincent delivered Pitt from the Spanish fleet, and the battle of Camperdown from the Dutch. Could he reconquer the Mediterranean? Since losing Minorca England had had no base within the Mediterranean: whence the importance she laid on the port of Toulon, which she captured only to lose again. Bonaparte, on his way to Egypt, conquered Malta, the best naval base of that time. But Bonaparte's fleet was destroyed by Nelson at the battle of the Nile, and this victory gave to England both Malta and the East. Leaning upon Malta and his Neapolitan allies, Nelson was able to exert pressure on Austria, whose Italian possessions he threatened. Once again, mastery of the Mediterranean would enable England to form a Continental coalition.

England lorded it at sea, but Bonaparte was still invincible on land. The First Consul and the Prime Minister now realized the limits of their respective powers. Peace was obligatory on both. But it was made difficult by the critical and doctrinaire attitude of England towards the French system. Only Fox appreciated the greatness of Bonaparte. The Tories viewed him merely as a sort of Corsican bandit; about him the most grotesque legends were current. In 1801, unable to secure the King's consent to the admission of Catholics to the House of Commons, Pitt resigned office. His successor Addington entered into negotiation, and in 1802 the Peace of Amiens was signed. It was a serious diplomatic defeat for England. She retained a few distant conquests, like Ceylon; but France remained in possession of the left bank of the Rhine and of Belgium, a state of affairs which was the less tolerable to England as Bonaparte immediately began to examine ways and means of making Antwerp a naval and military base. In the Mediterranean England abandoned Minorca and promised to restore Malta to the Knights, which would again have deprived her of any base. It had been necessary to make terms, as England needed a breathing-space, however short; but whereas to Bonaparte the Peace of Amiens was 'final', to Pitt it was only a truce.

A COAL MINE IN THE 1790'S before the green countryside was
wholly blighted by the coal and iron workings of the Industrial
Revolution. *Walker Art Gallery, Liverpool.*

France's acquisition of Louisiana, the expedition to San Domingo, and the alliance with Holland, finally brought English irritation to a head.

In point of fact, nobody observed the Peace of Amiens. England kept Malta; Bonaparte, despite his promise to respect the *status quo* in Europe, became head of the Republic of Italy, annexed Piedmont, imposed his protectorate on Switzerland, and took the chief part in the reshaping of Germany. After an ultimatum from Addington in 1803 hostilites were resumed. This time Bonaparte, planning to strike at England itself, assembled at Boulogne an invading force of 400,000 men, and fitted out a flotilla of flat-bottomed boats to convey this army across the Channel. Like the Duke of Parma with his Armada, he would have needed, for success, to have his transports shielded for at least a few hours by a squadron. But the French and Spanish fleets were blockaded in the ports of Toulon, Rochefort, Brest and Cadiz, by Nelson, Cornwallis and Collingwood. There they remained helpless until the summer of 1805, unable to obey the orders of the Emperor (as he had now become) to effect a concentration. In October, when Napoleon had abandoned his projected invasion of England, the defeat of the Franco-Spanish fleet at Trafalgar — the last great battle of sailing-ships — in which Nelson died, gave England for a full century the uncontested mastery of the world's seas. Two years later, in time of peace, the Danish fleet was seized at Copenhagen by the English, who thus completed the ruin of Europe's maritime forces.

At Trafalgar Napoleon lost his colonies, and all hope of getting control of the sea-route to India; but he was nevertheless master of Europe. In vain did Pitt, returned to office, conjure up coalition after coalition. After Austerlitz he had to recognize his powerlessness, and he died in 1806, worn out and broken-hearted. Master of Austria and Prussia, allied with Russia, Napoleon now sought to strike at England's naval and commercial power by indirect means, and forbade the Continental ports to admit any English ships. To this Berlin Decree which opened the Continental blockade, England retorted with Orders-in-Council, stopping all sea-borne traffic which did not pass through her own ports, even trade with the United States of America. On both sides these measures caused much hardship, and they brought about a war between Britain and the United States in 1812. As Europe could not dispense with English products, smuggling became universal, and was so profitable that severe penalties failed to check it. Such Continental industries as cotton, which depended on imported raw materials, were ruined, to the enrichment of their English rivals. England, on the other hand, went through a grave industrial and commercial crisis, and in 1810-11 there was serious unemployment in England, with menacing riots. If the Tsar Alexander of Russia had not broken the Continental blockade in 1811, England might perhaps have yielded.

But the Continental blockade brought about the downfall of Napoleon because it forced him, despite his anxiety for peace, to carry the war on and on. Having tried to bend Spain to his will, he found there a country of guerrillas, ' where either a large army starved or a small one was beaten '. British troops landed in Portugal — a country very useful to England as a landing-stage in Europe; led by Wellesley, later the Duke of Wellington, they forced the French to concentrate. In 1813 Spain was lost to Napoleon. Meanwhile he had to attack Russia, who was refusing to maintain the blockade. And there he lost the flower of his troops. Backed by English subsidies, Russia, Prussia and Austria, after the battle of Leipzig in October 1813, pushed Napoleon back into France; and there, notwithstanding the amazing victories of the campaign on French territory, he had to abdicate, in 1814. Whilst the Allies debated the fate of France at the Congress of Vienna, Napoleon, who had not been sent farther away than the island of Elba, returned, expelled the Bourbons without a struggle, and marched on Brussels. Wellington, with a small army of combined British and German troops, defeated him at Waterloo in 1815.

It was the aim of the sovereigns of Russia, Austria and Prussia, at the Congress of Vienna, to shut off with a wall of buffer states this nation which had so long intimidated them. They created a kingdom of the Netherlands (Belgium and Holland), which lasted in that form until 1830; they entrusted the safe keeping of the left bank of the Rhine to Prussia; that of the Alpine frontier to a kingdom of Piedmont and Sardinia; that of North-

THE HOUSE OF COMMONS IN 1793: Carl Anton Hiekel. The assembly is being addressed by 34-year-old William Pitt the younger, who had been in office as Prime Minister since 1783 and was to remain so until his resignation in 1801. In spite of the ritual symbols such as the Mace on the table, the assembly has an almost intimate air about it. *National Portrait Gallery.*

DEFENDING THE BREACH AT ACRE, MAY 1799:
W. Heath and T. Sutherland. British
resistance and plague in his army prevented
General Bonaparte from capturing this port-
town north of Haifa during his campaign
in the Levant. *Hachette*.

ern Italy to Austria. Talleyrand, in his efforts to
set limits on French sacrifices, found an unexpected
ally in the British emissary, Lord Castlereagh.
Once again, to maintain the balance of power,
after the triumph of a coalition inspired by herself,
Britain was taking the side of the vanquished. She
had obtained what she wanted — the Cape of Good
Hope, Malta, Ceylon; and above all, she had laid
low the man who had resisted her and had tried
to achieve hegemony in Europe. She could rest
content. But Napoleon himself she treated with
little generosity. After his second abdication he
threw himself on the hospitality of 'the most generous of his foes', who, however, left him until
his death on St. Helena, in a state of truly pitiable
destitution. This pettiness roused the indignation
of many Englishmen.

Freed now from its fears, the British government
would gladly have stood apart from European
affairs. But it could not. The victorious powers
had formed a league for the maintenance of the
treaty of Vienna and the principles of legitimacy;
and England, rather grudgingly, had to form part
of the Holy Alliance. It was not long before she
began to come into conflict with her partners. The
achievement of the Congress of Vienna may have
been more enduring than such diplomatic edifices
usually are, but during the nineteenth century it
crumbled away. The negotiators at Schönbrunn

had made full allowance for the two ideas which
seemed to them fundamental — legitimacy, and
European equilibrium. They had reckoned without
those nationalist sentiments whose growing strength
would, in thirty years time, burst through the
framework constructed in 1816.

About 1700 the inhabitants of England were
estimated at around five and a half million; the
figure rose slowly up to about 1750; and then suddenly, during the reign of George III, it doubled
itself, until in 1821 it reached fourteen million. A
larger population needed more food. And thus
came the need for increasing both the yield and
the area of cultivated land, and securing assured
profits for landowners. The great landlords, unfortunately, were alone to reap the profit from this
agricultural prosperity. The eighteenth-century
Parliaments were composed of these great landlords
and squires, and the laws which they enacted often
bore hardly on the country folk. Farmers holding
long leases were often supplanted by tenants liable
to eviction at six months' notice. All local rates
were raised. To become a magistrate, to hold rank
in the local militia, to obtain shooting rights, a
man had to be richer than ever. The old popular
institutions of the parish were replaced by the more
aristocratic ones of the county. At the time of the
French Revolution the justices of the peace became
harsher. And finally the great landlords were even

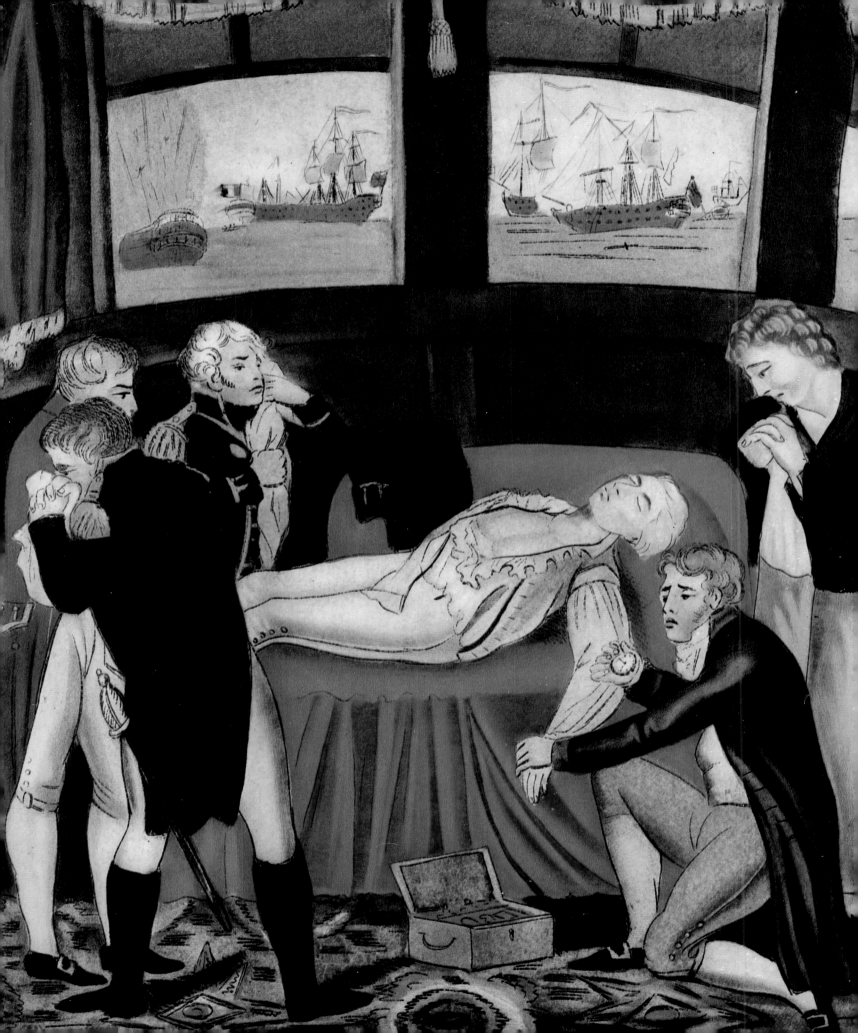

tempted to use their political and administrative power to expand their own estates.

At the beginning of the eighteenth century vast areas were still common land or open heath. Under George III landlords became more and more eager to enclose their fields; and in the process they acquired for their own use much of the peasants' ploughland and great stretches of commons, grazing and waste, as well. Their instrument was the private Act of Parliament. There were no fewer than 3554 such enclosure Acts during the King's reign, and about four million acres were thus made available for the new methods of farming. These enclosures made possible the formation of large farms with lands unified, the adoption of scientific methods, and increased productivity. England became one of the grain-producing countries of Europe. But the small peasantry suffered severely from this spoliaton. They lost heart in their toil, and drifted into idleness or drunkenness, or into the North Country towns where the swift growth of industry was causing a demand for workers. Then the excellent Elizabethan law was abrogated which forbade the building of a cottage without at least four acres of land; and this opened the way for the growth of those clusters of slum hovels which disgraced the large towns of England even into the twentieth century.

At a different period the yeoman would have resisted and clung to his soil. But besides the towns, the colonies were luring him. Canada, sparsely populated, and the prosperous American colonies, offered a refuge to the bolder farmers. Those who stayed at home entered the service of the landlords. The very name of yeoman began to be forgotten. During the Napoleonic wars the high prices of produce still permitted the survival of such of the small farmers as had been able to keep their land. Waterloo was their death-blow, and England then witnessed the almost total disappearance of that rural middle class which had so long been her military and moral backbone. The agricultural labourer himself, in the early part of the nineteenth century, was in dire plight. Wages had risen more slowly than prices. Formerly every village, and almost every house, had been able to live a self-supporting life. With the growth of large-scale industry the village craftsmen disappeared. Before long farmers were refusing, not only to give, but even to sell grain to their labourers. The divorce between production and producers created abstract economics totally unknown to the Middle Ages, and fostered the growth of the most hideous poverty.

Big-scale manufacture developed side by side with big-scale farming. With the disappearance of the gild system had begun the development of capitalism, or the exploitation of collective labour by a man of business. This tendency towards large undertakings was accelerated during the eighteenth century by the increased number of consumers in England, and by the opening up of new markets, especially in the American colonies, and by mechanical inventions. In the textile industry the invention of the mechanical shuttle (1733) increased the productivity of the weavers and the demand for thread. Then to meet the increased requirements of the weavers, it became possible to bring into simultaneous action a hundred spindles controlled by a single workman. Spinning thus became faster in output than weaving, and the invention of power looms met this new need. Then the steam-engine supplanted the power supplied by men or water, and coal-mines became the essential wealth of the country. The substitution of coal for charcoal in ironfounding led to the shift of the great English factories from the wooded south to the coal-bearing north.

All these developments in town and country called for improved means of transport. Over large parts of England during the eighteenth century travel was only possible on horseback. The trouble was that every parish was still, as in medieval times, responsible for its own roads; and local autonomy, useful enough in its day, was preventing the creation of a road system properly conceived by central authority. After 1760 fairly good results came from the system of turnpike roads, concessions being made to trusts which recovered their expenses by their right to extract payment from travellers using them — very much as is done on certain motor-roads on the Continent to-day. But little real progress in actual road-construction was made until after 1815. A Scottish engineer, John McAdam, conceived the idea of laying a water-resisting surface on roadways, and thanks to him the speed of the stage-coaches rose from four to seven, and then to over

CHELSEA PENSIONERS READ THE NEWS OF THE VICTORY AT WATERLOO. On the left is the Royal Hospital, Chelsea, much of it the work of Christopher Wren. Founded in 1682 by Charles II as a home for retired soldiers, it is still used for that purpose today. This painting, by David Wilkie, is dated 1822. (*Wellington Museum, Apsley House*).

ten, miles an hour, although these speeds were exhausting to the horses, of which very large numbers were used. In 1831, when coaching was at its heyday, about 150,000 horses were employed over some 3000 stages. (After the 1830's, coaching declined as railways began to spread.) It was also during the closing years of the eighteenth century that the Midlands and the North were threaded by canals intended mainly for the transport of coal. Concomitantly grew up the auxiliaries of trade — banking and insurance. Edward Lloyd's coffee-house in London, towards the end of the seventeenth century, was frequented by a group of men willing to insure shipowners against maritime risks. The institution thus begun came to be the greatest society of underwriters in the world; but with the usual English conservatism it retained for generations the name of Lloyd's Coffee House — and is still Lloyd's.

The industrial revolution prepared and necessitated a political revolution. The political map of England no longer coincided with the map of its population. The North, formerly sparsely populated, Jacobite and Catholic, was now swarming with radical miners and mill-workers. The growth of large industries created two new classes: the rich manufacturers whose fortunes, matching the expansion of new markets, were comparable to those of the great landed proprietors, and who became insistent on having their due share of influence; and the urban working class, very different from the old village craftsmen, more accessible to agitators because they were concentrated, and more

ready to claim political power because they were conscious of their strength. Between these 'Two Nations' (as Disraeli later named them) the current system of political economy raised a doctrinal barrier.

Every great social change finds its own theorists, who attribute transitory results to permanent causes. The theorist of the industrial revolution was Adam Smith, who wrote a book, *The Wealth of Nations*, which became the economists' Bible for over a century. In it he expounded the doctrines of *laissez-faire*, free competition, and trust in the spontaneous currents of economics. In the eyes of Smith and his followers, a benevolent Deity had so ordered the world that the free play of natural laws ensured the greatest happiness of the greatest number. This freedom might possibly cause temporary hardships, but a balance would in time be automatically restored. Such a theory soothed the consciences of the wealthy by representing poverty and unemployment as natural and heaven-sent remedies. Economic liberalism triumphed because it accorded with the temper of an age of expansion when all new producers were finding markets. It became dangerous as soon as the markets of labour, or of production, reached saturation point. Free competition then engendered disastrous evils, and England, like the rest of the Western world, was to see the beginnings of a protectionist reaction, holding views of State and autarchic authority which would have astounded Adam Smith.

The intellectual equilibrium sought in the eighteenth century by the wisest of the aristocracy and upper middle classes, as well as by men of letters, could not satisfy the much more numerous classes whose economic balance was overturned by the agricultural and industrial revolutions: they needed a religious or a political faith in order to escape from an intolerable actuality. The eighteenth-century theologians tried hard to show that reason and religion did not clash. Providence willed it that Christian morality should be the most certain path of temporal salvation. The Church of England at this time became a class Church. Nearly all its bishops belonged to aristocratic families, Whig or Tory, and reflected the party in power. The lesser clergy held their livings from patrons, who naturally gave them to men of their own social circle, and often enough to members of their own family, sons or nephews or cousins. The religious structure of the country thus doubled and amplified the political. In both, the main element was formed by the land-owning class, and the Church of England thus became linked with the local authority of the ruling classes, but lost most of its contact with the common people.

If the kindly and reasonable religion of eighteenth-century Anglicanism harmonized excellently with the more fortunate part of the nation, it brought no spiritual nourishment to the town toilers or country labourers, soured and perturbed as they were by dire want. The profound changes gave rise to a sense of injustice and instability. In days gone by, the dissenting or nonconformist sects had held sway among the populace with their more equalitarian teachings. But in the early eighteenth century the older of these denominations — Presbyterians, Independents and Catholics — had themselves grown humdrum. The middle classes and the poor contained countless souls craving for a more ardent religion, and as neither Anglicans nor dissenters could satisfy their need, a man was bound to appear who would give these great masses what they wanted. His name was John Wesley. As a young man at Oxford, he had been a latitudinarian, regarding faith as a reasoned consent. But such teaching did not fully satisfy the fervour of his spirit. There was some surprise in Oxford in 1726 when a few young men founded a Holy Club, whose members fasted, prayed, visited the poor, preached in the open air, and confessed their sins to each other.

Wesley and his friends were ridiculed, and dubbed 'Methodists'. The nickname was to become the name of a Church which to-day counts millions of adherents.

For several years Wesley led a life of intense activity. He first went off with his brother to the American colonies. The Christians in the Colonies did not like this aggressive religion, with its fiercely personal preachers. Wesley had to return to England rebuffed, without having yet found his true path. Then on May 24, 1738, in a moment of illumination, he saw the true faith, a living link and not a working of reason. From that day he had but one object in life — to bring men into that state of spiritual trance and total communion with God. Thereafter began a life of preaching. With his friend Whitfield, he preached in the fields, in barns, in working-class districts. At first he was often received with hostility by the crowds; but soon the news spread of the astonishing conversions which he wrought. His physical influence was extraordinary. The rational, aristocratic bishops of the time could only eye with scornful annoyance these open-air meetings and neurotic crowds. They closed their churches to Wesley, and refused to endorse his preaching or to ordain his preachers. It was only in the last years that Wesley, despairing of making his peace with the Established Church, resigned himself to ordaining his own ministers, and so, against his own inclination, founded the dissenting sect of Wesleyan Methodists, which, by 1810, could already show some 230,000 adherents.

The Methodist influence on the religious life of the English people was far-reaching. To thousands of men and women, and to those who most intensely needed it, religion once more became a living thing, in an almost primitive form. Inside the Church of England, the 'evangelical' influence permeated the whole of the Low Church party, whose clergy, like Wesley's preachers, made their appeal to the common people. The dissenting sects were startled by the headway made by the Wesleyans, abandoned their traditional Puritan anarchy, and formed church organizations. All religion became more emotional. And as this awakening absorbed the vital forces of the suffering lower classes, they were less tempted by revolutionary doctrines than the populace of the Continent. At the close of the eighteenth century, the aristocratic and upper classes in England may have been cynical, dissolute, and often atheistic, but the common people revered the Holy Bible.

Three important characteristics of the period between the Revolution of 1688 and the battle of Waterloo may be noted. First: the change from monarchic rule, under which Parliament had only a legislative part, to an oligarchic government in which Parliament, contrary to Montesquieu's belief, was also the source of executive power. That change took place because of the invention (or rather, the spontaneous engendering) of a Cabinet responsible to both Houses, which made possible the peaceful alternation of parties in power. Second: the struggle with France, aimed primarily at preventing a Continental hegemony inimical to England, whether controlled by Louis XIV or by Napoleon, aiming also at securing for England the mastery of the seas, and resulting indirectly in the almost unintentional formation of a new colonial Empire. Third: the agricultural and industrial revolution within the country, which by at once ruining the small landholders and accumulating a huge wage-earning class in the towns, made a political revolution inevitable. As Pollard has pointed out, every economic regime has a corresponding political one. The pastoral economy produces a family or tribal form of government; a primitive agricultural economy implies a feudal system, as the scattered tillers of the soil require protection; the age of merchants is the age of plutocracy; and the age of industry, during the nineteenth century at least, was to be that of democracy.

Power in eighteenth-century England had belonged to a mixed class, consisting of the aristocracy descended from a defunct feudalism, and of a new plutocracy. This class itself had split into the two great parties. In 1800 or thereabouts, out of the 658 members of the House of Commons, 487 were virtually nominated by that class. As we saw, this system of governance was accepted, because those who wielded power kept in contact with the rural classes, because local institutions to some extent mitigated its injustices, and because

this privileged order was open to talent, or at least to success. The system, highly unjust though it became, had the advantage of making the authority of Parliament accepted by the ruling class. And if Parliament, even when it became democratized during the nineteenth century, never had to face hostile prejudice from the ruling class, this was because during the eighteenth century they had become used to regarding Parliament as their own preserve. That is one reason, perhaps the most important, for the success in England of the Parliamentary system, which elsewhere failed for lack of such roots. But this aristocratic monopoly could not hope to survive when the industrial revolution, by massing the workers in the towns, compressed within narrow limits immense forces which had to find an open safety-valve, and if not, would have blown up the existing system. The House of Commons squires had neither life nor ideas in common with the workmen of Leeds or Birmingham. What could ' the parish ', in its true sense, mean to a slum-dweller? The population of England had doubled in sixty years, and the younger generations who peopled the great towns about 1815 had never known that rural life which created and explained the country's constitution. It was only natural that these generations should grow restive, irritable, and insistent on reform.

The Government was powerless to resist popular pressure, and if England escaped the vain and bloody shock of revolution and reaction, she owed this immunity to three forces: firstly, the power of opinion, which through the Press, the jury system, and the workers' associations, imposed the necessary reforms on an oligarchic Parliament; secondly, the existence in the Whig party (thanks to the enduring influence of Charles James Fox) of a liberal element proud enough of the privileges of birth to hold political privileges of less account; and thirdly, the currents of evangelism, which made for a gentler morality and diverted men's passions into other courses. The independence of the judiciary, the lofty liberalism of the Whigs, and a measure of Christian charity, all helped the country to traverse the most difficult tract in its history without civil warfare.

VII

From Aristocracy to Democracy

1816 to the Present Day

A LONG war, even if victorious, is naturally followed after the brief relaxation of triumph by a period of discontent and confusion. The years from 1816 to 1821 were dark ones in England. After the peace, prices fell. The fall in the price of wheat meant ruin to farmers, who had supposed high prices to be everlasting and tied themselves by onerous leases. Squires and farmers called out for reduced taxation. When a bad harvest suddenly sent wheat up again it was the turn of the working class to protest. The manufacturers accused the Government of forcing them to raise wages by a policy of 'dear bread'. In factories and manor-houses alike, prosperity was dead. A quarter of a million demobilized soldiers were vainly seeking work. As always happens in a period of rapid and many-sided invention, machinery was robbing men of their employment. Want and unemployment forced the poor rate up from five to nine million pounds sterling.

The interests of manufactory and manor-house seemed to be contradictory; but when popular agitation became violent, when the ricks blazed up after the mills, landowners and manufacturers were reconciled by alarm. Not being electors, the work-people in the towns and the labourers in the countryside were becoming rioters. None of their defenders had any chance of being elected to Parliament. Only freeholders having land of forty shillings value voted in the counties, and the list of parliamentary boroughs had not been revised since Tudor times, so that large towns of recent growth remained without representation. In such a plight, on whom could the townsmen count? Hardly on the King. Since 1810 the aged George III had been blind and insane. In practice the throne was occupied by his son, the Prince Regent (later George IV), for whom the English had little

or no respect. Prince George was neither bad nor foolish; he patronized the arts, and his polished manners made him, if not 'the First Gentleman of Europe', at any rate the prince among his own dandies. But he was selfish and petty, and in an age of prudent virtue his debauchery made him unpopular. Failing the intercession of a sovereign, could the people have entrusted their cause to ministers? A Tory Cabinet was in power, hostile to reform; and as for the Opposition, the great Whig Lords had not yet made alliance with the reformers. There remained only rebellion, the oldest and most undeniable right of Englishmen, a weapon all the more formidable as England had no great police system, and as the rapid growth of the cities had not allowed the local authorities to acquire experience of the mob. A plot to assassinate ministers, the so-called Cato Street Conspiracy, fostered by government police spies, brought matters to a violent head in both camps. The wealthy called for military rule and counted on the Duke of Wellington; the poor openly prepared for revolution. Five years after victory, England seemed to be on the brink of civil war.

She was saved by two unforeseeable circumstances: a scandal, and an economic recovery. The latter came, as usual, just when the economists despaired of it and were suggesting the most drastic remedies, including inflation. The scandal broke out when old George III died, and was succeeded by the Regent with the title of George IV. His wife, Caroline, who had for a long time been leading a rather shady life abroad, suddenly made up her mind, from vanity and in hatred of her husband, that she would be crowned Queen at his coronation. Legally she was within her rights; morally she was far from queenly. The King, highly vulnerable himself, would have been

THE PRINCE OF WALES, LATER GEORGE IV: Sir Thomas Lawrence. He was Prince Regent ▶ from 1810, when his father, George III, was declared insane, till 1820 when he ascended the throne. Before his official marriage to Caroline of Brunswick he had contracted a secret marriage with the lady of his choice, Mrs Fitzherbert, and was involved in a first-class scandal when the former returned from her pursuits abroad and insisted on participating at his coronation. (National Portrait Gallery). *Hachette.*

wise to avoid any moral debate. But in his determination to hold off Caroline, he showed such obstinacy and clumsiness that his ministers sometimes wondered whether he had inherited his father's madness with his crown. He even went so far as to engage in divorce proceedings before the House of Lords, undertaking to expose the Queen's dissolute life. London forgot electoral reforms to savour this indecency. The populace had sided with the Queen, and cheered her in the street. This infatuation, however, was shortlived, and the Queen herself died in 1821, to the vast relief of her husband.

Thanks to this diversion, tempers were cooled a little. The intransigent Tories had given way before some younger men in their ranks who wished to bring their party back into the reforming tradition of Pitt. Amongst these newcomers Robert Peel, Huskisson, and Canning were prominent. Peel, the son of a Lancashire manufacturer, owner of one of the seven largest fortunes in England, had been brought up, like Pitt before him, to be Prime Minister. At twenty-one he was found a seat in the House of Commons; at twenty-three he was a Secretary of State. Worthy of respect and winning respect, he was the arbiter between the advanced wing of the party, with such men as Canning, and the resisting wing, grouped round Wellington. As Home Secretary Peel did excellent work. In particular, he abolished the death penalty for numerous crimes and offences which did not deserve so ruthless a punishment. Huskisson meanwhile was giving relief to the manufacturers by suppressing the protective tariffs on raw materials, wool and silk; he would gladly have abolished the duty on corn likewise, but in this he clashed with the numerous and vigilant country gentlemen of his party. Finally, Canning, who took charge of the Foreign Office in 1822, pursued a 'liberal' policy from within a Tory ministry. And when in 1827, despite the wrath of the Holy Alliance, he gave recognition to the Greek rebels attacked by Egyptians and Turks, this Tory ministry became prime favourites of the liberal elements in every land.

Canning's death this same year caused a bewildering situation. Since 1815, whenever an English sovereign found himself in a quandary, he thought of 'the Duke'. The victor of Waterloo was venerated in the Tory camp, while the Opposition, after long fearing that Wellington wished to set up a military dictatorship, came to see that, like most great soldiers, he held civil war in horror and that in Parliament he was an honest, clumsy, not very dangerous adversary. The Duke feared all the fashionable reforms as much as the King did — Catholic emancipation, extension of the franchise, free trade. As he always gave way in the end, rather than engage in battle, he became despite himself the best ally of liberalism. It was under his ministry that Admiral Codrington, fulfilling old instructions from Canning without asking for new ones, destroyed the Turkish fleet at Navarino, although the Duke, in this matter, was favourably disposed to the Turks. Again, it was the Duke who accepted the abrogation of the Test and Corporations Acts, thus exempting dissenters from communion according to the Anglican rite as a condition of holding municipal or State offices. And it was likewise he who, having begun with the emancipation of dissenters, was brought face to face with the graver question of Catholic emancipation.

The right of Catholics to vote and sit in Parliament had been promised to the Irish at the time of the Act of Union (1800). Only the opposition of King George III, who made it a point of conscience, had prevented the promise from being kept. Thereupon the Irish had founded a league, raised funds, and chosen an eloquent leader in Daniel O'Connell. For several years Ireland breathed the air of civil war; the Catholic Association and the Protestant squires of the northeast were at daggers drawn. In despite of the law, O'Connell was elected in a Parliamentary contest, and the sheriff did not dare to declare either him or his opponent a duly elected member. Wellington grasped the danger of this situation. He was not personally hostile to Catholics; civil warfare seemed to him even more undesirable than change; he advised the King to give way, and in the end, though with difficulty, convinced him. Finally the Duke's prestige overcame all resistance within his own camp, and once again he carried out a victorious retreat. Catholic emancipation was passed in 1829.

King George IV died in June, 1830, and was succeeded by his brother, the Duke of Clarence, who reigned as William IV, an elderly and fairly popular man, with a long and honourable service in the navy behind him. He showed himself irresolute and not very intelligent, but impartial, and as a constitutional sovereign fairly sound. The year 1830 was one of revolutions in Europe. Charles X of France was supplanted by Louis-Philippe after the July rising. Belgium blazed up in protest against the union with Holland imposed on her by the treaties of 1815. In 1830 also, revolutionary agitation pervaded Spain, Italy, and even England, where a new peasants' revolt took place in the southern counties. The rural labourers claimed a minimum wage of fourteen shillings, which was just; but they did so collectively, which brought them within grasp of the Riot Act. After their suppression, three were hanged and four hundred sent to transportation. Many of these died of despair. But the insurrection showed up the real weakness of aristocratic rule. To most moderate minds among the middle classes, it was clear that electoral reform was a necessity.

After the overturning of the Wellington-Peel ministry, an old Whig leader, Lord Grey, long a supporter of reformist projects, consented to emerge from his rural retirement and form a coalition Government of Whigs and friends of Canning. A general election was held. True to family traditions, the Whigs had chosen to ally themselves with the reforming Radicals and the middle-class nonconformists, which made them a party of popular interests; and notwithstanding their 'rotten' boroughs the Tories lost their majority. In the counties, where freedom of voting was greater, sixty out of eighty-two members were Whigs. Immediately Lord Grey let it be known that the first aim of his Government would be a measure of electoral reform. The holders of 'rotten' boroughs were resolved to protect their threatened seats, and could count on the support of the House of Lords. The middle classes in the towns, on the other hand, favoured reform — the merchants, bankers, and people of independent means, who felt it anomalous and humiliating to have no vote. The Reform movement, between 1830 and 1832, was a middle-class movement, aiming at victory by lawful methods. The first bill, put forward by Lord John Russell, had a majority of only one vote in the Commons — not enough to force so important a measure on the Lords. In agreement with the King, Lord Grey decided to dissolve Parliament and hold an election.

He returned to power with a Whig majority of 136. The country felt that Reform was as good as gained, an drejoiced accordingly. In all classes of the population men were expecting wonders from a suffrage law. The middle classes hoped thereby to give platonic satisfactions to the common people, whose turbulence had been alarming them for quite fifteen years. As to the extent of the reforms, employers and employed would not have seen eye to eye; but regarding the need, their agreement was wonderful. It is difficult to bring men together for constructive action, but easy enough to league them against a minority. In the early nineteenth century the owners of the 'rotten' boroughs — three or four score families in all — fulfilled the role which a century later was to be held by industrial magnates and international financiers. Sydney Smith satirized the optimism: 'All young ladies imagine they will be instantly married. Schoolboys believe that currant tarts must ultimately come down in price; the corporal and sergeant are sure of double pay; bad poets will expect a demand for their epics; fools will be disappointed, as they always are.'

The Tories had supposed that the Whigs, men of their own class, would put forward mild projects of Reform. When Lord John Russell's bill appeared, they were stupefied and outraged. Boroughs having fewer than two thousand inhabitants were abolished; towns with a population of between two and four thousand were to lose one out of every two representatives; and the 144 seats thus left open were to be shared amongst the more important towns. London gained ten seats; Liverpool, Manchester, Birmingham and Newcastle each obtained two members. Broadly speaking, the distribution of seats favoured the industrial North at the expense of the rural South. It was obvious that this new balance of representative power would involve the suppression of the duties on corn. In the towns, the vote was given to all occupiers of houses having an annual value of £10 or over, and in the counties, to owners and tenants on a correspondingly wide basis. In fact, the

AN ELECTION SCENE IN MID-NINETEENTH CENTURY ENGLAND. An illustration from the French paper *La Mode*, of 10th July, 1841, from which it is evident that the expression of the Popular Will was generally regarded as a rather strenuous affair. The scene in which Mr Pickwick was reluctantly involved at Eatanswill may have been something like this. *Giraudon.*

bill would create an electorate of lower middle class townsmen and of small farmers. Factory workers and farm labourers were still unrepresented.

The Lords inclined to tolerate Reform in some attenuated shape, but were infuriated by this electoral revolution. In October 1831 they threw out the bill. Then, faced by popular agitation, they passed it in part, but not integrally. The clauses for the abolition of the 'rotten' boroughs were cut out. Lord Grey, being in a minority in the Upper Chamber, resigned. But when the Duke, who for all their disappointments was still the supreme hope of the Tories, tried to form a Government, the country rose. The tocsin was sounded from church towers, and work stopped in factories. The walls were plastered with posters calling upon Englishmen to withdraw their money from the Bank and so check the Duke. The Bank of England was the only institution held in greater respect than the Duke. The rebellion of depositors overwhelmed that of the great landlords. And when the King again summoned Lord Grey, the latter consented to take office only if the King gave him a

written promise to create, if necessary, as many peers as would secure the passage of the Reform Bill. The Duke and his friends abstained from attending the debates, and on June 4, 1832, in a half-empty House, the bill was at last passed into law by 106 votes to 27. The new Act was certainly far from being what is nowadays termed a democratic measure. By granting a few members to the industrial centres it certainly diminished to some extent the influence of the rural aristocracy. But it gave the suffrage to a larger number of farmers dependent on that aristocracy. The Whigs had served their party interest without seriously endangering their class interest.

For many years after 1832 the membership of the House of Commons changed little in character; but although men were slow to recognize it, the constitution had in fact been profoundly modified. Henceforward the last word in politics was with the electorate, and ministries came and went, not to the orders of parliamentary managers, but to those of the county and borough voters. And at once the Whigs and their new manufacturing friends had to proffer some reforms to the people who had expected so much from them. The most important, but most imperfect, was that of the Poor Law. At the time of the Reform Act, the condition of the poor in town and country was appalling. Disraeli and Dickens depicted these 'Two Nations' in their novels — the nation of the rich and the nation of the poor, living side by side, each cut off from the other. The rural labourer's cottage was often a mere hovel, round which ran children in rags and tatters. These villagers just contrived to keep body and soul together by eking out their wretched pittance with poaching and alms. Lord Grey's Government appointed a commission of inquiry, under the guidance of Nassau Senior and Edwin Chadwick, both men with dubious but firm preconceptions on the problem.

Senior believed that the best way to abolish poverty was never to help the poor. With serene, unwitting cruelty, he argued that if the poor know that they must either work or starve, they will work; if young men know that they will be helpless in their old age, they will save; if older men know that they need their children, they will take pains to secure their affection. Wherefore, no help should be given except to those who really have no family or means of existence. There must be no partial aid: all or nothing. For such as are old enough or strong enough to work — the workhouse. And lest the workhouse became a favoured haven, it was important, argued Senior, to make life therein less desirable than the life of the most hapless of independent workpeople. Considering what was then the lot of these, it seems almost impossible to evolve anything more wretched. But this cruel programme was put into operation and the workhouse became 'the Bastille of the poor', a loathed and dreaded place. In 1838 there were 48,000 children under sixteen living in workhouses, too often in company with adults of the basest type and even with half-witted creatures. After the passing of the Poor Law Administration Act (1834), the number of poor receiving parish aid was greatly diminished; expenditure fell from seven million pounds in 1831 to four and a half million in 1836. The commissioners were filled with pride in their achievement, but without justification. The result was due to the horror inspired by the work-houses and to the growth of industry.

Amongst other Whig reforms, two should be noted. Firstly, there was the Municipal Corporations Act of 1835, which replaced the old-fashioned system by more democratically constituted municipal bodies, elected by all payers of local taxation. The municipal corporations, with State aid, gradually came to administer means of transport, schools, and the supply of light and water. Secondly, there was the abolition of slavery in British colonial possessions. The history of this reform began in 1772, when Lord Mansfield laid it down in a judgment that the Common Law did not recognize the status of slave, which at one stroke freed some fifteen thousand negroes brought by their owners into the British Isles. It was more difficult to secure the abolition of the trade in slaves, which had been the basis of the fortune of ports like Bristol and Liverpool, and without which Nelson himself maintained that the British mercantile fleet could not live. It is to the honour of Parliament that, despite the pressure of the interests at stake, Bishop Wilberforce and Charles James Fox, with a powerful tide of Quaker and Methodist opinion behind them, and aided also by Pitt, managed to secure the prohibition of this traffic in 1807, at a time when the crisis of the Napoleonic wars was at its height. There remained the slaves in the British colonies, and on this point the West Indian planters continued the struggle with desperate obstinacy, spending vast fortunes on the purchase of 'rotten' boroughs. Upheld by liberal and nonconformist forces, the reform was finally voted in 1833.

Lord Grey resigned in 1834, partly because O'Connell and his group of Irish members made his life intolerable, but chiefly because there could be no enduring union between the moderate Whigs and the Radical nonconformists who had made up the victorious coalition of 1832. His place was taken, after a short interregnum under Peel, by Lord Melbourne, a Whig of the old school. A witty sceptic of eighteenth-century temper, he governed with something of Walpole's unobtrusiveness a country still perturbed by the backwash of the Reform agitation. The great event of his ministry was the death of King William and the accession of the young Queen Victoria, who was to reign from 1837 until 1901. She was welcomed by the English people, whom she saved from her uncle,

LONDON RUSH-HOUR IN THE 1820'S: E. Lami and H. Monnier. A view across Whitehall to Downing Street, with John Soane's newly completed Board of Trade building on the right. The southern end of Whitehall (Parliament Street, left) had not yet been widened. (Bibliothèque nationale, Paris).

LABOUR REFORM IN LANARK. A cotton-manufacturing town on the Clyde built according to the most enlightened modern methods of 1825. They embodied the ideas of Robert Owen who was in advance of his time in maintaining that the welfare of the factory worker was a national necessity. *Mansell Collection.*

CARDING, DRAWING AND ROVING: T. Allom. The Lancashire textile industries were among the first to become mechanised. *Mansell Collection.*

the Duke of Cumberland, the very unpopular brother of King William. For more than half a century her reign was to make loyalty a chivalrous duty. The young Queen was quick to show a tenacious will of her own, which amounted even to obstinacy. At first Melbourne had grounds for hoping that he would convert her to easy-going gaiety; but when she married her cousin, Prince Albert of Saxe-Coburg, she learned from him the professional sense of sovereignty and that respect for the domestic virtues which in years to come saved the British monarchy. It was under Queen Victoria that Englishmen came to regard the family life of the sovereign as something bound up with their own private family lives. The influence of Prince Albert's stiff morality, and the strictness of Court life, influenced the whole tone of English life as deeply, and at least as widely, as Wesley had done in an earlier age.

The Whigs had told the people that Parliamentary reform would end all their ills. The people had forced reform on the Lords, and the ills were worse than ever. The people were grumbling, and the Whigs tottering. The Tories had both weapons and leaders capable of depriving the Whigs of the favours of the new electorate. Party leadership had passed into the hands of Sir Robert Peel, who dropped the label of Tory and styled himself Conservative, a name better contrived to attract the middle classes. They were bound to like Sir Robert, a man closer to factory and shop than to manor or cottage. Alongside Peel, though opposed to him on occasion, a so-called 'popular' Conservatism had its representatives within the party, in the small 'Young England' group, whose spokesmen were an orator of genius, Benjamin Disraeli, son of a Jewish man of letters but baptized in the Anglican Church as a child, and Lord

John Manners, son of the Duke of Rutland. Disraeli and his friends condemned a doctrine which, instead of maintaining a natural hierarchy of classes involving rights and duties equally, allowed the automatic laws of economics to control the relations of employers and workers. They urged that salvation lay in a return to a society built up like that of the Middle Ages, wherein each man, be he lord or peasant, knew his place and accepted it. According to Disraeli and his associates, the role of a Conservative party was at once to save such elements of the past as still had vitality in them, and to prepare the future by a policy of generosity.

This clique of young gentlemen in white waistcoats, claiming to persuade the working classes into feudal ideas, seemed an oddity. The theories of Bentham, Malthus, Ricardo, Cobden, and James Mill were then accepted as articles of faith. All,

or nearly all, serious people believed with the utilitarians that human societies strove to achieve the greatest happiness of the greatest number, and could attain this only by allowing free play to the personal interest of the individual. Any State intervention should therefore be avoided. The slightest restriction on competition was deemed heretical. Prices should be fixed automatically by the laws of supply and demand; and customs barriers always distorted these. Actuated by the highest motives, men like Richard Cobden, manufacturer and statesman, the prophet of the Manchester School, strove to persuade the English people that their distress was caused by trade restrictions and protectionist duties, and in particular by the Corn Laws.

The anti-protectionist campaign was one of the first in England to be waged by those weapons of propaganda — in newspapers and speaking tours

— which were to transform political life during the nineteenth century. In public meetings the orators of the Anti-Corn Law Association displayed three loaves, different in size but costing the same in three countries — France, Russia, England. England's loaf was the smallest, and Englishmen were therefore being cheated. These demonstrations were particularly successful with manufacturers like those in Lancashire, who imported both their cotton and their corn. On the other hand, they alarmed the agricultural interests. 'Abolish the duty on wheat,' repeated the farmers and squires, 'and you will kill English farming.' 'That matters little to us,' retorted the Manchester School. 'If other countries are in a position to produce corn more cheaply than we can, let them plough and reap for us, and we shall spin and weave for them. All trade must be a cycle. We cannot sell if we do not buy. To bar our shores against imports would mean the end of our exports.'

The Conservative party, consisting largely of country gentlemen, was bound to be hostile to Free Trade and favourable towards maintaining the duties on corn. But Sir Robert Peel, its leader, showed dangerous sympathies with the opposing doctrine. He was a man of good faith, high intellectual courage, great administrative and financial skill, but domineering and not in close contact with the House. In 1842 he attacked the tariff, and reduced the number of dutiable articles from 1200 to 750. To make up for the losses thus caused in the Budget, he instituted an income tax of sevenpence in the pound on incomes above £150. In 1845 he further reduced the customs list to 450 heads. He was moving towards Free Trade by leaps and bounds. These successive reductions had astonishing effects. Not only were the State revenues undiminished, but they were actually increased by the augmented volume of trade and by the taxable profits. Peel was thus emboldened. But he had not yet ventured to touch agriculture, the citadel of his party. In 1845 and 1846 Ireland was twice in succession stricken by a failure of the potato crop. Before long Peel was using the word 'famine', because half of that over-populous island lived mainly on potatoes. A shortage of corn in England prevented help of that kind being sent to Ireland, and so the only solution, he said, was to abolish the duty on corn and at last authorize the free import of foodstuffs into Great Britain. Peel's decision came from instinct rather than argument. What the Tories called treason was in his view simply a pious conversion. The Queen and Prince Albert, Free Traders both, kept telling him that he was saving the country. Against him a group of Conservative Protectionists took form within his own party, the attack being led by two men of widely different character, Lord George Bentinck and Benjamin Disraeli. Nobody would have imagined that this young Jew, known only as a brilliantly sarcastic orator, would become the leader of the country gentlemen and overturn the

SUSANNAH AND THE ELDERS: H. B. A cartoon of 1837, the year of her coronation, showing 18-year-old Queen Victoria out riding with William Lamb, Viscount Melbourne, who was Whig Prime Minister, and (on the right) Lord John Russell who had played a leading role in the preparation of the Reform Bill of 1832. *Gernsheim Collection.*

CHARLES DICKENS. His early novel *The Pickwick Papers* is one of the best and most enduring comic works in the English language. His later novels, such as *Oliver Twist*, derived much of their inspiration from offended social conscience. His continuing popularity is due to the richness of invention with which he created a whole microcosm peopled with unforgettable characters. *Mansell Collection.*

all-powerful Sir Robert Peel. But so it befell. In a series of dazzling philippics, rich in imagery, Disraeli denounced the Prime Minister's 'treason'. The abolition of the Corn Laws was passed because, for that division in the House, the Whig and Free Trade opposition voted with Peel's supporters; but the same night saw the defeat of Peel by an alliance of ungrateful Free Traders and vengeful Protectionists.

For twenty years this split was to keep the Conservative party out of power, except for short intervals. Peel's friends never became reconciled with the men who had overturned their leader. Peel himself died as the result of a riding mishap in 1850. The leading Peelites, and in particular the most conspicuous of them, William Ewart Glad-stone, allied themselves with the Whigs and Liberals. The Conservatives were now headed by Lord Stanley (later Lord Derby), a great landowner of intelligence and culture, and devoid of personal ambition, and by Disraeli, who, notwithstanding his genius, was not for a long time accepted by his party as their leader, but ultimately secured their merited confidence. The government of the country was carried on by Lord John Russell, then by Lord Aberdeen and Lord Palmerston at the head of Whig and Peelite coalitions. The abolition of the Corn Laws had not ruined agriculture, as Disraeli and his friends had prophesied it would. For many years longer England imported only about a quarter of the grain she used. In spite of inevitable times of difficulty, the years

between 1850 and 1875 were a period of great
general prosperity, due to the increasing population, the development of railways, and the furnishing of the Empire overseas. But the swift development of industry had produced grave abuses.
The Irish famine had discharged into Liverpool
alone over 100,000 starving people whose advent
only intensified the squalor of the slums. When
Engels visited Manchester in 1844, he found
350,000 workpeople crowded in dank and dirty
little houses, breathing sodden, dustladen air. In
the mines half-naked women were employed as
mere beasts of burden, and children spent their
days in the darkness of a pit-gallery, opening and
shutting air-vents. In the lace industry infants
of four years old were employed.

Despite the *laissez-faire* prejudice, Parliament at
last intervened. A Factory Act of 1819 had controlled the employment of children under nine
years of age, who at the beginning of the century
had worked as much as fifteen or sixteen hours
daily in the cotton-mills. An Act of 1833 limited
the employment of workers under eighteen, and
set up the first factory inspectors. In 1847 the
hours of work for women were limited to ten,
and this soon brought a corresponding modifica-
tion for men. The textile industry in 1850 adopted

the Saturday half-holiday (a system widely known
abroad as the 'English week'). And this transformed the life of the English workman by enabling him to indulge his interest in sport on Saturday afternoons. The campaign for limiting hours
of work had been directed by Lord Ashley (later
Lord Shaftesbury); and in 1842, after the publication of a report which inspired shame and dis-
gust in the public conscience, he also pushed
through legislation to prevent the employment of
women and children under nine in the mines. By
these more humane laws, by the general prosperity in which they shared, and also by the attraction
of the nonconformist chapel, large numbers of
English workmen were diverted from movements
of a revolutionary character. It was in England
that the co-operative societies and trade unions for
bettering conditions were brought to birth. The
trade unions had existed since the eighteenth century, but they were not strictly legal. They became
so in 1824. One of the most conspicuous was
the Amalgamated Society of Engineers, founded
in 1851, and counting 30,000 members in 1865,
at once a trade union in the strict sense and a
mutual benefit society. Its first head, William
Allen, was the typical trade unionist of the
Victorian period.

The administration of the new laws touching factories, mines, and sanitation, and Peel's creation of a regular police force in 1829, necessitated the growth of that central bureaucracy which England, a country of local government, had previously lacked. In 1815 the Home Office had only eighteen officials. With the Post Office, railways and factory inspection, the number of officials rose to 16,000 in 1853. The question of the recruitment of the Civil Service is never an easy one to solve in a democracy. If posts are at the disposal of politicians to reward their partisans, no government can keep a steady control over its servants. In America the 'spoils' system, which upsets the whole administration of the country after every election, and in France the abuse of political recommendation, are examples of dangerous error. One reason for the success of England during the nineteenth century was the creation of an excellent Civil Service, non-political in character and taking no direct part in politics. During the first half of the century, the reign of political influence throve. The old Whigs held on to the gift of place as one of the attributes of power, and when an open system of examination was laid down as essential for the Civil Service, this new-fangled idea shocked them profoundly. They were soon to realize that it gave good results. Civil Servants showed themselves loyal executives for every successive government, whatever its party colour, and by keeping scrupulously aloof from partisan disputes ensured the continuity of national traditions.

After Canning, the great Foreign Secretary for twenty years was Lord Palmerston, who was not a Whig but had supported the Reform movement and so quarrelled with the Tories. Public opinion in England favoured the cause of peoples struggling for liberty, and Palmerston accordingly sided with the Hungarians and the Italians, and supported the Sicilians against the King of Naples, and the Sardinians against Austria. In any international discussion Lord Palmerston's usual argument was the British fleet. He thus annoyed the Court, which he embroiled with other Courts, perturbed the peace-loving, who feared that this bluff might one day lead to war, but delighted the average Englishman, who beheld his flag honoured without fighting. But when Palmerston allowed himself to approve the *coup d'état* of Napoleon III in 1852,

without consulting the Queen or the Cabinet, he was obliged to hand over his portfolio to Lord John Russell. The incident, however, only increased his popularity, and not long afterwards he himself became Prime Minister.

The fact remains that Palmerston's masterful policy did not involve Britain in any hostilities, whereas the vacillation of Lord Aberdeen produced the Crimean War. The famous Eastern Question was primarily the question of Turkey. Many European statesmen in the mid-nineteenth century believed that the Ottoman Empire in Europe could not survive much longer. 'We have a sick man on our hands,' said the Tsar to the British ambassador, 'and we must not let him disappear without settling the succession.' The Tsar's idea of the settlement was that he himself should take the Balkan provinces, whilst he offered Egypt and Crete to Britain. If Britain and Russia could agree in this matter, he said, it mattered little what anybody else thought or did. But Britain desired the convalescence of the sick man more than his inheritance, and viewed with anxiety the growing strength of Russia, an Asiatic power formidable to India, an autocratic power hostile to liberal nations. France, on her side, had recurrent quarrels with the Tsar concerning the Holy Places, of which both countries claimed to be protectors. The storm broke when the Tsar demanded that the Sultan should entrust him with the protection of all Christians in the Levant. The British ambassador in Constantinople, Stratford Canning, joined France in encouraging the Sultan to resist this. British foreign policy became strangely confused. Lord Aberdeen, the Prime Minister, wanted peace; the Foreign Office wanted peace; the ambassador in Constantinople may have wanted a diplomatic victory; public opinion, ruffled by the Tsar's arrogance, wanted war. For the first time an attitude was imposed on the Foreign Office by an emotional campaign in the country. This was one consequence of a widened suffrage and the freedom of the Press. On March 27, 1854, France and England declared war on Russia, who had invaded Turkish provinces. French and British ships sailed up the Bosphorus and forced the Russian fleet to take refuge in Sebastopol.

Public opinion had the war it clamoured for. Was public opinion right? Admittedly the Tsar

VICTORIA AND ALBERT INSPECT THE FRENCH FLEET. This painting by François Biard commemorates the visit of a French naval squadron to Portsmouth, October 1844. In forty years the pattern of alliances in Europe had undergone a considerable change. (Musée de Versailles). *Bulloz, Paris.*

could not be allowed to slice up the Ottoman Empire to suit himself, but he might perhaps have been prevented by a more dexterous diplomacy. It was a paradoxical success — the triumph of sentimental liberalism making England the ally of one 'despot' — Napoleon III — to support another despot — the Sultan.

British campaigns had generally opened with a spectacular lack of foresight, and the Crimean War was the most brilliant of these exhibitions. The medical and commissariat services were so far beneath requirements that, in a war employing only small numbers of troops in the field, 25,000 British soldiers died, whilst the country spent, in vain, seventy million pounds. Fortunately the new power of the Press stirred up public opinion. Lord Aberdeen, attacked by every party, had to resign, and his place was taken by Lord Palmerston, who had the good fortune to come on to the stage when circumstances were at last turning in the Allies' favour. After a lengthy siege Sebastopol was taken (1855). Napoleon III, already reconciled with Russia, was anxious for peace in order to

pursue his other great projects, and especially to further the unity of Italy. Lord Palmerston would have liked to bring Russia to her knees and force her away from the shores of the Black Sea. Had his views prevailed, the war might have lasted for many a long year, and for very remote and ambiguous objects. But already a volatile public opinion was wavering, and beginning to wonder whether it had not backed the wrong horse. In 1856 the Treaty of Paris was signed, known to the malcontents as the 'Capitulation of Paris'. It was decided that the Ottoman Empire would be left intact, and that Russia should no longer be entitled to have a fleet in the Black Sea. The Sultan promised certain reforms, and to show more benevolence towards his Christian subjects; and a whole generation of Englishmen believed that the 'sick man of Europe' had been made a better man. Disillusion was at hand: the check to the Tsar's European ambitions resulted in his turning towards Asia, which implied danger to India, and the Sultan's conflicts with his Balkan provinces were to cause disturbance in Europe for over half a century.

One remote and unforeseen consequence of the Crimean War, in England, was women's suffrage. At the time when the medical services were in a state of collapse in Russia, the only person who proved capable of reorganizing them was a woman, Florence Nightingale; and this brought into currency entirely new ideas of the education of women and of their place in society, which paved the way for the women's suffrage movement.

During the Crimean War, Napoleon III had been insistent that the Sardinians should be authorized to join the Allies. The romantic strain in the Emperor of the French had been attracted by the idea of nationalism. He was eager to help the Italians to liberate themselves from Austria, and to make the House of Savoy, which ruled over both Sardinia and Piedmont, the pillar of the new Italy. Palmerston and English opinion favoured the idea, but the Court was suspicious of the Emperor. Prince Albert kept saying that Napoleon was a conspirator, and that this was the key to all his actions. In 1859 Napoleon III embarked on his Italian campaign. Anxious though he was to liberate Italy, he nevertheless wished to keep that country divided so as to make his own power felt there, and in particular he wished to preserve the temporal sovereignty of the Pope. Palmerston and his Foreign Secretary, Russell, forced Napoleon's hand and lent their support to the Sicilian expedition of Garibaldi, thus facilitating the total attainment of Italian unity. The aim of this policy was threefold: to satisfy liberal and Protestant opinion, to ensure the friendship and gratitude of the new Italy (Anglo-Italian friendship was to last unbroken from 1860 until 1935), and to prevent France from acquiring too much authority beyond the Alps. Palmerston had been alarmed by the annexation to France, after a plebiscite, of Nice and Savoy; and he took pleasure in beating Napoleon III with weapons of his own forging.

When the Southern States of America, in 1860, declared their intention of secession from the

Union, England was in two minds about this grave issue. A certain number of Radicals and dissenters sided with the anti-slavery campaign waged by the Northern States, but London's fashionable world, the small aristocratic clique which controlled British policy, was wholeheartedly in favour of the South. There indeed manners were more agreeable and accents more refined; thence, also, came the cotton which England urgently required. In 1861 and 1862, with Lancashire stricken by a veritable cotton famine, Palmerston's Government was on the point of recognizing Southern independence. Only the decisive victories of the Northern armies in 1863 prevented this rash step. But the attitude of the English newspapers had deeply wounded the Northerners, whose annoyance almost brought open war when the British Government authorized the building in England of ships supposedly for mercantile purposes; several disguised warships, such as the *Alabama*, were put in the service of the Confederates and wrought havoc in the Northerners' trade. For many years this episode poisoned the relations of the two countries; in the course of the next fifty years, moreover, North America received a flood of Slav, Latin and Irish immigration, and ceased to be a predominantly Anglo-Saxon community, becoming the great melting-pot of races that it continued to be until the war of 1914.

At no stage in human history did scientific invention so rapidly alter manners, ideas, and even landscapes, as in the first part of the nineteenth century. Man seemed to have mastered Nature. Steam was replacing the strength of men's arms, of animals, of the wind. In 1812 a steamboat puffed its way up the Clyde; in 1819, the first steamship crossed the Atlantic; in 1852 the *Agamemnon*, the first armour-plated screwdriven warship, was launched. In 1821 Stephenson built his first locomotive engine; in 1830 the Duke of Wellington opened the railway between Manchester and Liverpool; in 1838 Prince Albert, having come from Windsor to London by rail, asked the driver at the end of the journey kindly not to go so fast next time. The boldest minds were impressed by the vastness of the railway-stations and the busy districts growing up round them. Companies had been formed to exploit the invention; men from every walk of life — retired officers, merchants, schoolmasters — were becoming directors of railway companies. Speculation in shares, which had been only a transitory sickness in the eighteenth century, was now becoming a regular occupation; in many large enterprises, the joint-stock company (foreshadowed by the older colonial companies) was supplanting the individual and responsible master. The Victorian era in England, like the age of Louis-Philippe across the Channel, was the reign of the middle classes. Enriched by the application of scientific discovery, they might at that time have assumed power by force, had it not been that the Whigs surrendered the aristocratic citadel to them without a blow. The alliance of the Whigs and the middle classes had deep and lasting effects on England's moral standards. Many of the wealthy men who formed the new industrial oligarchy sprang from nonconformist stock. Even those among them who no longer held the faith of the Puritans retained a Puritan austerity, and this blend of moral strictness with commercial success was not fortuitous. Religion, indeed, proved frequently to be a direct occasion and secret of worldly success: Thomas Cook, who founded the famous travel agency, was a Baptist missionary who began by organizing excursions for temperance meetings and Sunday schools; the Cadbury and Fry families were Quakers and built the most prosperous and beneficent chocolate-works, cocoa being a powerful ally of preaching in the struggle against

'strong drink'. In deference to their political allies, the Whigs abandoned their cynicism, and, outwardly at least, their pleasures. Together with Free Trade and electoral Reform, the Whigs, reluctantly no doubt, had added Virtue to their programme.

The Queen herself, wedded to the prudish Albert, had been transformed. Her Court had become serious and domestic. Novels and plays took on a tone suitable for a youthful Queen, a virtuous wife and mother, and vice and crime were banned from literature, unless veiled with sentimentality or humour. To impress the mass with a sense of their safe respectability, the ruling classes assumed, if not always the reality, at least the conventions and semblance of respectability. And to a great many, these appearances became habits. The blend of solemnity, reserve and strength which was characteristic of that age, reappeared in the black frock-coats and high collars and ties of the men, as it did in the legendary black silk gowns and bonnets of Queen Victoria, And whilst the Whigs, in this alliance, sacrificed their free-living ways, the bourgeoisie abandoned their radicalism. The Victorian middle class professed an essentially conservative form of snobbery, accepting the structure of aristocratic society, and respecting that framework all the more as it offered chances for outsiders to take their place inside it. Middle-class people seemed to regard themselves as spectators enjoying the spectacle of a sumptuous life presented to them by excellent actors on a superb stage. Thus the great English families still preserved for many years longer their noble parks, their almost royal state, their Wren or Inigo Jones mansions, without having to face any vehement opposition. This upper-class life, widely tolerated and fabulously rich, is all the more astonishing

INAUGURATION OF THE GREAT EXHIBITION, 1851. The scene, painted by Henry Selous, shows the royal family gathered in the Crystal Palace, surrounded by British and foreign dignitaries. The Power behind the Exhibition, designed to celebrate British industrial progress, was Prince Albert. (Victoria and Albert Museum). *Hachette*.

◀ A TRAIN ON THE LIVERPOOL AND MANCHESTER RAILWAY, opened in 1830. The world's railways trace their origins back to those in the North of England where the requisite supplies of coal and iron, as also the inventive genius of Watt and Stephenson, were to be found. *Hachette*.

because the lot of the poor was then so deplorable. Mortality in the working-class quarters of the large towns was appalling. In the East End of London it was double what it was in the West End. Rural England, indeed, was not altogether dead. In 1861 the proportion of urban to rural population was as five to four; not until 1881 did the town population become double that of the country district. But the rural population itself did not recover its equilibrium. The farm worker was henceforth better off on the great estates, where 'the Dukes' built sound cottages, than on small properties which, except in periods of high prices, were hard put to it to make both ends meet. As for the urban workers, their lot grew slowly better throughout the long reign of Victoria. The worst period was at the beginning of the century. Until Peel's time, the people's foodstuffs were expensive. Free Trade lowered the cost of living, and in the early '50's wages began to rise.

And so Progress became the faith of all the Victorians, rich and poor. Science filled them with a religious awe. Lyell's *Principles of Geology* and Darwin's *Origin of Species* shattered the Biblical theories and gave their contemporaries the illusion of having discovered, from the evolution of living creatures, laws as exact as those of the material world. Philosophy itself became materialist. This era of universality, of faith in scientific and material progress, of pacifism and industry, found its perfect expression in the Great Exhibition of 1851, organized by Prince Albert with truly German solemnity and thoroughness. The vast size of the Crystal Palace, the enthusiasm of the crowds, the atmosphere of national reconciliation after the turmoils of Reform and Chartism, deeply impressed the English people, many of whom, on that occasion, took their first railway journey and for the first time beheld their capital city. Inevitable reactions appeared against social and scientific materialism. Not only did the Methodist movement make further headway, but the Anglican clergy worked devotedly at the evangelization of the new industrial towns. The Oxford Movement, which began about 1833, strove to invest the Anglican faith anew with the historic and poetic glamour of Catholicism. Its most famous figure, John Henry Newman, himself became a convert to the Church

LONDON DOCKSIDE WAREHOUSE IN 1872: Gustave Doré. Commerce flourished but so did a particularly bleak style of industrial architecture: towering brick walls shutting out light and air. (Bibliothèque nationale, Paris). *Hachette.*

BESSEMER CONVERTER. Sir Henry Bessemer's discovery, in 1856, of a process for converting pig-iron into steel was a leading factor in the great expansion of mechanical and civil engineering — notably railway, bridge and ship construction — during the latter half of the century. *Mansell Collection.*

of Rome, and in his later years a Cardinal. Carlyle led the charge against utilitarianism; Ruskin attacked the ugliness of industrialism. Finally there was Charles Dickens, in himself the most redoubtable wave of attack, who did more than all the professional philanthropists to teach the England of his day that true generosity which is fundamentally imaginative. But even Dickens, to make his realism acceptable, had to blur its outlines with humour and sentiment, and provide happy endings for his tragic stories. For such was the Victorian compromise.

The Reform of 1832 satisfied the middle class, but left the working classes with no means of expression. The new masters of law-abiding England, who in any case had maintained their former masters in power, felt no desire to enlarge the electorate further; but the most far-seeing statesmen in both parties, Gladstone in the Liberal, Disraeli in the Conservative camp, believed this to be the only remedy. Each party desired the honour and the fruits of a new Reform. A group of about thirty Whigs were determined to bar the road against any new advance of democracy, and in 1866 refused to vote for Gladstone's Reform measures. Lord Derby and Disraeli then overturned Russell and Gladstone. Regaining power in a minority, they proceeded to give the Conservative party a modern colour, no longer hostile to any change as the old Tory party had been, but prepared, if new conditions demanded it, to renovate the old national institutions (the monarchy, the House of Lords, the Church of England) even although they staunchly upheld them. Disraeli's efforts to educate his party were successful, and to him the Conservative party owed a new and prolonged youth. Making concessions to the Liberals on points of detail, he induced the Commons to pass the new Reform Act of 1867. As in the Act of 1832, the vote still depended on the ownership of a house, or on a sum of rent, but the limits were lower, especially in the boroughs, and more than a million new voters were added to the electorate, mostly from the urban working class. In the long run, the Conservatives had no reason to regret their move, but the next election (1868) brought a Liberal victory.

When the Conservatives returned in 1874, Lord Derby, in failing health, handed over the Premier-

ship to Disraeli. About the same time Gladstone became the undisputed leader of the Liberal Party, and the two men who, since the fall of Peel, had always differed from each other now found themselves in direct conflict. Two philosophies, two mental attitudes, were at grips. On one side, solemnity, earnestness, conscious rectitude; on the other, brilliance, wit, and — under the guise of superficial frivolity — a faith no less living than Gladstone's. The latter believed in government by the people, wished to receive his inspiration from the people, and declared his willingness to accept all the reforms desired by the people, even if they should destroy the oldest traditions of England. Disraeli believed in government *for* the people, in the necessity of keeping intact the framework of the country, and would concede reforms only in so far as they respected certain essential institutions linked with unchanging traits of human nature.

Gladstone was Prime Minister from 1868 to 1874, Disraeli from 1874 to 1880, and then Gladstone returned from 1880 to 1885. During these eighteen years great changes took place in Europe. Neither Gladstone nor Disraeli was able to realize that the balance of power was about to be upset by the new power of Prussia; and they did not react when confronted by the Austro-Prussian war, nor by the Franco-Prussian war, which achieved the hegemony of Prussia and brought about the creation of the German Empire. Russia in her turn denounced the Treaty of Paris, which had ended the Crimean war, and reorganized her Black Sea fleet. Here again Gladstone let things take their course. But the danger of concessions is that they whet the appetite and boldness of those who take advantage of them. Disraeli's foreign policy, however, was bold; it was more dramatic, and also more dangerous than Gladstone's. Whereas the Liberal leader desired peace at any price, took up a disinterested view even regarding the Empire, and desired to see his country endowed with a moral rather than an imperial prestige, Disraeli and his friends declared themselves imperialists. The conception of Empire, eclipsed since the death of Chatham and the loss of the American Colonies, was reborn in the romantic imagination of Disraeli. Against the wishes of the majority of his party, who distrusted changes whatever they might be,

he brought the Queen, who ardently desired it, to assume the title of Empress of India. In 1875 he secretly bought from the Khedive, for £4,000,000, 177,000 shares in the Suez Canal. The majority of the shares remained in French hands, but Britain thus acquired a share in this undertaking, of high importance to her as determining in future the shortest route to India and China. In that same year, Disraeli, a tired and aging man, went to the House of Lords as Lord Beaconsfield. Europe continued to be perturbed over the conflict between Turkey and her Christian provinces, which Russia, to obtain them, defended. There was nothing that Disraeli dreaded more than to see the Russians in the Mediterranean. In his view the prime axiom of British policy was to maintain free communications with India. By land, this communication was possible only through a friendly Turkey; by sea, it must now be kept through the Suez Canal, which would be highly vulnerable if the Turkish provinces in Asia were in hostile hands. He therefore sided with Turkey. But when atrocities were committed by the Turks in Bulgaria, Gladstone kindled British opinion against

them by pamphleteering and speech-making which Disraeli found absurd, but which touched the religious masses by their fervour. The wave of feeling was such that Disraeli had to abandon intervention. Before long Russia was able to force the Treaty of San Stefano on the Turks. Turkey-in-Europe disappeared almost completely, and an expanded Bulgaria gave the Russians access to the Mediterranean. Lord Beaconsfield held that this treaty was unacceptable to Europe and sent an ultimatum to Russia. Exhausted by the war, and alarmed by the arrival of troops from India and the dispatch of the British fleet to Constantinople, Russia bowed. This negotiation in the Palmerston manner, the fleet first with diplomacy following up, was refreshing to British pride. The Congress of Berlin in 1878 revised the Treaty of San Stefano. Bulgaria was bisected, Bosnia was promised to Austria, and Britain obtained Cyprus. The Treaty of Berlin seemed a complete triumph for Beaconsfield, who was rewarded with the Garter. In point of fact Cyprus was never of much use to Britain; Turkey continued to maltreat the Christian subjects restored to her, and it was the Bosnian problem which precipitated the war of 1914. In 1879 the hostility of Russia precipitated a clash on the Indian frontier. When a war followed against the Zulus in South Africa, the public began to feel that Disraeli's Imperialist line had its dangers. In 1879 Gladstone again conducted a great oratorical campaign with prodigious success. He told the electors that it was no longer a question of approving this or that political measure, but of choosing between two systems of morality. For five years past they had heard of nothing but the interests of the British Empire — and with what result? Russia was aggrandized and hostile, Europe in ferment, India at war, Africa stained with blood. Gladstone's lofty and religious doctrine impressed his devout audiences with an almost awful admiration: they seemed to be hearing the divine word, to be gazing upon a prophet inspired. In the election of 1880, Disraeli and his party were swept away.

Gladstone was sincere in his hatred of force, but he found himself constrained to use it. The first troubles rose in South Africa. There had been clashes there between the Dutch farmers and the English settlers ever since England annexed the Cape during the Napoleonic wars. In 1877 they had further annexed the Dutch republic of the Transvaal, and in 1881 the Boers revolted, overwhelming the small British army of occupation at Majuba Hill. Gladstone bowed to the force of circumstance and restored Boer independence. In Ireland, meanwhile, a rebel, republican, anti-English party was secretly gathering strength. In the House of Commons, the Government was constantly harried by the eighty Irish members, partisans of Home Rule, led by the brilliant, enigmatic Parnell. In Ireland itself Parliamentary action was backed up by a policy of direct action which culminated in murder. The peasantry refused to pay rent. Gladstone vainly tried to support their cause by a Land Act which gave special tribunals power to adjust leases; and, also unavailingly, he released Parnell and some of his associates who had been arrested for incitement to lawlessness. Within a few days violence was again abroad. Public opinion in England was outraged and the Cabinet was forced to

THE EGYPTIAN CAMPAIGN. The British ▶
occupied Egypt in 1882 to fill a power
vacuum. Modern weapons of war, such as
this armoured train equipped with light
artillery, facilitated the conquest though
three years later the British troops were
shut up in Khartoum and annihilated by
the Mahdi and his Dervishes. A drawing
by William Overend in the *Illustrated London
News*, 12 August 1882. (Bibliothèque
nationale, Paris). *Hachette.*

W. E. GLADSTONE (1809-1898), leader of the Liberal Party and
four times Prime Minister. It is a significant trait of character
that this champion of reform felled trees on his estate, Hawar-
den, with his own axe, whereas Disraeli at Hughenden refused
to let a single tree be cut down. *Victoria and Albert Museum.*

put forward fairly effective repressive measures.
After the Transvaal and Ireland came Egypt. The
Khedive's bad administration had led Britain and
France to undertake a joint control of finance and
the administration of the Egyptian Debt. After
the massacre of some Europeans in Alexandria, the
French Government, with more timidity than wisdom, withdrew the French fleet. Gladstone would
willingly have done likewise, but the Press and
public forbade him. British troops entered Cairo.
Theoretically, this occupation of Egypt was temporary, and it was jealously scrutinized by France.
Actually, Sir Evelyn Baring (later Lord Cromer)
was soon administering the country under the nominal sovereignty of the Khedive. A British army
of occupation remained 'provisionally' in Egypt.
When a Moslem fanatic proclaimed himself as the
Mahdi in the Egyptian Sudan, rallied the Dervishes
and drove out the Egyptian soldiery, the British

General Hicks was dispatched there, and his force
was cut to pieces. Gladstone decided to evacuate
the Sudan, and rashly entrusted the operation to
General Gordon, an extraordinary personage who
had won a great reputation during the campaigns
in China, a man as fanatical in his own way as the
Mahdi. Instead of evacuating the Sudan, Gordon
shut himself up in Khartoum and called in vain
for reinforcements. When Gladstone at last decided
to send them, it was too late. The Mahdi massacred
the General and his garrison of 11,000 men. Gordon
had all the virtues necessary to become a national
hero. His death brought the Government down.
But the murder was not avenged until Kitchener's
expedition in 1898.

At home, Gladstone had been removing some
of the last of the country's religious inequalities.
He disestablished the Anglican Church of Ireland,
which the Catholic Irish had no reason to maintain;

and he opened the Universities of Oxford and Cambridge to nonconformists, who since 1836 had had access to the younger University of London. Forster's Education Act of 1870 gave England at last the embryo of a national system of schools. The upper and middle classes sent their sons to the public schools or grammar schools; the common people in England for a long time had only the schools maintained by the Church. At last the Forster Act of 1870 set up State schools in villages and districts wheret here was no non-ecclesiastical school. The new schools were Christian, but not sectarian. It was in 1891 that education became compulsory; and in 1912 it became gratuitous for all. In 1877 Disraeli had given the vote to the urban working class; in 1884 Gladstone gave it to the agricultural labourer. Bills for a secret ballot and to stifle electoral corruption had ended the plutocratic control of polling. After 1884, out of

seven million adult males, five million were on the register. Almost the only exceptions now were those sharing their masters' houses (servants) or their fathers' houses (sons living with their family), and all women. Local government was now mainly carried out by elected bodies, and the justices of the peace had lost the administrative power which they had held since Tudor times. Within fifty years England had passed, with no great upheavals, from oligarchy to democracy. But at the same time the independence of the House of Commons had been weakened. Under the old aristocratic system, a rich landlord in his own borough (or his nominee) knew himself invulnerable; and his vote in Parliament was free, because the Prime Minister had no hold over him, unless by corruption, which honourable (or extremely rich) members resisted. But under the democratic system all seats became uncertain; no member could be absolutely sure of re-election by a wide and capricious electorate, and a threat of dissolution therefore became the whip which the Prime Minister cracked to bring straying members to heel. A Liberal association founded by Joseph Chamberlain at Birmingham became the pattern of what was called, from American usage, a 'caucus.' The parties became powerful organizations, each choosing its candidates, collecting election funds (provided, on occasion, in exchange for titles), and setting forward its chosen leader as the Premier to be summoned to office by the sovereign. Barring some unforeseeable accident, a grave personal mistake or a party split, a Prime Minister with an electoral majority was now increasingly certain to retain power for the duration of a Parliament. In this way, as an unforeseen outcome of electoral reform, the executive was increasingly strengthened, and the English system became more akin to the American, although it was freed from the dangers raised under the American constitution by the twofold currents of Presidential and Congressional elections.

The two great traditional parties seemed now to be part of the eternal verities; and it would have been a bold man who foretold that one day a Labour party would come into power. English Socialism, from More to Morris, had been utopian and ineffectual. A German Jew, Karl Marx, who had lived in London since the Revolution of 1848, published there his book, *Capital*, in 1864, which became to socialism what *The Wealth of Nations* had been to Liberalism. He described therein the results of free competition, which were quite unforeseen by Adam Smith, and declared that, just as the middle classes had ousted feudalism, so one day the proletariat would expropriate the bourgeoisie. But the class war found few recruits in the prosperous England of these days. It required the long and distressing slump which began in 1875, to bring into being a Social Democratic Federation, though this played a far smaller part in the activities of the working class in England than did the practical trade-union leadership of Keir Hardie or John Burns. Socialism in England always took peculiar forms. It had been reformist and paternal with Robert Owen, aesthetic with Ruskin; it was intellectual, paradoxical and temporizing with the Fabian Society; emotional and evangelistic with Ramsay MacDonald. Fabian collectivism was dif-

ferentiated from Continental socialism by two characteristics: it assailed ground rent and large landed estates rather than industrial capital, and it clung to the principles of representative government rather than urging direct rule by the voting masses. Fabian ideas, not very many years after the Society's foundation, were to inspire the social and financial policy of advanced Liberals like Lloyd George.

After the loss of the American Colonies, it was common enough to find Englishmen denying the economic value of colonies. This indifference explains the surprising generosity with which England twice, in 1802 and in 1815, restored to France and Holland colonies which her maritime supremacy had enabled her to conquer. But some obscure instinct checked the negotiations at certain points, and they retained at least the framework of an Empire. India and Canada were still the two main pieces. The Cape of Good Hope, taken from the Dutch in 1796, was held as a useful stage on the passage to India. Gibraltar, Malta and the Ionian Islands dominated the Mediterranean. In the Antipodes, transported convicts had made the first Australian settlements in the later eighteenth century. Thus the groundwork of the future British Empire was unmistakably sketched out; but nobody supposed that one day these scattered territories would form a Commonwealth of Nations, self-governing, but united by bonds freely accepted.

Nevertheless, if the new Empire were not sooner or later to follow the American example, it must obtain some form of autonomy, at least in those parts where large communities of the white race had grown up. The English colonist, who quite often had left the mother-country to escape from religious or social restrictions, was not the man to surrender in exile the right to share in the government of his new country. A fortunate accident created the first Dominion; success encouraged imitation; and so the Commonwealth of Nations was born. The said accident was the existence in Canada of a French population which, since 1791, had maintained a legislative assembly almost entirely French in speech and sympathies, whereas the executive power was in the hands of a British Governor, with a Council composed of British officials. In 1837 a rebellion broke out in French Canada and spread into the provinces. It was easily put down, but the Whigs were wise enough to send over to Canada a statesman not afraid of experiments, Lord Durham. After a few months in residence he drew up a remarkable report on the Canadian situation. His conclusion was the necessity of trying to unite both provinces more closely, and of setting up in both some form of ministerial representation. He had no desire to touch any of the Crown prerogatives, but the Crown would have to submit to the necessary consequences of representative institutions and govern through the intermediary of those in whom the representative body put confidence. To many of Lord Durham's contemporaries these ideas seemed revolutionary. They held that this meant the breaking of every bond between colony and mother-country. The risk, however, was accepted. The new Governor-General, Lord Elgin, bravely formed a ministry of reformist Canadians, who then held a majority in the country, and several of whom had taken part in the recent rebellion. The experiment was successful. Confidence fostered loyalty. Thenceforward the principle of self-government was admitted. Theoretically nothing had changed, as the form had to be respected. The British Government retained the right of appointing the ministers. In practice they made their choice only from amongst the men who held the confidence of the Canadian Chambers. Thus the greatest colonial revolution was accomplished with no theorizing and no noise. It was a very British solution.

The different States composing Australia and New Zealand also became entitled, between 1850 and 1875, to provide themselves with liberal constitutions. But the solution was more complicated in countries where small numbers of white colonists lived side by side with numerous natives. In these cases it would have been dangerous to grant all rights of control to the white minority, which might misuse its power to oppress the natives. In South Africa a still more awkward problem was raised by the presence of two European races. The original colonists at the Cape, at the time when England occupied that country, were Dutch farmers; these Boers had emigrated first into Natal, and then into the Orange and Transvaal republics which they founded. In 1881 the Boer rising wiped out the British forces at Majuba Hill, and Gladstone had thereupon abandoned the Transvaal. But British penetration of South Africa was carried on by a chartered company, the animating force of which was Cecil Rhodes, the Clive of this continent. When gold and diamond mines were shortly afterwards discovered in the Transvaal, a flood of British immigrants poured into the Dutch republics, where they were granted mining or trading concessions, but not civic rights. In 1895 Dr. Jameson, a friend of Rhodes, acting under the latter's inspiration, organized in time of peace an armed raid into the Transvaal to overturn the existing government. Repulsed and captured, Jameson gravely compromised the British Government, whom the Boers suspected of having encouraged the raid.

During the second half of the nineteenth century, Africa was sliced up by the European Powers. Between 1853 and 1873 Livingstone explored the region of Lake Tanganyika; then Stanley crossed the whole continent. While the new territories were being opened up, Germany, Belgium, France, and later Italy, all quarrelled over them. Officially, Britain for a long time stood aloof from the African game. It was the great Companies — not only Rhodes's British South Africa Company, but also the Niger and the East Africa — which founded the new British colonies of Rhodesia, Nigeria, Kenya, and Uganda. This curious reversion to the Chartered company system is attributable to the advantage found by the Imperial Government in allowing capitalist enterprise to bear the cost of exploration and pioneering work. If the undertaking was a failure, it was abandoned. If it succeeded, the Imperial Government supplanted the Company. Thus, piece by piece, there grew up in Africa an Empire of such magnitude that Rhodes was able to envisage a railway running from the Cape to Cairo without ever leaving British territory. The only barrier across this line was German East Africa, which Britain was ultimately to acquire after the War of 1914-1918.

In India the East India Company, almost despite itself, had continued the conquest of that country after the collapse of the Mogul Empire. It brought over a body of officials who battled as best they could against anarchy and famine. The Reform advocates of 1832 had been anxious to apply their principles in India, too, and an Indian Charter of 1833 laid it down that any subject of His Majesty could fill any post, whatever his race, birthplace, or colour. It was a bold theory, and difficult of application. In 1857 a terrible mutiny broke out amongst the native Indian troops to whom the Company, like the Roman Empire of old, had entrusted the security of the country. After fearful massacres of women and children by the rebels came a ruthless and efficacious suppression. The British Government itself took over the administration of India, and the European garrison was increased to 75,000 men. The great period of conquest was by now over. Fresh campaigns in Burma and on the Eastern frontiers led to the final delimitation of territory in 1885.

Queen Victoria respected Gladstone, but deemed him dangerous: in her view, he had weakened his country's authority in the world. Since the death of Gordon, many of Gladstone's supporters had also lost faith in him, notwithstanding his astounding eloquence. In the election of 1886, after a short Conservative interregnum, he came back with a small majority, holding power only by the support of the Irish Nationalists. Soon it was rumoured that Gladstone had bought their support by a promise of Home Rule for Ireland. And it was true: in April 1886 the Prime Minister introduced a bill to grant Irish autonomy and set up an Irish Parliament in Dublin. Joseph Chamberlain, Lord Hartington, and numerous Liberal leaders protested; if need be they would have accepted a federalist solution, but they refused a separatist handling of the Irish problem. Before long these Unionists, as they then came to be called, left the Liberal party, and, without as yet joining the Conservative party, pledged themselves to support the latter against Gladstone. The Prime Minister appealed to the country, but the polls went against him. Four hundred Unionists were returned to the House, three hundred and eighteen of whom were Conservatives. The Gladstonians were routed, and Lord Salisbury, at the head of the Unionist coalition, took office.

Robert Cecil, Marquess of Salisbury, regarded the affairs of mankind with a deep, aloof wisdom. In the days when he served under Disraeli he had condemned the romantic visions of his leader as severely as he did the idealism of Gladstone. He detested the lofty moral arguments with which most politicians buttress their selfish interests, and regarded human societies as fragile organisms to be interfered with as little as possible. When he left office after twenty years, he had solved neither the social problems nor the Irish question; but he had prevented them from causing any disorder during that period. In foreign policy, as in his conduct of home affairs, he tried to avoid emotion and to think in ' chemical ' terms, striving to feel neither sympathy nor antipathy towards foreign nations. A solitary in his private life, he accepted for his country ' a splendid isolation '. And this attitude remained possible, even reasonable, so long as Lord Salisbury remained in office, that is, until 1902. Thereafter came the time when England was menaced and, as in Pitt's day, had to find an army on the Continent.

Salisbury's long rule was broken only by a brief interregnum. At the election of 1892 the majority in the House of Commons once more consisted of Gladstonian Liberals and Irish Home Rulers. At the age of eighty-three the indomitable Gladstone once more pushed a Home Rule Bill through the Lower House. But it was rejected by the Lords, and the measure was not sufficiently popular to justify a decisive battle with the Upper Chamber on that ground. Gladstone's retirement through illness and old age put the premiership into the hands of Lord Rosebery from 1894 to 1896; but the Liberal party was uncomfortably divided between his supporters and those of Sir William Harcourt, and the role of the Conservatives became easy. This time the Liberal Unionists — Lord Hartington (later Duke of Devonshire) and Joseph Chamberlain — consented to enter the Government alongside Salisbury and his nephew Arthur Balfour.

It was a time of conflicting imperialisms, of jealousy and intrigue. In America, a frontier dispute between Venezuela and British Guiana brought the President of the United States to remind the world of the Monroe Doctrine, and might have led to war if Salisbury had not accepted arbitration. In Africa, French military expeditions, pushing up the valleys of the Niger and Congo, were annexing vast territories which cut off the British Colonies from their hinterland. France had then no reason to renounce Egypt, which she hoped to enter by way of the Upper Nile, and a mission under the command of Commandant Marchand found its way across Africa towards the Sudan. Britain, for her part, had not renounced Morocco. The Siamese frontier, Madagascar and Newfoundland were also

BRITISH CAVALRY ENCAMPMENT, BOER WAR. A photograph taken during the advance on Pretoria which fell in June 1900. The fight between the British and the Dutch settlers in South Africa ended on such amicable terms, in 1902, that the adversaries could make common cause in the World War which broke out twelve years later. *Sirot Collection.*

points of friction between the two countries. This latent hostility became acute when General Kitchener, after defeating the Mahdi, avenging Gordon and occupying the Sudan, came face to face with Marchand's column at Fashoda. The Conservative newspapers in London had a dangerous attack of war-fever; the Liberal editors spoke gravely of the moral duty incumbent on Britain to reconquer the Sudan for the Egyptians. Both countries mobilized their fleets. Britain hurriedly moved her ships, which were dangerously scattered, the Mediterranean fleet being partly at Malta and partly at Gibraltar, and therefore liable to be cut in two by the French fleet from Toulon. The German Emperor, William II, hoped that this war would break out. But Delcassé, at the French Foreign Office,

deemed it wise to yield and thus prepare the way for a reconciliation between the two countries. During the years that followed this episode England's name was hated in France.

Truth to tell, it was hated all the world over at that time, for England was going through one of those periods of vainglorious prosperity which are as dangerous to nations as to individuals. The Imperialist doctrine, propounded by Disraeli in the middle 'seventies to somewhat protesting Conservatives, was becoming a national religion. Just as the Great Exhibition of 1851 marked the apogee of England's industrial prosperity, so the Diamond Jubilee of 1897 crowned her Imperial glory. The Queen and Lord Salisbury had agreed in making this festivity a private celebration of Empire. No foreign sovereigns attended, but from all the Britains overseas came princes, statesmen and soldiers. For some years past a poet of genius, Rudyard Kipling, had been voicing the feelings of all those Englishmen who, scattered over the globe, strove to uphold in every clime the solid qualities of the British character as it had been shaped by the public schools since the days of Dr. Arnold. To this moral race Rudyard Kipling supplied moral grounds for cherishing their own renown; conquest became in their eyes an Imperial duty, and they were called upon to take up 'the White Man's burden'. Another man of genius, Joseph Chamberlain, the Radical who had become the ally of the Conservatives, urged at the Colonial Office that poverty and unemployment were best combatted by the development of Imperial trade. He tried by every means to imbue the Dominions, the Colonies, and the mother-country with the sense of unity sung by Kipling. Within three years of the glorious Jubilee procession, however, the most powerful Empire in the world was being held in check at the southern end of the African continent by two small republics of farming folk — the Transvaal and the Orange Free State. England and Europe alike were astounded when the conflict lasted for over a year. It exposed the weakness of the British army, the faulty organization of the War Office, and also the enmities which Britain's policy of Imperialist self-seeking had roused against her all the world over. When the victories of Roberts and Kitchener at last enabled a victorious peace to be signed with the Boers, its terms were conspicuous for their moderation. Both republics were annexed; but Britain granted the vanquished farmers a generous indemnity which enabled them to rebuild their farms and replenish their fields, and when the Boer generals came to London a few months later they were welcomed with an enthusiasm that surprised them. In 1906 both republics received a measure of responsible self-government, and in 1910 the Union of South Africa was set up, comprising the Cape Colony, the Orange Free State, and the Transvaal Republic.

Queen Victoria did not live to see the Boer War ended. She died early in 1901, after a reign of sixty-three years, the happiest reign perhaps in England's history, in the course of which the country had accepted without civil strife or grave suffering a revolution far more profound than that of 1688, while the kingdom was becoming, not only in name but in fact, an Empire. She had restored and enhanced the royal dignity, besmirched by the later Hanoverians. Thanks to her, constitutional monarchy had become an accepted, tested, desirable form of government. Except in the far-off days of her girlhood, she had always been wise enough to yield when she found herself in conflict with her ministers; but she retained and insisted upon her three essential rights — to be consulted, to encourage, and to warn. In this way the sovereign, especially after a long reign, was able to exercise a moderating influence upon ministers, who could not but respect her. Early in her reign, and again about 1870, when as a 'professional widow' she seemed to lose interest in the realm, waves of republican feeling rose here and there; but when Victoria died, the country's attachment to the monarchy was as firm as, perhaps firmer than, it had been in the days of Elizabeth. And her son and grandson, by their firm grasp of the craft of kingship, kept that feeling warm and rooted it still more firmly.

King Edward VII, on his accession, was nearly sixty. The new king had sound sense, *bonhomie*, and tact. Widely travelled, he knew Europe and the statesmen of foreign countries, and realized also the limitations of Britain's power. Whilst having many friends in Paris, even among Republican statesmen, he was the object of nothing less than hatred on the part of his nephew William, the German Emperor since 1888. In the end, after several public and private affronts, the uncle himself came to have an obvious dislike of his nephew. The antipathy between these two men played a secondary, but very real, part in the development of European politics between 1900 and 1910. In particular, the Kaiser's longing to astound the English and beat them on their own ground hastened the construction of a great German navy which ere long began to alarm England.

The South African War had shown the more clear-sighted of the English that 'splendid isolation', from being a source of strength had become a danger. The extent of the Empire was such that England might at any moment be obliged to use a large part of her strength in some distant quarter of the globe. If one of her enemies chose such a moment to strike at her in India, in Egypt, or even at home, who would come to her defence? Two powers were outstanding as possible allies — Germany and France. When Salisbury's place in Downing Street was taken by his nephew Balfour, and the Foreign Office was in the hands of Lord Lansdowne, a reconciliation with France became more practicable: all the more so because the statesmen of both countries were alarmed by the power of Germany and anxious for a more friendly relationship. Steps to achieve this were taken after a visit to Paris by King Edward VII in 1903, which transformed the emotional atmosphere of the negotiations. The essential point was the abandonment by France of any claim to Egypt, in exchange for Britain's recognition of French interests in Morocco, the country bordering on Algeria. The agreement concluded in 1904, the starting-point of an Entente Cordiale, was remarkable in that it satisfied both parties. All the old disputes, in Newfoundland, Africa and the Far East, were settled. Both governments promised mutual diplomatic support against the claims of a third party in the fulfilment of this agreement. The German government had observed this *rapprochement* between Britain and France with perturbation and, in regard to Morocco, where German interests were involved, with annoyance. But they awaited a favourable opportunity for protest. This seemed to come with the Russo-Japanese War in 1904. Russia, in spite of the Tsar's hesitancy, had for about ten years been drawing nearer to France. After her defeat she ceased, for a time at least, to count as a military power. Since the Dreyfus Affair France had apparently been so deeply divided by domestic strife as to make her incapable of withstanding foreign conflict. The moment seemed favourable to get rid of Delcassé, whom Germany regarded as the architect of a coalition designed to oppose her. The landing of the German Emperor at Tangier, followed by a thinly veiled ultimatum, roused fears of war. Lansdowne offered Delcassé not an alliance, but a tightening of the bonds uniting the two countries. Rouvier, the French Premier, was alarmed by Germany's threats and preferred to capitulate. Delcassé was thrown overboard. For some weeks British statesmen wondered whether the Entente Cordiale had been a wise policy. Such were the events of May and June 1905.

But in England, meanwhile, the swing of the pendulum had come. The education policy of the Conservative ministry had caused discontent amongst its Radical-Unionist allies. Aware of the gathering storm, Chamberlain sought to avert it by launching a new idea — that of Tariff Reform, a programme of preferential tariffs designed to tighten the trade bonds between the Colonies and the mother-country. But to protect Canadian wheat, Australian sheep, Indian cotton, meant the re-opening of the whole Free Trade Controversy. England had waxed rich and fat on Free Trade, and to its principles she owed a century of contentment, abundance and variety of foodstuffs, and markets for her manufactures. The appeal to Imperial sentiment made little impression on the electorate; it even displeased them, because the enthusiasm of the early stages of the Boer War had been succeeded, as the war dragged on, by a wave of pacifist and anti-Imperial feeling. All the Free Traders in the Cabinet handed their resignations to Balfour. Unionism was disunited.

The Liberal party now had some difficulty in forming a ministry. To avoid quarrels, the old leaders were set aside and the Prime Minister was Sir Henry Campbell-Bannerman. He died, however, in 1908, and his place was taken by Asquith, a great parliamentarian who was also a man of indisputably fine character. The Foreign Office was given to Sir Edward Grey, a descendant of the famous old Whig family. The harsh irony of fate willed it that this Liberal Cabinet, peace-loving in tone and hostile to Imperialism and military and naval expediture, inherited, as Gladstone did in 1880, a situation which demanded firmness. Hardly had Grey settled into the Foreign Office when he had to concern himself with the Algeciras Conference, convoked to deal with the fate of Morocco, and had to authorize the conversations between the General Staffs of France, Belgium and his own country. Algeciras ended without catastrophe, von Bülow having yielded before the firm attitude of Britain and the hostility of Europe at large. But between 1906 and 1914 alarms came thick and fast. The German navy was increasing so rapidly that the day could be seen when it would equal, then surpass, the British navy itself. The balance of power in Europe was upset. However peace-loving the Liberal ministry might be, it recognized its

EDWARD VII, who was almost 60 when he came to the throne. His worsening relations with his nephew, Kaiser Wilhelm of Germany, and his improved relations with France (Entente Cordiale) were not without influence on political developments in Europe. *W. and D. Downe.*

SUFFRAGETTES ARRESTED OUTSIDE BUCK-INGHAM PALACE, MAY 1914. The militant campaigners for female suffrage succeeded in exasperating the Government by their methods. The vote was extended to women over 30 in 1918; the age limit was subsequently reduced to 21 years, as for men. The extent to which suffragette methods contributed to the victory is debatable. *Radio Times Hulton Picture Library.*

responsibility for the country's security and knew that without the mastery of the seas Britain was doomed. An agreement with Russia, supplementing that of 1904 with France, grouped these three powers in a Triple Entente. Germany, in all good faith, declared that she was 'encircled'. Lord Haldane reorganized the Army at the War Office, created the Territorial Army, and formed a General Staff. Admiral Sir John Fisher, supported by Winston Churchill at the Admiralty, strove to re-group the unduly dispersed fleets and to get a powerful fighting fleet into the North Sea.

This armaments race swallowed up the resources which the Liberal Government had planned to devote to social reform. Its supporters were re-sentful. To go to the polls without some popular agitation to rehabilitate the party would have been to court disaster. Lloyd George, a young, aggress-ive and spellbinding Welshman, was now Chan-cellor of the Exchequer; he found an advantageous opening for such an agitation in a revival of hos-tilities against the House of Lords. The Liberals had good reason for resenting the Upper Chamber, which had rejected its most cherished measures, notably Welsh Disestablishment, the development of nonconformist schools, and Irish Home Rule. But in a country so loyal to tradition, the defeat of the peers depended on their being put unmis-takably in the wrong. Lloyd George put forward a body of new taxes and social legislation which he styled the People's Budget, for which he appro-priated some of the ideas of the Fabians, imposing fresh taxation on large landed estates and on 'un-earned increment'. In 1909, as Lloyd George desired, the lords threw out this Budget and Par-liament was dissolved. The election campaign showed how conservative Edwardian England re-mained. The Liberals lost a large number of their seats. Asquith returned to power in very much the same position in the Commons as Gladstone had stood. He could pass his Budget only with the support of the Irish Nationalists, and had to obtain this by a promise of Home Rule. But if this promise were to have any validity, the veto of the House of Lords must be abolished, as the peers would certainly never vote for a dismemberment of the Empire. How could the Lords be induced to vote their own abdication? This was possible only by the method of 1714 and 1832: a threat to create a batch of new peers. Such a threat in itself re-quired the support of the King; and the King would certainly not grant it without a fresh election. Prudently the Lords passed the Lloyd George Budget. The party struggle was interrupted by the death of Edward VII in 1910, but feeling ran too high for the quarrel to be left where it was. Another election repeated the situation of a Liberal-Nationalist majority, and the new King, George V, obliged the House of Lords, by a threat to create new peers, to vote the limitation of its own powers. Since 1911 any financial measure passed by the House of Commons becomes law after one month, even if the Lords refuse to accept it. As regards other legislation, the Lords retain a suspensive veto; but after three favourable votes in three successive sessions of the Commons, the Upper House is obliged to yield.

This just law was passed in a cloud of hatred, and these political battles between 1911 and 1914 were more violent than any which England had known for years. Lloyd George had set class against class, even Church against Church. Amongst the coal miners and railway workers powerful trade unions were confronting the autocratic organizations of employers. It was a time

of numerous strikes. The Labour party, which had only had two members in 1901, had fifty in 1906. Allied with the Liberals, it pushed forward useful laws for the safeguarding of working-class interests. Meanwhile women, eager to secure for their sex the right of the Parliamentary vote, abandoned peaceful agitation, and tried now to alarm, rather than to convince, the male. Further, the Home Rule Act of 1912 met with impassioned resistance from the Ulster Protestants, who declared that they would never consent to be separated from Britain and vowed to defend themselves, if need be, by armed force. Their leader, Sir Edward Carson, formed a provisional Ulster government, and organized an army. To avoid civil war, Asquith proposed giving Ulster six years' respite. But Carson stood fast: Ulster, he said, would not agree to a death-sentence with six years' respite. In 1914 the peril was imminent. The Act was due to come into force. It required only the assent of the Crown. On July 21, 1914,

the King in person opened a conference between representatives of the Government, the Opposition, Southern Ireland, and Ulster. After three days, seeing no hope of agreement, this conference broke up. On the same day Austria dispatched her ultimatum to Serbia.

In Europe as in Britain, a period of comparative tranquillity was beings ucceeded by one of feverish unrest and excitement, animated by philosophies of violence. The static conservatism of the Holy Alliance, the ineffective idealism of the revolutionaries of 1848, had been supplanted by the realist politics of Cavour and Bismarck, and by the ruthless class warfare prophesied by Karl Marx and Georges Sorel. Liberalism might be in power in Britain, but its idealist, reformist, rational and moral doctrines were checkmated at every turn by frenzied women suffragists, by impatient strikers, malcontent Irishmen, rebellious officers. And it was at this juncture that, for four years, the most terrible of foreign wars interrupted the painful, unconscious travail whereby the old nation was giving birth to a new England.

Once again, a European sovereign was aspiring to hegemony in Europe, and was anxious to build a fleet capable of opposing the British Navy; and once again the policy of the balance of power obviously required Britain to oppose such claims. The successive Ententes with France and Russia, after 1905, were a defensive gesture. But although the Conservatives, the Admiralty, and a few clear-sighted Liberals like Winston Churchill, discerned a traditional danger ahead, the British Government at this time was essentially pacifist. Accordingly, no formal promise had been given to either France or Russia before August 1914. The immediate cause of the war of 1914 (an ultimatum from Austria to Serbia following the murder of the Austrian heir-apparent) could not in itself affect the British electorate. It required the German invasion of Belgium, in defiance of treaties of neutrality, to release that emotional wave which, arising to swell a wave of realism, swept England into almost complete unanimity. In any case, even if Germany had respected Belgian neutrality, Britain would nevertheless have been forced before long to enter the war. She had given no direct pledge to France, but many of her statesmen felt that neither her honour nor her interest could allow

France to be crushed. Still less could she tolerate what William of Orange or Pitt would never have allowed — the presence of Germany at Antwerp or Calais. Asquith and Grey were resolved to resign if Britain remained neutral. The violation by Germany of the Belgian frontier determined the dispatch of an ultimatum to Berlin on August 4, 1914 and that night war was declared.

Although the Great War shows certain recurrent characteristics of Continental wars involving England in the past (the guarding of sea-routes, a Continental coalition, subsidies to allies, and the dispatch of an expeditionary force to Flanders), there were several new features. In the first place, and for the first time, the masses of men set in motion were such, and the dangers were such, that Britain was forced against all her instincts to fall back on conscription for her armed forces. The main body of British citizens, hitherto screened by professional soldiers and sailors, felt for themselves the evils of war. Secondly, Britain's maritime resistance was very nearly shattered by the submarine. At the start of the war, the British fleet easily enough assured the transport of the expeditionary force. But gradually the number and the active range of German submarines increased. In 1914 there were on the high seas about 8000 merchant ships, half of them under the British flag. Between 1914 and 1918 Germany sank 5000 of that total. At first the losses were made up fairly well by the shipyards, but in 1917 the rate of torpedo destruction rose rapidly and fresh building lagged behind. If remedies had not been found, the Allies might have collapsed about August 1917, for lack of transports.

It was this situation, fully visible to the Germans, which decided them to torpedo ships at sight, even under neutral flags, and at the risk of bringing in the United States on the Allied side, as indeed happened in 1917. The submarine menace was thwarted by the organization of convoys screened by destroyers, by the use of armed vessels disguised as merchant ships, and by blocking the Belgian coastal bases used by the German submarines. In 1918 the submarine danger was so far obviated that the transport of forty-two American army divisions was carried out with a loss of only two hundred lives. Although the one great naval battle of the war, that of Jutland, was

«OVER THE TOP»: JOHN NASH. When the Germans invading
France were stopped at the Battle of Marne, September 1914, the
contending armies were forced into trench warfare for the next
four years. The death toll in this war was enormous. Here
British infantry are seen leaving their trenches to make an assault
at Marcoing, on the left bank of the Scheldt, December 1917.
(Imperial War Museum, London). *Hachette*.

indecisive, Britain kept the mastery of the seas, as the German fleet, in spite of some remarkable exploits by isolated ships, could not leave its base. Without the British Navy, the food supply of the Allies would have broken down.

The first aim assigned by the British Government to its expeditionary force in France was the protection of the Channel and North Sea ports. This could not be completely attained as the Germans captured Antwerp, Ostend and Zeebrugge; but the first battle of Ypres saved Calais and Boulogne. When the Western front had become stabilized by continuous lines of trenches from the Channel to the Swiss frontier, many able minds both in France and in England were bent upon the problem of outflanking this line by making some other front the scene of the military blow. Some suggested Salonika and a vigorous campaign in the Balkans, which would rally to the Allied cause certain hesitating nations, such as Greece, Bulgaria and Rumania. Others advised a landing in the Dardanelles, to force the Straits and get supplies through to Russia. Both plans were put into execution, but as regards the second, despite heroic efforts and immense losses, the peninsula of Gallipoli defied capture. The Allies had to revert to the sanguinary tactics of frontal attack against fortified positions. To relieve the French army, fiercely attacked at Verdun, the British fought the costly battles of the Somme in 1916. Until June, 1918, fortune was undecided on the Western front. The new weapon of tanks, which if used in mass might possibly have broken the German line, was tried too soon and on too small a scale. The tank was the most original invention of the War, and the most effective reply of the shock-troops to the improvements in projectiles. To modern infantry the tank is what armour was to the medieval warrior. And another new aspect of the war of 1914-1918 was the fourfold part played by the aeroplane — for reconnaissance, bombardment, pursuit, and direct attack on infantry.

The resoluteness of all the peoples of the British Empire was unbreakable. By voluntary enlistment, then by conscription, they raised eight million men. All the Dominions, and India herself, rallied to the help of the mother-country. Only in Ireland a minority — but as events proved, a potent minority — showed recalcitrance, although at the outbreak of war Irishmen were moved by the fate of Catholic Belgium. The Easter rising of 1916 in Dublin had to be suppressed by armed force, with considerable loss of life on both sides. The Sinn Fein rebels in years to come became the governing power in Ireland.

To meet the enormous expenses of the war, the rate of income tax rose to six shillings in the pound, and the super-tax on large incomes went higher still. Food had to be rationed. The Government tried to make restrictions weigh equally on rich and poor; war burdens were shared much more equitably than under Pitt; and the common liberties were respected as far as seemed possible. A united nation sustained the war until it was won, not because leaders forced them to do so, but because the people themselves believed it to be a just war. A coalition Cabinet formed in 1915 entrusted the Ministry of Munitions to Lloyd George, who succeeded Asquith as Prime Minister after a later ministerial reconstruction. The conduct of the war was handed over to an inner War Cabinet of five members, presided over by Lloyd George. An Imperial War Cabinet was also summoned which brought together the Dominion Premiers and Indian representatives. These innovations did not outlast the war itself.

Possibly Germany would not have been beaten at all without the intervention of the United States against her. The German command's attack on the point of juncture between the French and British armies in March 1918, nearly succeeded in separating them and driving the British back to the Channel coast. On March 26, at Doullens, Marshal Foch was given supreme command of the Allied armies. The German onslaughts were still formidable, but the rapid arrival of the American divisions afforded relief to the Allies and made possible the formation of substantial reserves. The failure of the German attack in Champagne, followed by Mangin's attack at Villers-Cotterets on July 18, marked the moment when ' hope changed sides '. On August 8 began the counter-offensive of the British, Canadian and Australian forces, and thereafter until November 11, when an armistice was declared, the forward movement of the Allies was continuous, their triumphs uninterrupted. Defeat in the field and revolution at home drove the Kaiser into exile in Holland. In the German fleet,

where orders had been received late in October to make a last desperate sortie, the sailors mutinied and refused to obey the order. Rather than leave their ships in British hands the German officers sank their surrendered vessels at Scapa Flow, and England was rid of that nightmare, a rival fleet in Europe. This, to her, was a prime objective of the war. She had achieved others: Mesopotamia, Palestine, the German colonies in Africa had all been conquered by her armies or those of her allies, and these territories would now, in various guises, be incorporated in her Empire or gravitate around her.

It was natural enough that so complete a victory, rounding off so stern a war, should open the doors to an 'orgy of chauvinism'. The 'khaki' election soon after the armistice gave Britain a House of Commons elected on a programme of retribution. Lloyd George, by adding to claims for war damage a claim for the cost of war pensions, raised the reparations demanded from Germany to a ludicrously swollen figure. It was no longer easy to calm them down. The Peace of Versailles was a bad peace. On the pretext of the selfdetermination of peoples, the so-called Big Five sliced up Europe with little or no regard to its traditions, history, or economic life. France, refused the Rhine frontier by Lloyd George, found herself promised in compensation a treaty of alliance which was never ratified. Italy, who had been given definite pledges when she entered the war on the

Allied side, was treated by British and Americans with an ill-will which bordered on enmity. And Germany herself, by a treaty too indulgent for its sternness and too stern for its indulgence, was cast into desperation.

This conflict had disturbed the world more widely and deeply than even the Napoleonic wars. Ancient States had vanished, and new ones been brought into being. While Russia became a Communist State, Italy and Germany fell under dictatorships, and corporative or totalitarian States supplanted the parliamentary regimes. These transformations affected England less than might have been thought possible. Nevertheless, she underwent profound political and economic changes. In domestic politics the most conspicuous of these changes was a new Representation of the People Act, which made adult suffrage really universal. Passed during the war years, a symbol of national unity, the Act of 1918 gave the Parliamentary vote to all men over twenty-one and to all women over thirty, thus bringing eight million new voters on to the register, six million of whom were women. This was supplemented by another measure passed a few years later which made the voting age the same for women as for men. A second political fact of importance was the virtual disappearance of the Liberal party, which, counting its Whig forerunners, had endured for three centuries. In the election of 1924, the Labour party became preponderant over the Liberals. Af-

ter that date the latter dwindled continuously, and by 1936 it could muster only a handful of members. The main political problems having been virtually settled to the general satisfaction, it was the problems of labour, unemployment, and the division of wealth that became paramount. The Labour party, buttressed by the trade union movement, was more representative than the Liberals of the views of the working classes in general.

As after Waterloo, the war of 1914-1918 was followed by a serious industrial slump. The causes of upheaval were the same as in 1816: the sudden demobilization of large numbers of men who could not recover their place in an altered economic machine; the phenomenal development of mechanical processes which had been stimulated by the needs of war; and a Budget inflated by the colossal debts incurred during the conflict. For some years it almost looked as if Britain were doomed. The running start she had made ahead of her rivals

during the nineteenth century had been lost. Her industries were inferior in equipment to those of Germany and the United States, and were furthermore handicapped by higher wage-rates than those of the Continent; the trade unions refused to allow these rates to be touched. Her trade was affected by the disappearance of consumers in an impoverished world which tended to make its units more and more self-sufficing; and on account of this shrinkage in international trade her merchant marine lay idle. In order to preserve her role as the world's banker, Britain tried until 1931 to maintain the gold-value of the pound sterling; and this monetary policy, theoretically defensible but in practice harmful, was responsible for increasing unemployment still more.

In 1926 an attempt to lower miners' wages led to a general strike. Newspapers ceased to appear, and the Government issued a small official newspaper, the *British Gazette*, and for the time being

WORKERS' DEMONSTRATION, 1932. A great economic recession followed the end of the First World War. Unemployment figures reached critical proportions, especially in the Midlands and the North, and the country was demoralised. Those who could not earn their living had to depend on the bounty of the Government, the Dole. *Fox Photos Ltd.*

POLITICAL DEMONSTRATION, Hyde Park, 1938. Neville Chamberlain had proved his worth as Chancellor of the Exchequer during the early '30's, but as the Nation's leader he was not a success. Public opinion did not support him over his policy of appeasement towards Nazi Germany. Once war had been declared Churchill was called in to give the country the leadership it needed. *Radio Times Hulton Picture Library.*

annexed the wireless broadcasting service. Thus controlling public opinion, supported by the majority of the country, and helped out by numerous volunteers who co-operated with the police and ensured the food supply for the large towns, the Conservative Government, under Stanley Baldwin, defeated the strike.

With the numbers of unemployed standing at over one and a half million, the unemployment insurance system broke down and had to be replaced by a subsidy method of relief, known as the dole, which threw heavy burdens on the Budget. A Labour Government under Ramsay MacDonald, which came to power in 1929, was no more successful than the Conservatives had been in overcoming the slump and the problem of the workless. Both in America and Europe capitalists were losing faith in Britain's future. There was a flight of gold from London. At this pace, bankruptcy was not far ahead. MacDonald came to feel that a

National Government would inspire more confidence, and without having been defeated in Parliament, which in any case was not sitting, he tendered his resignation to the King (1931). He was at once entrusted with the formation of a coalition Cabinet with a strong Conservative element, over which he presided until 1935, when the Conservative leader, Stanley Baldwin, took his place, retaining the National form.

Between 1931 and 1935 the rapid re-establishment of British economic stability surprised even the most optimistic. It was due in great measure to the cool heads of the people themselves, but also to an energetic Chancellor of the Exchequer, Neville Chamberlain. The methods used were simple. Firstly, Britain abandoned the gold standard of the pound. Prices in England dropped to levels lower than those of countries still on the gold standard, and thus favoured export trade. The fluctuations of the pound had been followed by the Scandinavian countries, South America, and to some extent by the United States, and a sterling bloc thus came into existence within which London was able to continue as a supreme banking centre. Secondly, Free Trade was finally abandoned. At the Ottawa Conference in 1932 British statesmen invited the Dominions to make economic agreements with the mother-country. But the Dominions were not enthusiastic, and this failure obliged British ministers to look elsewhere for a solution of their problems in an internal reorganization. Protective tariffs enabled manufacturers in many fields (at heavy cost to France and Germany) to recover British markets; and great efforts were made to revive home agriculture and stockbreeding. Thirdly, the Budget was balanced, thanks to the courageous acceptance of economies in expenditure and of fresh taxation.

Having successfully compromised in the matter of production and consumption, by compromise also England was able to preserve her Empire. During the war, Canada, Australia, New Zealand and South Africa had poured forth men and money to help the mother-country. But they had agreed to do so as separate States. In the newly founded League of Nations they demanded representation distinct from that of Great Britain. The second Statute of Westminster in 1931 declared that the British Parliament would no longer be entitled to legislate for the Dominions; that the rights of making peace or war, as also of negotiating treaties, would appertain to the Dominions in so far as their concerns were in question; and that the Dominion Prime Ministers would derive their authority direct from the Crown. The Crown was thenceforth the sole official link between Britain and the nations composing the British Commonwealth. By the treaty of 1921 Ireland likewise had been given a separate status, as the Irish Free State, although Northern Ireland was excepted and retained a close British connection. Between 1922 and 1931, under Cosgrave's presidency, Ireland accepted this position, but when Eamon de Valera succeeded him, the bonds were gradually loosened. Ireland no longer acknowledged the link of the Crown, was not represented at British ceremonies, and acted as an independent State. In 1926 Britain signed a treaty with Egypt which assured that country her freedom, and British troops, leaving the fortress of Cairo, defended only the Suez Canal.

George V and Queen Mary had enhanced the prestige of the monarchy by the simplicity and dignity of their life; and Edward VIII himself, at the outset of his reign in 1936, was invested with an almost universal sympathy. Before Edward's reign had lasted ten months, however, his subjects at home and overseas became aware, by persistent rumour and through the American newspapers, that their King proposed to marry an American, Mrs. Ernest Simpson, who was about to obtain her second divorce. The Prime Minister, Stanley Baldwin, was beset by messages of warning and anxiety. He requested an audience of the King and laid before him the dangers of any such decision. The sovereign's right to marry a foreigner, as so many of his ancestors had done, would not have been questioned; but a vast majority of his subjects, refusing to admit the idea of his marriage with a woman twice divorced, required the King to choose between his crown and this marriage. Edward VIII himself desired abdication. 'I am ready to go,' he had told Baldwin. After his abdication on December 11, 1936, when he was succeeded by his brother under the title of George VI, he broadcast a message to his former subjects from Windsor, in which he explained his action and declared his loyalty to the new sovereign.

British foreign policy after the war of 1914-18 conformed to the country's traditions. England still strove, as for four centuries past, to maintain the balance of power in Europe. Just as she upheld France against the Continental allies after Waterloo, so after 1919 she was afraid of enfeebling Germany excessively, and in the international conferences frequently fought Germany's battle. French demands that the League of Nations should be organized to defend its decisions, if need be, by force, were countered by successive British Governments with the idea of moral constraint — an ineffectual method when applied to nations like Germany and Italy, where totalitarian regimes had come to power. But when Italy in 1935 overran Abyssinia, a wave of sentiment rose in England, reinforcing a sudden revival of the Imperial sense, and then, for the first time, it was Britain who proposed the application of the sanctions provided for by the pact. The sanctions proved inadequate in their scope

THE EVACUATION FROM DUNKIRK, 1940: Richard Eurich.   A
British expeditionary force, sent across to the Continent in 1939
to help the French contain the German advance, was outflanked
by the fast-moving German armoured columns. Every ship that
could be mustered was sent across the Channel, in May 1940,
to evacuate the trapped army. The Germans hampered but were
unable to prevent the rescue operation, thanks to the cover-action
of the R.A.F., the Royal Navy and the French forces. (National
Maritime Museum, Greenwich). *Hachette.*

and merely encouraged Italy to throw in her lot with Germany; Neville Chamberlain, who succeeded Baldwin in 1937, embarked on a 'policy of appeasement'.

Such an approach to upstart leaders who acknowledged only force was bound to fail. Encouraged by a naval treaty with Great Britain and by the impunity with which France and Britain had let him remilitarize the left bank of the Rhine in 1936, the German leader, Hitler, undertook a series of unopposed encroachments. In March 1938, Austria was annexed. Then came the turn of Czechoslovakia. Chamberlain and his colleagues believed that if Germany were give satisfaction on certain points she would be prepared to co-operate in the maintenance of order in Europe. At the Munich Conference in September 1938, Britain and France abandoned Czechoslovakia. 'I bring you,' said Chamberlain on his return, echoing the words of Disraeli, 'peace with honour.' Winston Churchill's comment on this was: 'England and France had to choose between peace and dishonour. They have chosen dishonour; they shall have war.' His assessment proved right: at Munich Hitler had gauged the weakness of the democratic states and was now wholly reassured. In spite of his promise to respect what was left of Czechoslovakia, he decided, in March 1939, to retract his pledge and invade the whole country.

Hitler had not reckoned with the effect that such a violation would produce on Chamberlain. The statesman who had tried so hard to conciliate Germany now turned sharply against her. Since everything pointed to Poland as the next likely victim, he informed the Polish government that in case of attack Britain would furnish Poland with all the assistance in her power. There was no avoiding a new European conflict. Poland was invaded on September 3 and Chamberlain announced to the Commons that war had been declared. It was Winston Churchill, a man of genius and imagination, who stood at the helm during the stormy years that followed and brought his country through to victory.

More than the Napoleonic wars, and far more than the 1914 war, the second World War was for Britain a matter of life and death. Protected by her fleet, her armies, her wealth and her allies, she had from the time of the Norman Conquest been secure even at the height of her struggles. Her battles had been won on the continent of Europe or on the high seas. But from 1920 onwards the development of aviation largely deprived her of the benefits of insularity.

When the war began Poland and France were Britain's allies, but she had been unable to give them sufficient help either on land or in the air. A long period of pacifism had weakened her war-potential. It needed Churchill at the seat of authority to give her war-production the powerful impetus that it lacked. Poland, weakly supported and ill-equipped, could hold out for only one month. France, relying on the Maginot line, was making ready to fight a defensive war; but the line did not cover her northern frontier, which was crossed by Hitler's armies in May, 1940, after they had violated the neutrality of Holland and Belgium. Large French forces, and the bulk of the British Expeditionary Force, were cut off from their bases by the rush of German armoured divisions to the sea. Within a few days the confusion caused by the Luftwaffe with its mastery of the air, by the tanks which attacked headquarters staffs far to the rear, and by the hordes of civilian refugees blocking the roads, was such as to render any counter-attack, or even any large-scale re-deployment, virtually impossible.

It was in these circumstances that a fleet of more than a thousand vessels of all kinds and sizes crossed to Dunkirk by day and by night, in the face of air attack, to rescue the broken allied armies. Close on 350,000 men, of whom nearly a third were French, were brought off under the protection of the heroic French divisions and of the British fighter squadrons. When France, her armies completely disorganized, signed an armistice, Britain found herself alone, facing the imminent peril of invasion with none but obsolete land-weapons. She went stoutly to work, creating a new army, smothering beaches, cliffs and roadways with all manner of defence-works, and devising a sea-wall of flames to be fed by a huge network of petrol-pipes. Not for an instant did she give way to despair. She had never known defeat; she refused to believe in the possibility now. Exiled Governments came to her from Norway, Belgium, Poland and Czechoslovakia, and from France came General de Gaulle and his volunteers. British scien-

CHURCHILL BROADCASTS TO THE NATION, 1940. At this time, when Britain's chances of resisting invasion, let alone those of defeating Germany, were slim, the Prime Minister did not attempt to minimise the dangers facing the isolated country. He imbued the British with the will to resist which saw them through till the tide of war turned. *Keystone*.

tists performed miracles, sustaining the armed forces with new inventions and brilliant improvisations, among them Radar. Churchill, who showed himself to be a Prime Minister worthy of Pitt, was the voice of the nation and a source of inspiration to all those who served it. 'Upon this battle depends the survival of Christian civilization...'

The Battle of Britain opened with an attack from the air. Goering, who believed he had absolute air supremacy, hoped by means of heavy air bombardment so to shatter the defences and morale of the British as to make the subsequent invasion a simple matter. The R.A.F. fighter force was heavily outnumbered, but German losses were so heavy that the enemy in the end had to abandon his attempt to become master of the British sky.

But thereafter Britain had to pass through a long and painful period of defeats. Submarine warfare caused her terrible shipping losses which new construction could not overtake. Crete was occupied by the Germans after the first aerial invasion in history, and this gave rise to fears for the safety of Egypt. In the desert, between Tripolitania and Alexandria, the Italian divisions were reinforced by Rommel's *Afrika Korps*, and the British troops holding Tobruk were surrounded. But instead of exploiting his African and east-

European successes Hitler, in June, 1941, committed the supreme folly of attacking Russia. President Roosevelt, for his part, was in the meantime giving Britain immense material aid in the form of 'lend-lease'. This American aid partly re-equipped the Eighth Army which, under General Montgomery, won the victory of El Alamein in 1942, thereby saving Egypt.

The United States entered the war in December, 1941, following the Japanese attack on Pearl Harbour. The early stages of the war in the Pacific brought a succession of disasters for the Western Powers. America lost the Philippines, Britain lost Singapore and Burma, Holland lost Java and Sumatra, and Australia found herself with the Japanese army at her door. But it was clear that America's huge productive capacity must eventually turn the scale. In the European theatre, the plan upon which the British and Americans agreed was for the occupation of French North Africa as a base for further operations. In November, 1942, Allied forces landed in Casablanca, Oran and Algiers. The still-numerous French *Armée d'Afrique* soon joined them, and in a concerted effort they crushed not only the German army in Tunis but also the *Afrika Korps* which, retreating before Montgomery's Eighth Army, was caught between two fires. This total surrender of the German

[273]

LONDON IN FLAMES AFTER THE AIR
RAID OF 29 DECEMBER 1940. The
London docks were a prime target of
the Luftwaffe which aimed at knocking
Britain quickly out of the war by
crippling its transport and industry.
The area round St. Paul's was set on
fire by a rain of incendiary bombs. The
Cathedral itself did not escape damage.
Keystone.

[274]

THE PRIME MINISTER INSPECTS THE BOMB DAMAGE, LONDON
1940. Both the Royal Family and the Government
remained in London throughout the bombing, a powerful
factor in upholding morale in the capital. *Keystone*.

and Italian forces in Africa was the first major victory of the Western Allies.

The time had come for the re-conquest of Europe. From Tunisia the Allies advanced to Sicily and thence into Italy itself. The question arose whether the main attack was to be delivered from the Mediterranean, as advocated by Winston Churchill, or from Britain against the coast of Normandy, as advocated by Roosevelt and Stalin, who had their way. The huge and elaborately-mounted operation was launched on June 6th, 1944, and was rapidly successful. The German reply was a renewed attack on Britain, and in particular on London, by means of pilotless aircraft, known as 'flying bombs', which were launched from sites in the Pas de Calais area of northern France. This new weapon the V1, (Vergeltungswaffe Eins), had been meticulously prepared by the Germans, but its development had not gone unperceived in Britain. By bombing the specially constructed launching-ramps, as well as the railways and storage-depots, the R.A.F. greatly reduced the scale of the attack, which nevertheless did heavy material damage. More than a million houses were wholly of partly destroyed in London and the surrounding districts. Casualties, however, were lower than had been feared, and by the time the Allied armies over-ran the launching area, thus

putting an end to the attack, various methods of intercepting the bombs had still further reduced the number reaching the target. A second 'revenge weapon' was also employed by the Germans, the V2, consisting of a stratospheric rocket with a heavy explosive charge, travelling at supersonic speed. Against this no defence could be devised, but the number discharged was relatively small. It seems certain that if the Germans had been in a position to launch this offensive earlier they would have gravely hampered the invasion preparations.

While the British and Canadian armies advanced into Belgium, the Americans penetrated to the east and the French Leclerc division entered Paris. A further landing had been effected in the south of France on August 15th and had progressed northward without difficulty. By September the Allied armies were in a position to attack the Siegfried Line, against which, however, a direct frontal assault was likely to prove extremely costly. Before attempting it, therefore, Eisenhower sought to turn the German flank by means of a surprise airborne attack in Holland. This manoeuvre failed and the fighting continued throughout the the winter, although the steady destruction of German heavy industry by British and American air-attack placed the final issue beyond a doubt. Eventually the armies of the West made contact

WOMEN WORKING IN A NAVAL SHIPYARD. To fill the gaps in the labour force women undertook to replace men in the factories and on the land. The new role women were called on to play during the war contributed much to the social changes in the post-war years. *British Embassy Press Library, Paris.*

BRITISH ARTILLERY IN THE LIBYAN DESERT, ▶ MARCH 1941. British troops were dispatched to North Africa in 1940 to prevent the Axis forces from thrusting eastwards from Libya and seizing Britain's vital oil supplies in the Middle East. The fortunes of war fluctuated for two years in the North African campaign until General Montgomery's decisive victory at El Alamein, October 1942. War Office Photograph, *Crown Copyright Reserved.*

with the Russian forces. Hitler committed suicide, and on May 7th, 1945, Germany signed a treaty of unconditional surrender. The defeat of Japan remained to be completed, but this victory, too, was on the way. It was achieved in August, 1945, by the use of atomic bombs.

The part played in the common victory by America and Russia, and also by the European resistance movements, had been great indeed; but to Britain belonged the glory of having fought alone through the darkest days of the war. She emerged from the conflict with a well-warranted sense of pride, but she also came out of it exhausted. Her people had grown accustomed to restrictions which before the war they would never have endured. The less-favoured classes had seen that controls and rationing made for economic equality. War conditions had made it necessary to satisfy the basic needs of the whole population

before any kind of superfluity could be enjoyed by the more privileged. The British had thus grown familiar with the idea of a national minimum standard of life which it was the duty of the State to maintain. The functions of the State had also been greatly extended in the sphere of industrial control. Planning on a world-wide scale had been needed to sustain war production. And so by logical stages the conviction gained ground that a degree of socialism, adapted to the habits of the nation, might ensure a greater extent of social justice in time of peace. Hence the victory of the Labour Party in the 1945 General Election when Mr. Attlee replaced Winston Churchill as Prime Minister. Clement Attlee was a parliamentarian of great experience, a moderate and conciliatory statesman who succeeded in preserving the unity of the nation while introducing socialist measures. His Chancellor of the Exchequer, Sir

Stafford Cripps, imposed on the country a regime
of severe austerity. The British were fully aware
of the importance of protecting their currency, and
moreover they have always shown an admirable
sense of responsibility when faced by the need for
collective sacrifice.

The nationalisation of industries encountered
more opposition, however. The railways, taken
over by the State during the first World War, had
been financially regrouped and restored to private
ownership in 1921. The Labour Party put nationalisation in the forefront of its programme. Upon
coming into power it gave a first evidence of its
intentions by nationalising the Bank of England.
The nationalisation of the coal industry followed.
Similar bodies were created for the administration
of rail and road transport, gas, electricity and civil
aviation. Broadcasting had long been in the hands
of the B.B.C., an independent corporation, free to
determine its own programmes, but one which
in the last resort is answerable to Parliament. By
1950, 22⅓ per cent of all workers were employed
in the nationalised industries. The Labour Party
projected a further programme of nationalisation,
including that of the Iron and Steel Industry; but
it fell from power in 1951, before these new measures could be introduced. Despite all restrictions, the nation's import requirements after the
war were so great that the trade balance remained
unfavourable. Gold and dollar reserves in the
sterling area fell so heavily during 1949 that it
became necessary to devalue the pound, which was
reduced from 4.03 dollars to 2.80 dollars.

The Empire presented problems of the utmost
gravity. The peoples of the British Commonwealth had proved their solidarity during the war,
those of British origin freely affirming their ties
with the Mother Country. But in South Africa,
where the population was more mixed, a local
nationalism was stirring, and India was no longer
disposed to accept a British administration. Britain showed great wisdom in voluntarily loosing
bonds which could not in any event have been
maintained. She resolved to withdraw all her civil
administrators and troops from India, and on
August 15th, 1947, India became two independent
sovereign States, Pakistan and the Union of India,
both of which joined the Commonwealth. In

1948 Ceylon received Dominion status and Britain abandoned her protectorate over Palestine; in 1949 Eire withdrew from the Commonwealth, ceasing to acknowledge the suzerainty of the Crown, and became a republic. By gradual stages Britain withdrew her troops from Egypt, accepting the evacuation of the Sudan and even of the Suez Canal. Certain of the Commonwealth nations, Canada, Australia and New Zealand have been prompted by reasons of proximity, economic solidarity and national defence to draw closer to the United States. Canada, possessing a huge common frontier with the States, has concluded trade and monetary agreements with that country, and Australia and New Zealand have entered into defence treaties with her. This approach to America on the part of nations considered to be wholly British has come as a shock to many Englishmen. Since the ending of the war the whole question of Anglo-American relations has been both delicate and difficult.

There are two reasons for this. In the first place, Washington is today the incontestable centre of world-power in the West. The British may regret the fact, but they are sufficiently clear-sighted to recognise it. They know that Britain's position in the world can only be maintained by good relations with the States in both the economic and the military spheres. The change, however, has come about too rapidly not to wound the susceptibilities of the more ardently patriotic among them. It was a shock to many when an American was selected for the post of Admiral of the Atlantic, and a still greater shock to see America assume the political leadership in the Middle and Far East. Many Englishmen believed, not without reason, that Britain, with her long experience in those regions, still retained a greater competence. Nevertheless the British have realistically accepted the new balance of forces while striving to pursue their traditional policy — for example, in China, where they are on better terms than the Americans with the Communist government. And in the second place, the British during the past ten years have been very much afraid of being dragged by America into a third world war arising partly out of ideological differences. They have done their utmost to apply the brakes. In 1950 Attlee flew

to Washington to counsel prudence over Korea, and later Churchill and Eden went to confer with President Eisenhower during the crisis in Indo-China. Since then the two countries have reached a better understanding, partly because the British Government has been able to speak with greater authority now that the nation has acquired the status of an atomic Power, and partly because Russian advances in nuclear science have made the Americans more cautious. It is true that the English, by nature inclined towards compromise, take a more favourable view than do the Americans about some sort of agreement with the Russians and Chinese, but, by and large, the relations between Britain and the United States are very close. Their shared conviction that the peace of the world depends on their remaining united has always enabled them to reach agreement after a period of tension.

Britain's attitude towards Europe has disappointed many Europeans who had hoped, especially after Churchill's words at Strasbourg, that England would be quick to join the six Western European nations. This belief showed a faulty understanding of Britain who has always considered herself, as we have had frequent occasion to remark in the course of this history, a neighbour but not an integral part of continental Europe. The Channel may have lost the defensive value it possessed before the days of aircraft and guided missiles, but a nation cannot in the course of a few years lose a habit of mind ten centuries old. Moreover Britain had always replied, in answer to European solicitations, that her close link with the Commonwealth prevented her from committing herself too deeply on the Continent. The imperial preference set her apart from the other European nations in the commercial sphere. The formation,

however, of a European consumers' market of a hundred and sixty million people could not fail to affect her. Here too she hoped to find a compromise. Sir Oliver Franks, in defining his country's position, once used the parallel of a club that accepts country members without asking them to undertake the duties performed by town members. Great Britain, he said, wanted 'Country membership' of the club of Western Europe. She was willing to pay a subscription and accept certain obligations, but she did not want to become a 'regular member'.

From the military point of view, however, she is firmly committed to the Western camp. For many centuries she was the invariable adversary of the strongest continental Power, maintaining the balance by throwing her weight, now into one side of the scales, now into the other. This policy is no longer feasible; nor is it possible for the present to imagine Germany becoming as formidable as the Soviet Union. Britain is a member of N.A.T.O. and has even consented — a most notable break with tradition — to maintain troops permanently on the Continent.

The General Election of 1951 restored the Conservative Party to power with Winston Churchill at its head. The Government's majority was as narrow as that of its predecessor, the new House of Commons being composed of 320 Conservatives, 295 Labour members and 6 Liberals. It was a re-affirmation of the two-party system, which ensures the smooth working of parliamentary government. In Britain as in the United States chances of a third party are extremely small, and it is better that this should be so. The Conservative Government showed wisdom in not undoing the reforms introduced by the Labour Government, which would have provoked a dangerous reaction in the country, but it did not pursue the policy of nationalisation. A period of relative prosperity and increasing exports made it possible to relax the policy of austerity, but after fifteen years of privation the country, not unnaturally, was disposed to demand and consume more. In 1955 the shrinkage of reserves obliged the Chancellor of the Exchequer to restrict hire-purchase sales and raise the Bank Rate. Nevertheless, Britain has been able to maintain a strong hold on world markets thanks to the high quality of its industrial production.

The modern world has seen the birth of a new source of power — atomic energy. This was developed in the first instance for warlike purposes, and for a number of years it appeared that it would be monopolised by the United States and Russia. But Britain has always possessed excellent physicists, and she has set up a very large research centre at Harwell, in Berkshire. She has produced atomic bombs which have undergone successful tests, and also guided missiles. No country has a greater need of powerful atomic reactors for peaceful purposes. British coal resources cannot last for ever; many of the seams at present being worked are difficult of access, and the country possesses few sources of hydro-electric power. The Government has embarked on a vast programme. In twenty years a large part of the power used in Britain will be derived from atomic fission. Moreover the country has played a leading part in the production of radio-active isotopes. It is remarkable that this land of tradition, with its mediaeval universities, should continue to be among the leaders in the race for scientific discoveries.

In 1952 King George VI died. He left behind him the memory of one of the best of English monarchs, and the Crown continues to enjoy immense prestige in modern Britain. The Sovereign remains the sole link between the free nations of the Commonwealth. King George VI was succeeded by his elder daughter, who became Queen Elizabeth II. As Princess Elizabeth, the Queen had in 1947 married Prince Philip Mountbatten, who was created Duke of Edinburgh, and who has borne himself with a notable distinction in the difficult role of Consort. They have three children, Charles, Prince of Wales born in 1948, Princess Anne, born in 1950, and Prince Andrew, born in 1960.

In 1953 Winston Churchill, whose state of health and advanced age did not permit him to remain in power, handed over the reins of office to Anthony Eden, who was then Foreign Secretary. The new Prime Minister first became Foreign Secretary in 1935, but after battling in the cause of collective security resigned his office owing to differences of opinion with Neville Chamberlain, who was then head of the Government. Eden was a man of character and a supporter of the 'three unions', with the Commonwealth, with Europe and with the

United States. In 1955 he brought about a General Election as a result of which the Conservatives were returned to power with an increased majority.

The international situation was dangerous. The Soviet Union, skilfully exploiting the grievances of the Arab countries, was trying to incite them against the West. She succeeded in Egypt. On July 26, 1956, Colonel Nasser, head of the Egyptian government, announced that he was nationalizing the Suez Canal. This was a heavy blow for Britain and France. Confused negotiations followed during which efforts were made to find a compromise, but they proved fruitless partly because the United States, still believing in the possibility of keeping Egypt in the Western camp, did not support her allies, and partly because Egypt, assured of Russian support, refused to make any concessions. Britain and France assembled an expeditionary force at Cyprus with the object of reoccupying the Canal Zone. The attack was launched in November and the military objectives would have been achieved, with the help of the Israeli army, had political pressures not intervened: there was the strong disapproval of the United States, who were neither consulted nor given prior notice about the attack, the condemnation of the United Nations for resorting to force, and above all, a direct threat of reprisals by Russia. Public opinion in France was exacerbated by Nasser and largely supported the Government. In England, on the other hand, not only the Labour opposition but many of the Conservatives also criticized the Government's measures. In the twelve hours which followed Bulganin's ultimatum, England decided to withdraw her troops. It was the first time since the war that a British government had tried to 'go it alone' without the U.S.A. The experience had proved that the West was powerless unless united, and resulted in closer consultation between London and Washington. Sir Anthony Eden, who had been suffering from a serious liver complaint, tendered his resignation, and the Queen summoned Harold Macmillan. In the 1959 General Elections the Conservative party was again returned to power.

Britain's colonies acquired their independence in an atmosphere which was marked on the whole by orderliness and goodwill. South Africa however, once a British Dominion, was isolated from the other states by her racial ideas, similar to those held in the southern states of the U.S., and decided to become a totally separate republic. In Cyprus, whose population had engaged in a long and bitter struggle against Great Britain, a constitution was finally worked out by negotiation and established in a treaty between the United Kingdom, Greece and Turkey on one side, the Republic of Cyprus on the other. The Prime Minister, Archbishop Makarios, requested that his country be admitted to the Commonwealth for a five-year period. The solution of the Cyprus question is a good example of what can be achieved by patience and a spirit of compromise.

Britain meanwhile had an important role to play in the East-West conflict. Prime Minister Macmillan took part in a summit conference of the Big Four in Paris, May 1960. The English had placed great hopes on this meeting but Mr. Khrushchev's sudden intransigence brought it to a premature close. The dialogue was resumed that September in New York at the U.N. General Assembly where the Prime Minister's quiet humour helped to thaw the atmosphere. When the Soviet leader took off his shoe and thumped it on the table, Mr. Macmillan's only comment was: 'If this continues, I shall be obliged to demand a translation.' It was there too that he made an approach to Nasser which was ultimately to result in the resumption of diplomatic relations between Great Britain and the United Arab Republic in 1962.

In October 1961 the British Government decided to make official application to join the European Economic Community and sent Mr. Heath to Brussels to negotiate terms. The problems of entry were complex, not least because, as we have frequently indicated, the conception of a close link with the Continent flies in the face of every Englishman's inherited traditions. However, to cope with a new situation a new attitude was necessary. Furthermore, the industrial and commercial prosperity of the Six, contrasting with Britain's own economic difficulties, was a constant invitation for her to participate in their success. The chief obstacle was the reluctance of the Commonwealth countries to sacrifice the prefential tariffs which their agricultural products have always enjoyed in the British Community. The Six, however, who had their own problem of agricultural surpluses, would not consent to admitting

England as a member of their economic club unless she accepted all the clauses of the Rome treaty. The discussions proved long and difficult. They were inhibited not only by the opposition of many of the Commonwealth prime ministers, but also by that of the Labour Party which meant to make this an issue at the next General Election. The Conservative Government, however, did not waver in its course. 'There can be no doubt,' said Mr. Heath, 'that the success or failure of these discussions will determine the future shape of Europe. They will affect the way of life, the political thought and even the character of each one of our countries...'

It would indeed represent an immense change if Great Britain became economically and politically a Continental power; this change will, nevertheless, most probably (1962) come about, for it is vital to the prosperity of British industry and sterling currency. For the third consecutive year the budget showed a deficit due to an increase in spending and to the fact that some essential industries were no longer sufficiently competitive overseas, though this state of affairs should be remedied once access to the European market gives them scope for greater productivity. Plans for a tunnel or bridge across the Channel are being studied; when either of these projects materialises Britain will have the most palpable link with the Continent.

While attempting to draw closer to Europe, Britain has no wish to lose her privileged position relating to the United States. Since her nuclear programme must necessarily be limited for financial reasons she has to rely all the more on her American partner. The Prime Minister has main-

tained the closest relations with President Kennedy from the moment of his inauguration. He has remarked on the perfect *entente* between the two countries and suggested that the two leaders and their administrations, far from trying to take advantage of each other at the bargaining table, act in close consultation, on an equal footing, with a view to attaining mutually acceptable goals.

It has been said with justice that if in France 'plus ça change, plus c'est la même chose' in Britain the reverse is the case and the less things change the less they are the same. In the shadow of time-honoured ceremonial, of wigs and golden coaches and fairy-tale princesses, a rapid evolution is taking place. The process of social levelling, which is today an almost universal trend, has been very marked in Britain. The majority of the ancestral castles, and many of the great country houses surrounded by their parks, have become the property of the National Trust or else have been converted into public institutions. The rate of Income Tax no longer permits the private maintenance of vast estates. Domestic servants are rare and often unprocurable. A simple mode of life has been adopted by a steadily increasing section of the British people, dress requirements are very much less rigid than they once were and the spectacular growth of the television industry has been responsible for a notable change in social habits. The Television Act of July, 1954, projected the establishment of an Independent Television Authority. The reasons given for the Government's authorizing the creation of a television network separate from the B.B.C. and financed by advertisers were not economic but arose out of the conviction that, since television is destined to exercise an increasing influence over the minds of the people, its control cannot be allowed to remain in the hands of a single authority, no matter how excellent that authority may be. Television played a noteworthy part in the General Election of 1955, and there can be little doubt that the personal attractions of statesmen will henceforth have a greater political importance than they have had in the past. The Press is not very different from what it was before the Second World War. The British people buy more newspapers than any other (611 for every thousand inhabitants, as opposed to 353 in the United States). A Sunday paper, *News of the World*, holds the world circulation record with 8,000,000 copies, while among the dailies the circulation of the *Daily Mirror* greatly exceeds 4,000,000.

The public schools and universities have followed the general trend and opened their doors more and more widely to all classes. Scholarships and State and County grants are numerous, affording entry into even the most ancient and exclusive colleges. Science has an honoured place in all British universities, and the number of Nobel prizewinners in physics, chemistry and medicine bears witness to the excellence of their laboratories, many of which receive subsidies from the State. Radar was first developed in Britain. Professor C. T. R. Wilson invented the 'cloud chamber' which bears his name and which was instrumental in the discovery of the positive electron and the meson. This device was perfected by Professor P. M. S. Blackett, who has played an important part in the sphere of nuclear physics, as has Professor Lindemann (Lord Cherwell), Winston Churchill's scientific adviser. British scientists have always shown an aptitude for the composition of literary works which, while of high technical importance, have been so written and conceived as to bring them within the grasp of a large lay public. Professors Jeans, Eddington and Whitehead have advanced theories of the universe extending beyond the confines of accepted knowledge.

The history of England is that of one of mankind's outstanding successes. It is the history of how certain Saxon and Danish tribes, isolated on an island on the outer rim of Europe, merging with the Celtic and Roman survivors and organized by adventurers from Normandy, became with the passing centuries the masters of one-third of this planet. It is instructive to probe the secret of a destiny as fortunate and impressive as that of ancient Rome.

The racial blend was aptly measured, the climate healthy, and the soil fertile. Local assemblies had implanted in village communities a sense of public debate, and also of compromise. But these customs would doubtless have fallen into desuetude, as happened elsewhere, had it not been for the conquest by the Normans. To the strong authority of the Conqueror and his successors both Norman and Angevin, the English owed the benefits of sound justice and their heightened respect for law. Shielded by the sea from their Continental neighbours, and thereby set free from the fears which paralysed so many statesmen in France, they were able with comparative safety to improve upon their original institutions. By a sequence of fortunate chances they slowly discovered certain simple conditions which assured them at once of their security and their liberty.

In the time of the Saxon kingdoms, the English sovereigns collaborated with a Council, and strove to obtain for their acts the approval of the most powerful men in the land. Their successors did likewise, and England never knew an absolute monarchy. When the effective forces shifted from their proper place, sovereigns or skilful ministers consulted and rallied the several 'estates' of the realm. The best ecclesiastics were their ministers; the barons, then the squires, became their officials; the burgesses and notables became their 'faithful Commons'. As political maturity advanced, the lords, knights, smaller landowners, merchants, artisans and farmers were in turn called upon to participate in the responsibilities of power, until at last, not many years ago now, the working-class party itself became 'His Majesty's Opposition', and then assumed power. Having thus transmuted successive groups of potential malcontents into active collaborators, the rulers of England were able to grant the people a measure of freedom which expanded as their sense of security deepened.

Two supremely valuable virtues ensured a tranquil evolution in England — continuity and flexibility. Balfour once remarked that it was better to do something absurd which had always been done, than to do a wise thing which had never been done before. To-day, as always, England is ruled by precedent; the monarchy, Parliament, the universities, are all faithful to medieval tradition and usage. But the adaptive powers of the English people are equal to their conservatism. The ancient institutions always acknowledge and accept the newer powers. There has never been a real revolution in England. The short lived risings which mark the stages in her history were only passing waves on a great sea, and the 'glorious Revolution of 1688' simply an exchange of signatures. Chance results have been made use of by England's statesmen, rather in the way that great artists seize and perpetuate a fortunate expression or feature. We saw how the association between knights and burgesses, and then the deliberate abstention of the clergy, led to the formation of a Parliament composed of two distinct Houses. Before long the Kings depended for their financial resources on that Parliament's good will. In France or Spain sovereigns might forcibly raise taxes imposed without consent. But the English soon realized that their freedom was bound up with the maintenance of two protective axioms: no perpetual taxation, and no royal army unduly strong. Here they clashed with, and defeated, the Stuart dynasty. With Parliament victorious, it remained to find a means of drawing forth an executive power from this legislative assembly. An opportune chance, in the accession of the Hanoverian dynasty, made possible the system of a Cabinet responsible to the Parliamentary body. Finally, the prudence of the aristocracy and the political shrewdness of its leaders led to the peaceful transformation of a country gentlemen's club into a great national assembly. Thus came about the slow formation of a mode of government which is not, as Europe often believed it was, an abstract system with universal validity, but an amalgam of devices which, in that particular country and for particular historical reasons, have proved successful.

An insular and remote situation brought about a religious breach with Rome, and this rupture was in its turn an initial cause of the formation of a British Empire. Prolonged religious conflict created a type of courageous, resolute Protestant, who yielded to nobody, and preferred to quit his own country and settle in distant lands to which he gave an Anglo-Saxon population. The survival of this Empire was assured by the mastery of the seas, which England wrested from Spain, France, Holland and Germany in succession, gaining that supremacy because, thanks to her geographical position, she was able to concentrate so much of her resources upon her fleet. That Empire might well have disappeared, at one time or another, if not by conquest from without, at least through explosion from within. But the loss of the American colonies gave home Governments a lesson in moderation. England had evolved Parliament and the Cabinet; encountering by chance the idea of an Imperial federation of free States, she applied it by common sense. Within the Empire, as in its home boundaries, the British Government now hardly desires to maintain its authority save by consent of the peoples governed.

The modern world confronts Britain and the Commonwealth with a new problem, more difficult of solution than any of those which she has successfully solved in the past. She finds herself in company with huge nations whose population and resources are superior to her own. Many of the countries which hitherto bought her products or her services are now in a position to supply themselves. Certain of the Commonwealth nations may be drawn into the sphere of influence of other groups. In these circumstances, can Britain remain one of the great world-Powers? The British Empire as Kipling saw it no longer exists, but it has been replaced by something no less splendid or valuable. The essential change lies in the fact that the British peoples are no longer in a position to select their allies or to live in a state of isolation. It is for them to achieve a last compromise between the national independence which is so dear to their hearts and that international solidarity which is the condition of their survival.

Index

Numbers in italics refer to the captions to illustrations

[294]

DATE DUE

GAYLORD	PRINTED IN U.S.A.